PAUL JENKINS

ANDY CLARKE

# REPLICA

## VOLUME 1

## THE TRANSFER

DAN BROWN

MARCELO MAIOLO

CLAYTON COWLES

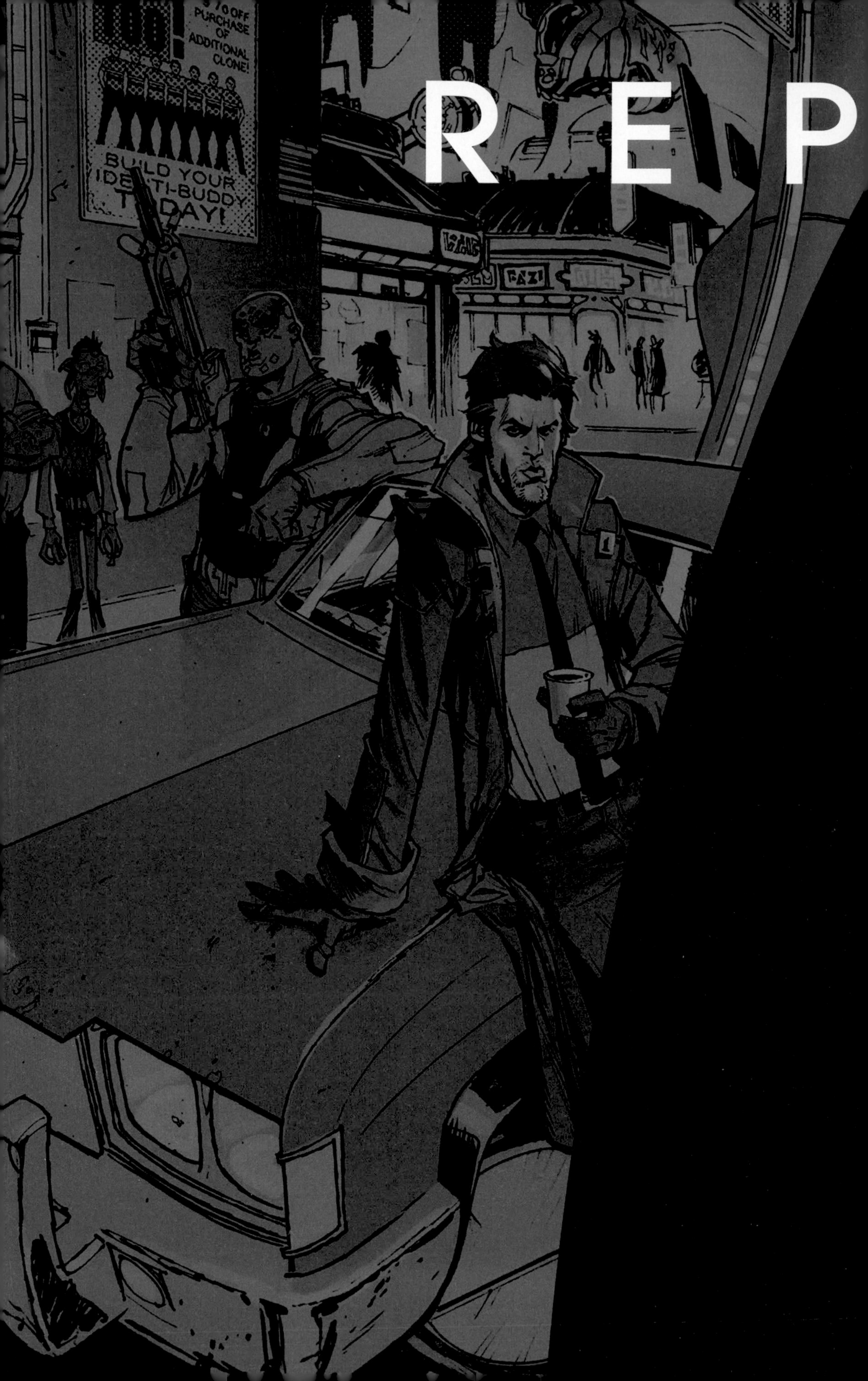
R E P
PURCHASE
OF
ADDITIONAL
CLONE!
BUILD YOUR

# LICA

## VOLUME 1

### THE TRANSFER

**PAUL JENKINS** creator & writer

**ANDY CLARKE** artist

**MARCELO MAIOLO** (#1) & **DAN BROWN** (#2-5) colorists

**CLAYTON COWLES** letterer

**ANDY CLARKE** w/ **MARCELO MAIOLO** front cover

**ANDY CLARKE** w/ **MARCELO MAIOLO** (#1-2) & **DAN BROWN** (#3-5) original covers

**ANDREW ROBINSON** & **PHIL HESTER** variant covers

**JOHN J. HILL** book & logo designer

**MIKE MARTS** editor

## AFTERSHOCK™

**MIKE MARTS** - Editor-in-Chief • **JOE PRUETT** - Publisher • **LEE KRAMER** - President
**JAWAD QURESHI** - SVP, Investor Relations • **JON KRAMER** - Chief Executive Officer
**MIKE ZAGARI** - SVP Digital/Creative • **JAY BEHLING** - CFO • **MICHAEL RICHTER** - Chief Creative Officer
**STEPHAN NILSON** - Publishing Operations Coordinator • **LISA Y. WU** - Social Media Coordinator

AfterShock Trade Dress and Interior Design by **JOHN J. HILL**
AfterShock Logo Design by **COMICRAFT**
Proofreading by **DOCTOR Z.**
Publicity: contact **AARON MARION** (aaron@fifteenminutes.com) &
**RYAN CROY** (ryan@fifteenminutes.com) at **15 MINUTES**

**AFTERSHOCKCOMICS.COM** Follow us on social media 🐦 📷 f

# INTRODUCTION

### BY **PAUL JENKINS**

In case you're wondering, Trevor Churchill is me, Paul Jenkins.

These days I'm a novelist, a studio head, a director and writer of animation, a videogame creator, a comic book writer, a teacher and who-knows-what else. Not a day goes by that I don't wish I could clone myself fifty times.

The problem is, I'm pretty sure the clones and I would not get along. Because I'm kind of an asshole. I have bad habits, like always needing to be the driver of a car (can't be a passenger since I broke my neck). I play golf far too quickly and I sneeze a lot. Can you imagine fifty of that idiot? Believe me, one is more than enough.

But, you know, I'd like to think that's why Trevor is such an endearing character. We all have a little bit of Trevor in us – trying to do the right thing and never succeeding, barely suffering the fools around us, and never taking no for an answer. Truth be told, I actually like the guy after having written him for a while.

Now, to business: I did so much less of the work than the rest of the creative team, and so this is a great place to shout them out, or whatever it is you kids do these days. Thanks to Andy Clarke, without whom Vorgas and Veet would not be nearly as hilarious. I'm always amazed when I can give an artist certain humorous parameters and find they accomplished far more than my words ever could. Andy, you are a bloody little genius. Thanks also to Dan Brown and Clayton Cowles for their amazing work – you guys are true professionals, and deserve all the recognition you can get. This book is yours, too.

And thanks to Joe and Mike and all the AfterShock team, all of whom need about fifty clones of themselves. I know they appear to be an obvious money laundering front for the Chinese Mafia, but I'm getting more and more convinced these guys are legit and I am contractually obliged to say so.

Thanks for picking up our book. I know you will love it. And if you don't, you only have yourself to blame.

Which would be a lot easier if there were fifty of you.

**Paul Jenkins**
**Atlanta, 2016**

# 1

## “BY THE BOOK”

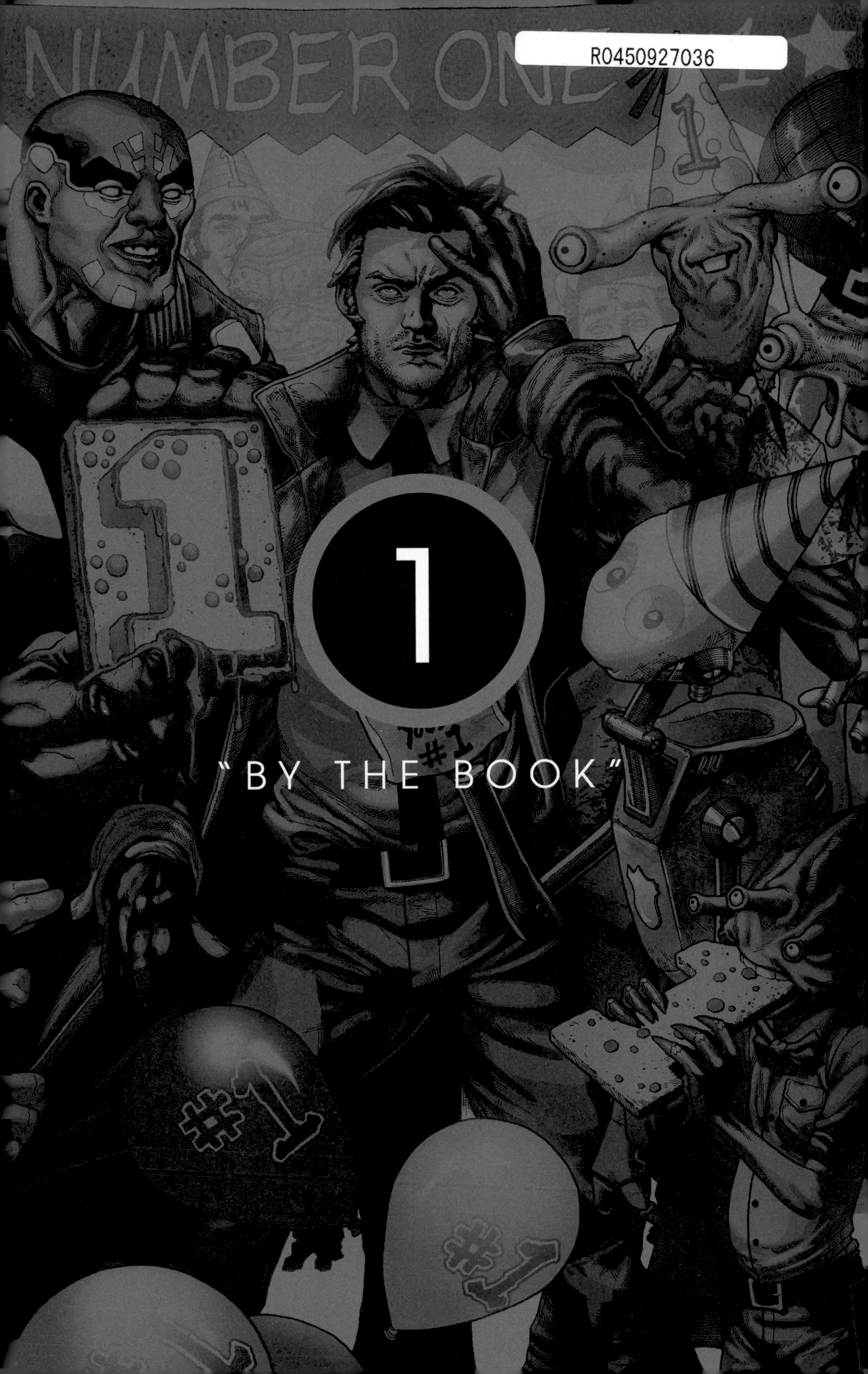
NUMBER ONE
#1
#1
#1

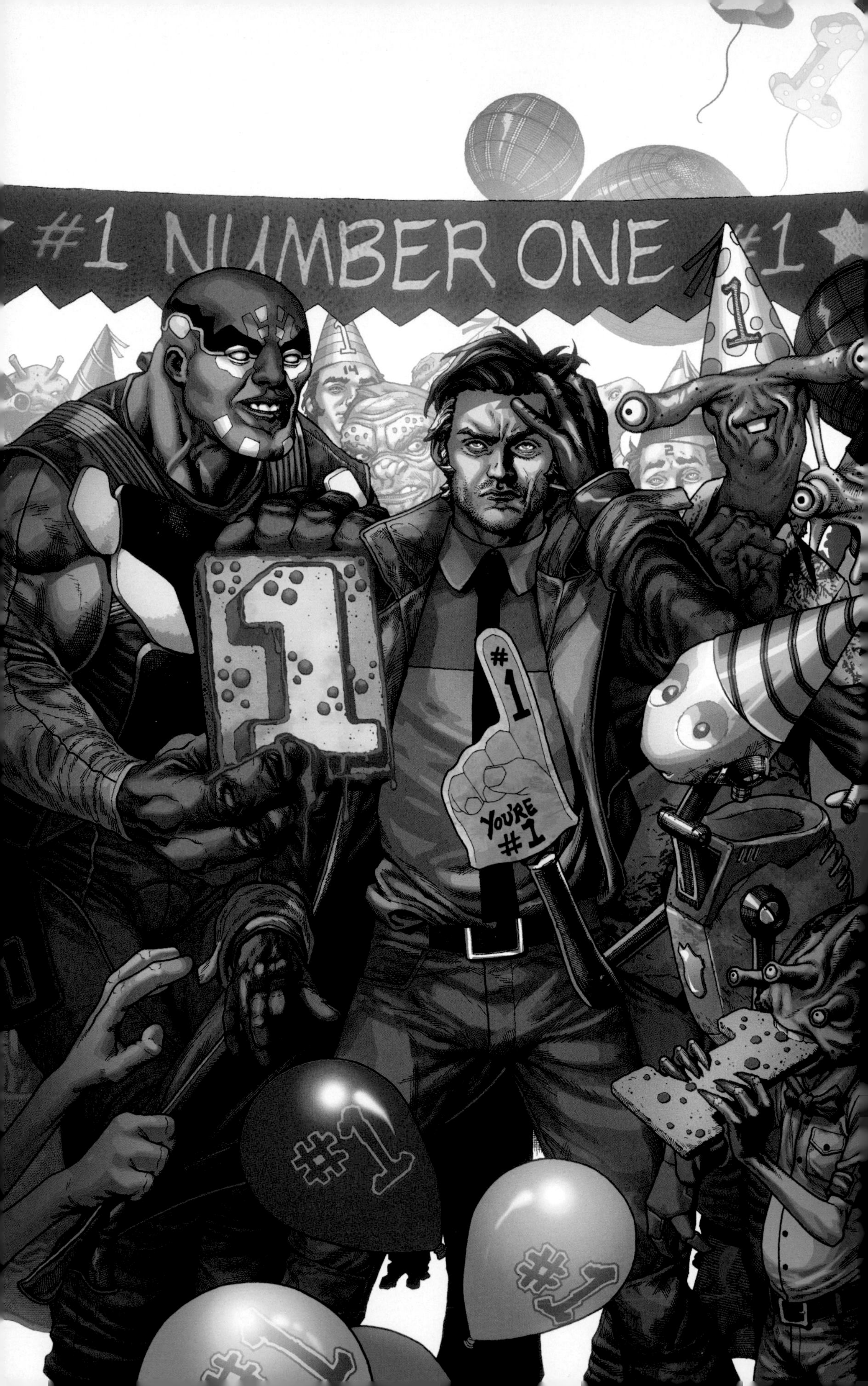
#1 NUMBER ONE #1
#1
YOU'RE #1

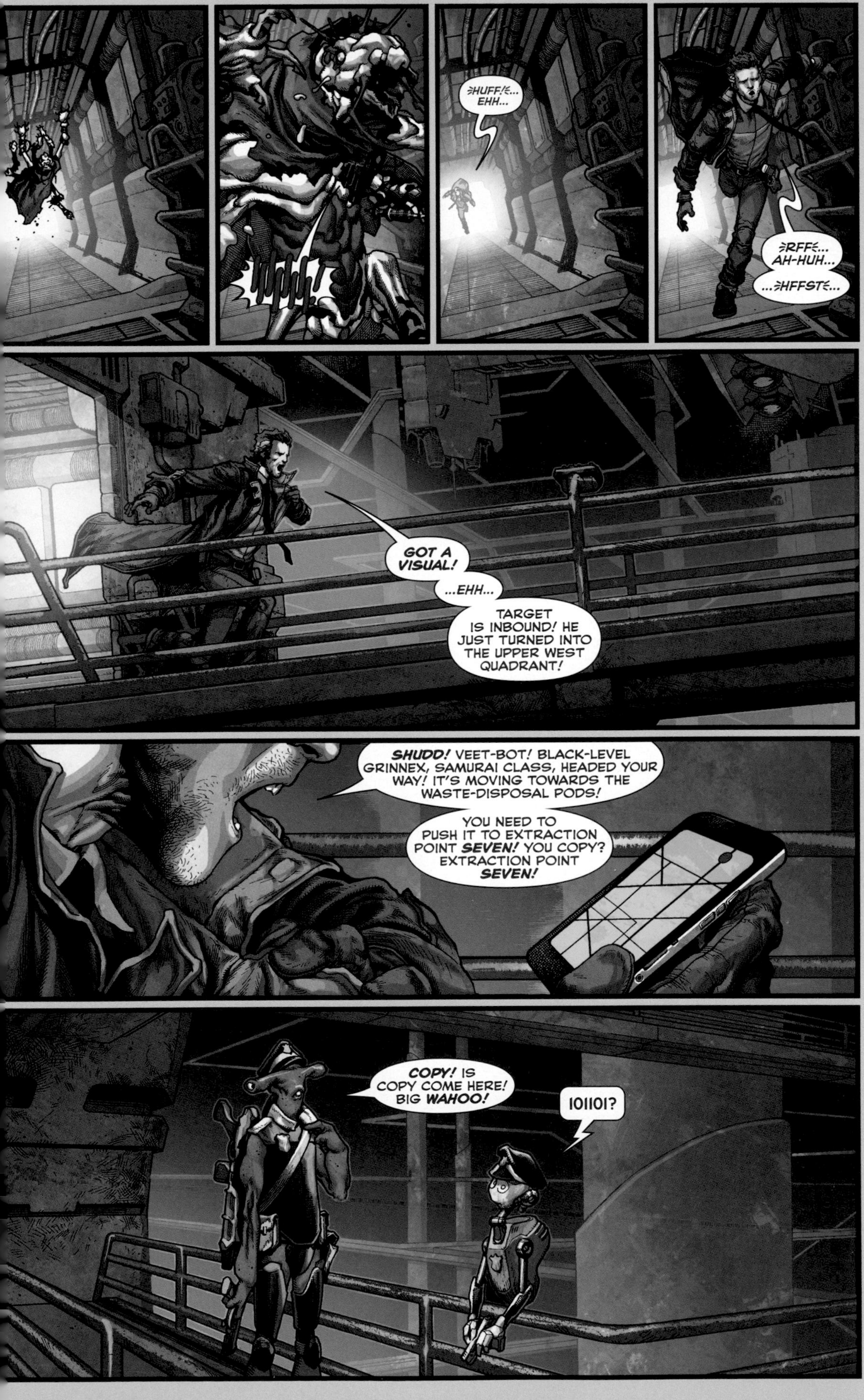

THWAK!
⋟HUFF!⋞... EHH...
⋟RFF⋞... AH-HUH...
...⋟HFFST⋞...
GOT A VISUAL!
...EHH...
TARGET IS INBOUND! HE JUST TURNED INTO THE UPPER WEST QUADRANT!
SHUDD! VEET-BOT! BLACK-LEVEL GRINNEX, SAMURAI CLASS, HEADED YOUR WAY! IT'S MOVING TOWARDS THE WASTE-DISPOSAL PODS!
YOU NEED TO PUSH IT TO EXTRACTION POINT SEVEN! YOU COPY? EXTRACTION POINT SEVEN!
COPY! IS COPY COME HERE! BIG WAHOO!
101101?

LOOK! IS COPY! NUMBER SEVEN! IS *COPY!*

OIIO! *OIIO!*

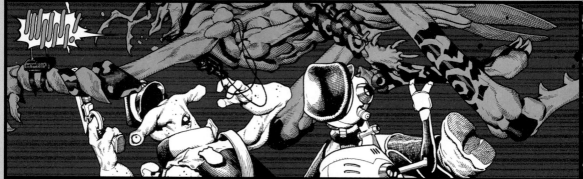

VVRRRh!

NEGATIVE! *NEGATIVE!* SHUDD, YOU TELL THAT METAL BUCKET IF IT SO MUCH AS *THINKS* OF DISCHARGING A WEAPON, I'LL PUT YOU *BOTH* ON THE SCRAP HEAP! YOU HEAR ME?

TARGET IS A GRINNEX SAMURAI ACOLYTE WITH FULL DIPLOMATIC IMMUNITY! WE NEED TO BRING THIS GUY IN WITHOUT A SCRATCH! GO WITH *CONTAINMENT* PROTOCOL!

ONE-ADAM-ONE... TREVOR, THIS IS SUB-LIEUTENANT *WEEZIK* OF THE SHADARR REPORTING: THE TARGET IS IN VISUAL RANGE AND MOVING TOWARDS THE EXTRACTION POINT, AS REPORTED!

PERFECT. LET'S TAKE THIS SUCKER *DOWN.*

OKAY, PEOPLE... WE DO THIS EARTH-STYLE: TARGET IS AT A DEAD END AND HEADED FOR EXTRACTION POINT SEVEN. WE NEED A LOCK ON ITS POSITION.

HAS ANYONE SEEN *VORGAS?*

OCULARS ON VORGAS? *ANYONE?* IS COPY COMING! CAN YOU READ MY WORDS? OVER.

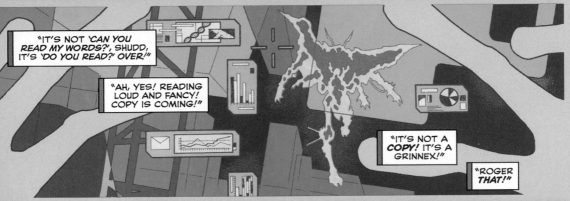

"IT'S NOT 'CAN YOU *READ MY WORDS?*', SHUDD, IT'S '*DO YOU READ?*' OVER!"

"AH, YES! READING LOUD AND FANCY! COPY IS COMING!"

"IT'S NOT A *COPY!* IT'S A GRINNEX!"

"ROGER *THAT!*"

ONE-ADAM-ONE! TREVOR, THIS IS *DOREMI*--I'M AT THE EXTRACTION AREA.

I CAN SEE THROUGH THE ENTIRE GRID WITH THIS WEARABLE TECH YOU HUMANS LICENSED FROM THE GHNN'DAR! IT'S *REMARKABLE*--

*MMF.*

NOTE TO SELF: MUST FIX PROXIMITY SENSORS.

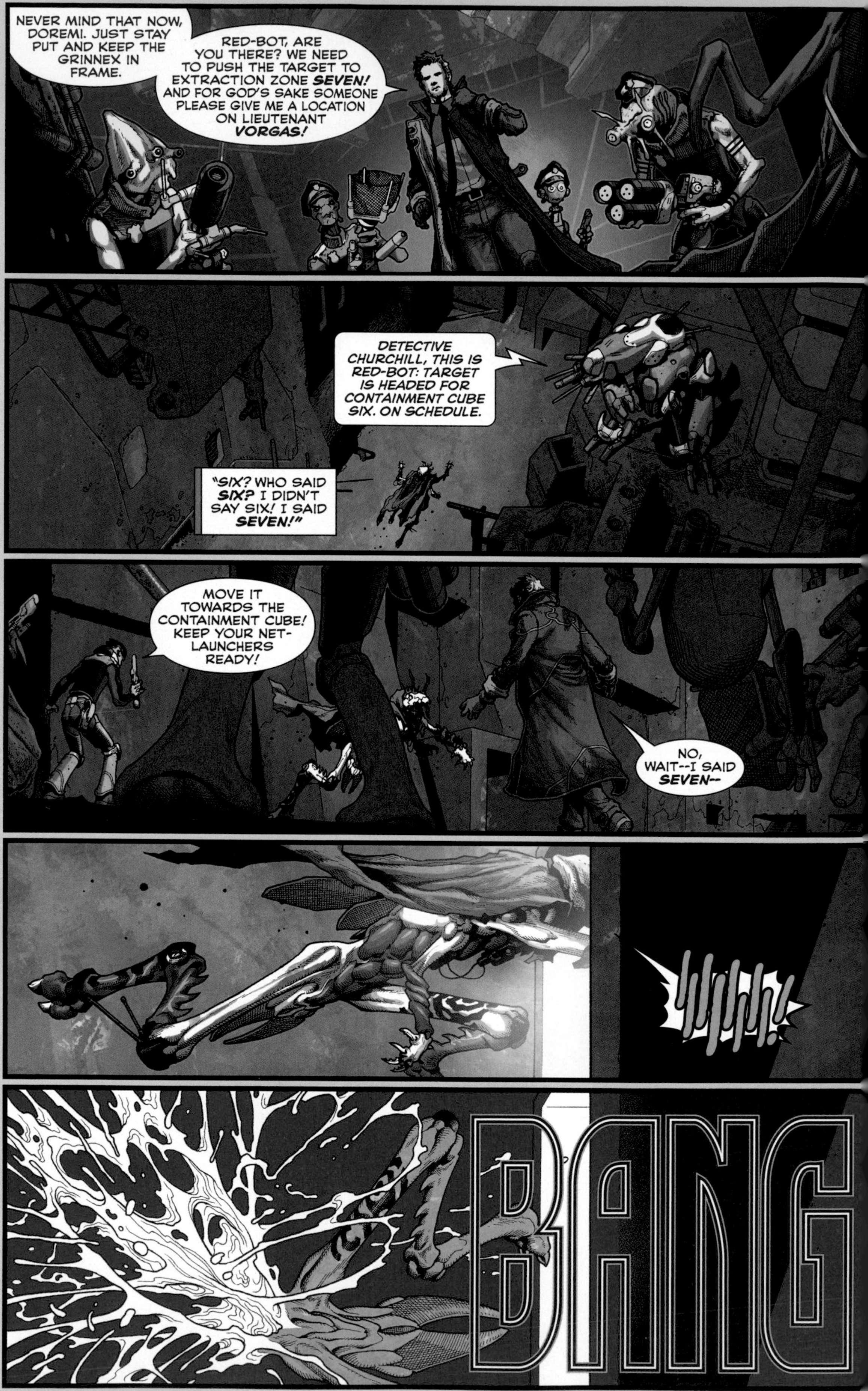
NEVER MIND THAT NOW, DOREMI. JUST STAY PUT AND KEEP THE GRINNEX IN FRAME.
RED-BOT, ARE YOU THERE? WE NEED TO PUSH THE TARGET TO EXTRACTION ZONE SEVEN! AND FOR GOD'S SAKE SOMEONE PLEASE GIVE ME A LOCATION ON LIEUTENANT VORGAS!
DETECTIVE CHURCHILL, THIS IS RED-BOT: TARGET IS HEADED FOR CONTAINMENT CUBE SIX. ON SCHEDULE.
"SIX? WHO SAID SIX? I DIDN'T SAY SIX! I SAID SEVEN!"
MOVE IT TOWARDS THE CONTAINMENT CUBE! KEEP YOUR NET-LAUNCHERS READY!
NO, WAIT--I SAID SEVEN--
BANG

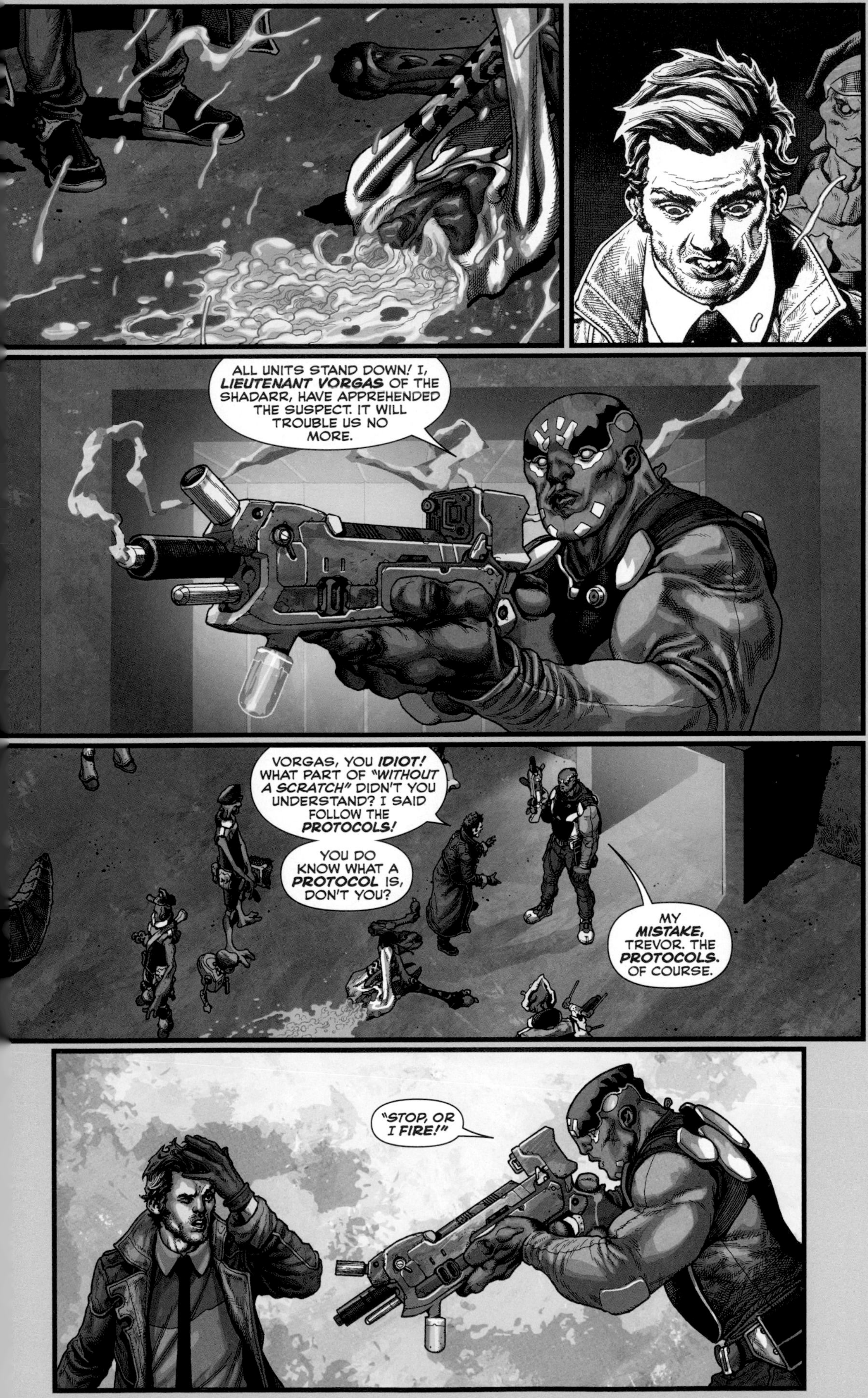
ALL UNITS STAND DOWN! I, LIEUTENANT VORGAS OF THE SHADARR, HAVE APPREHENDED THE SUSPECT. IT WILL TROUBLE US NO MORE.
VORGAS, YOU IDIOT! WHAT PART OF "WITHOUT A SCRATCH" DIDN'T YOU UNDERSTAND? I SAID FOLLOW THE PROTOCOLS!
YOU DO KNOW WHAT A PROTOCOL IS, DON'T YOU?
MY MISTAKE, TREVOR. THE PROTOCOLS. OF COURSE.
"STOP, OR I FIRE!"

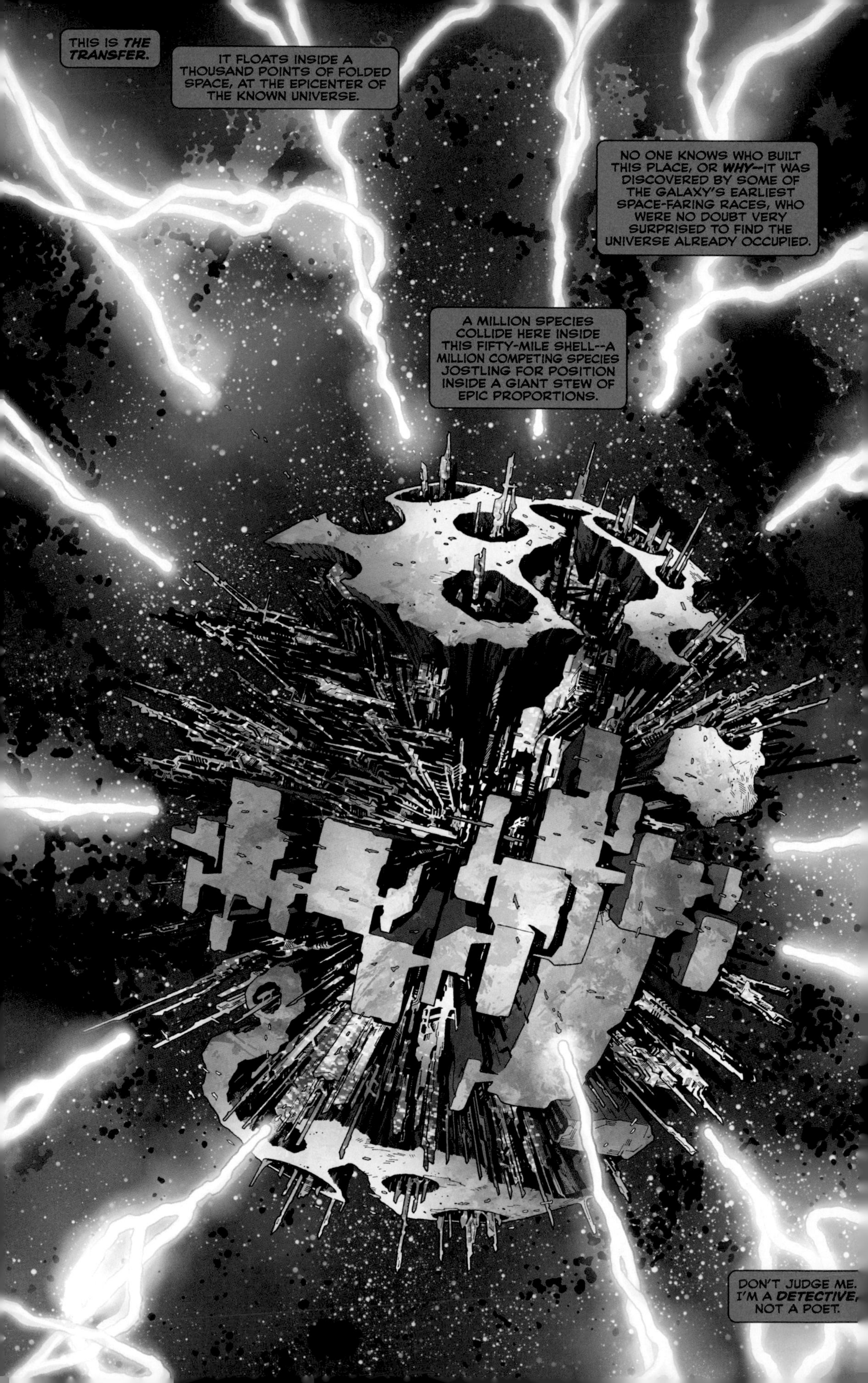
THIS IS THE TRANSFER.
IT FLOATS INSIDE A THOUSAND POINTS OF FOLDED SPACE, AT THE EPICENTER OF THE KNOWN UNIVERSE.
NO ONE KNOWS WHO BUILT THIS PLACE, OR WHY--IT WAS DISCOVERED BY SOME OF THE GALAXY'S EARLIEST SPACE-FARING RACES, WHO WERE NO DOUBT VERY SURPRISED TO FIND THE UNIVERSE ALREADY OCCUPIED.
A MILLION SPECIES COLLIDE HERE INSIDE THIS FIFTY-MILE SHELL--A MILLION COMPETING SPECIES JOSTLING FOR POSITION INSIDE A GIANT STEW OF EPIC PROPORTIONS.
DON'T JUDGE ME. I'M A DETECTIVE, NOT A POET.

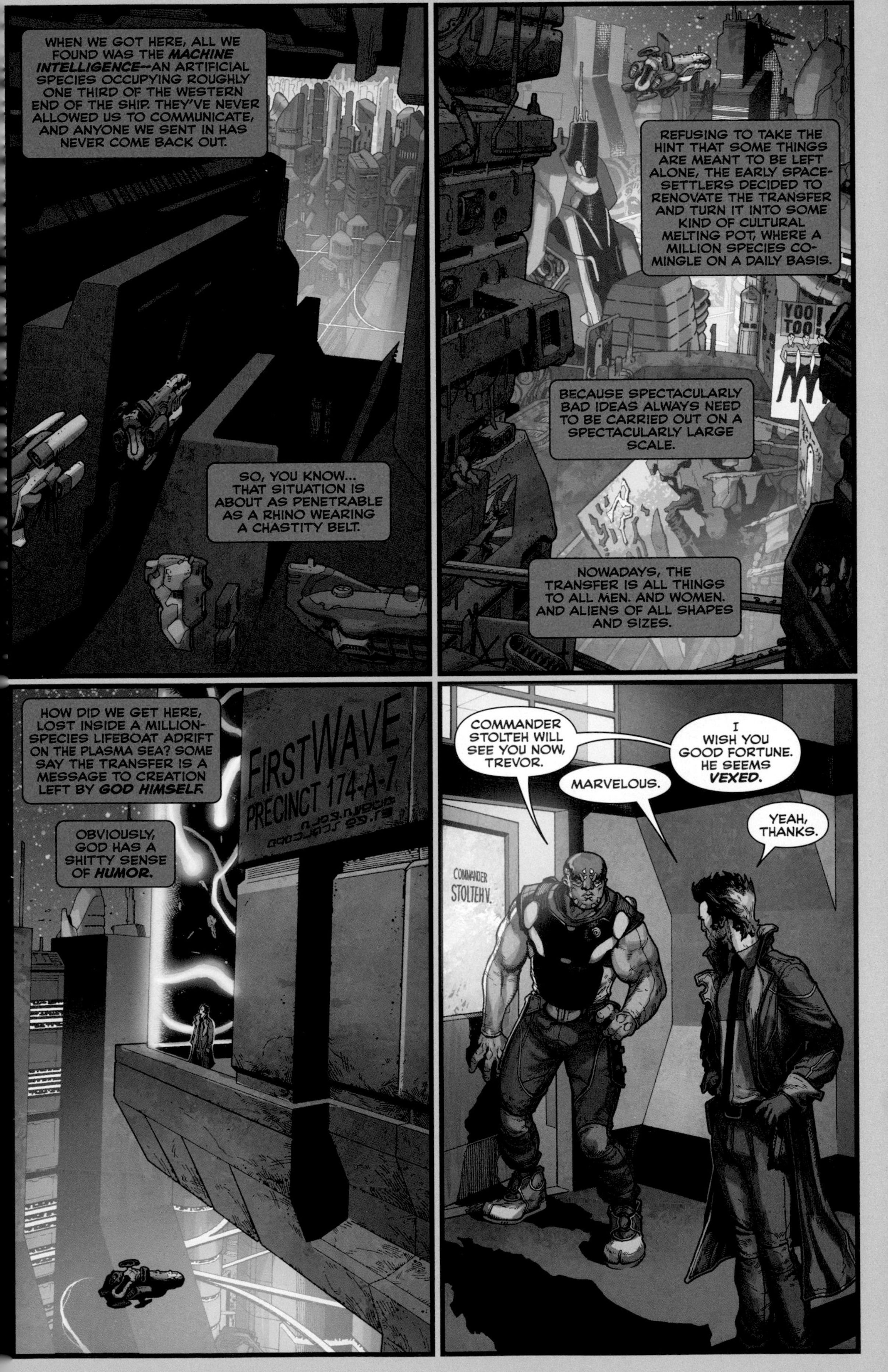
WHEN WE GOT HERE, ALL WE FOUND WAS THE MACHINE INTELLIGENCE--AN ARTIFICIAL SPECIES OCCUPYING ROUGHLY ONE THIRD OF THE WESTERN END OF THE SHIP. THEY'VE NEVER ALLOWED US TO COMMUNICATE, AND ANYONE WE SENT IN HAS NEVER COME BACK OUT.
SO, YOU KNOW... THAT SITUATION IS ABOUT AS PENETRABLE AS A RHINO WEARING A CHASTITY BELT.
REFUSING TO TAKE THE HINT THAT SOME THINGS ARE MEANT TO BE LEFT ALONE, THE EARLY SPACE-SETTLERS DECIDED TO RENOVATE THE TRANSFER AND TURN IT INTO SOME KIND OF CULTURAL MELTING POT, WHERE A MILLION SPECIES CO-MINGLE ON A DAILY BASIS.
YOO! TOO!
BECAUSE SPECTACULARLY BAD IDEAS ALWAYS NEED TO BE CARRIED OUT ON A SPECTACULARLY LARGE SCALE.
NOWADAYS, THE TRANSFER IS ALL THINGS TO ALL MEN. AND WOMEN. AND ALIENS OF ALL SHAPES AND SIZES.
HOW DID WE GET HERE, LOST INSIDE A MILLION-SPECIES LIFEBOAT ADRIFT ON THE PLASMA SEA? SOME SAY THE TRANSFER IS A MESSAGE TO CREATION LEFT BY GOD HIMSELF.
FIRSTWAVE
PRECINCT 174-A-7
OBVIOUSLY, GOD HAS A SHITTY SENSE OF HUMOR.
COMMANDER STOLTEH V.
COMMANDER STOLTEH WILL SEE YOU NOW, TREVOR.
I WISH YOU GOOD FORTUNE. HE SEEMS VEXED.
MARVELOUS.
YEAH, THANKS.

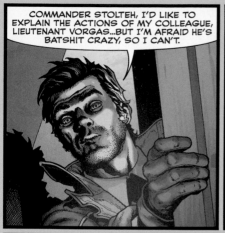

COMMANDER STOLTEH, I'D LIKE TO EXPLAIN THE ACTIONS OF MY COLLEAGUE, LIEUTENANT VORGAS...BUT I'M AFRAID HE'S BATSHIT CRAZY, SO I CAN'T.

DETECTIVE TREVOR CHURCHILL OF THE TERRAN CORPORATION. *JOIN* ME.

TELL ME, WHAT DO YOU SEE OUTSIDE THIS WINDOW?

"LOTS OF LIGHTS, COMMANDER."

"INDEED. EACH ONE REPRESENTING SOME FORM OF ALIEN INTELLIGENCE."

"EXCEPT FOR *VORGAS*, SIR. HE'S AN IDIOT."

"A MILLION DIFFERENT SPECIES, DETECTIVE. TEN BILLION LIFEFORMS. AND IT IS OUR JOB TO *POLICE* THEM."

IT IS NOT, HOWEVER, OUR JOB TO SHOOT GRN'#X*IAN ACOLYTES THROUGH THEIR THORASSIC CAVITIES. I TRUST YOU HAVE AN EXPLANATION?

NO, SIR. THAT'S WHY I'D LIKE TO BE *REASSIGNED*. EFFECTIVE IMMEDIATELY.

REQUEST *DENIED*.

OKAY. I'D LIKE TO RECOMMEND LIEUTENANT VORGAS FOR A COMMENDATION AND A PROMOTION. AND A *TRANSFER*.

YOU'RE NOT GETTING OFF THAT LIGHTLY, CHURCHILL.

I UNDERSTAND YOUR CULTURAL DIFFERENCES ARE CREATING TENSION BETWEEN YOU AND VORGAS.

HE'S NOT USED TO TERRESTRIAL POLICING METHODS--

PLUS, HE'S DUMBER THAN A BOX OF ROCKS WITH THE ROCKS TAKEN OUT, SIR. DON'T FORGET THAT.

"TREVOR, *LISTEN* TO ME-- *FIRSTWAVE* WAS NEVER CREATED TO ESTABLISH THE RULE OF LAW OVER A MILLION SPECIES WITH A MILLION DIFFERENT SETS OF LAWS.

YOO TOO! 50% OFF DEALS!

BUILD YOUR IDENTI-BUDDY TODAY!

"THE BEST WE CAN HOPE FOR IS TO STOP PEOPLE FROM KILLING EACH OTHER. WHICH ISN'T HELPED BY SHOOTING A GRN'#X*IAN DIPLOMAT IN THE THORAX."

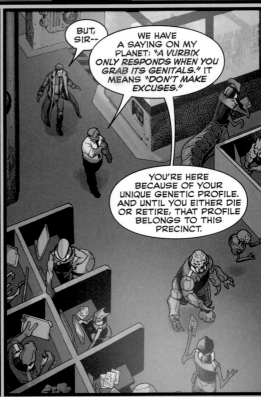

BUT, SIR--

WE HAVE A SAYING ON MY PLANET: *"A VURBIX ONLY RESPONDS WHEN YOU GRAB ITS GENITALS."* IT MEANS *"DON'T MAKE EXCUSES."*

YOU'RE HERE BECAUSE OF YOUR UNIQUE GENETIC PROFILE. AND UNTIL YOU EITHER DIE OR RETIRE, THAT PROFILE BELONGS TO THIS PRECINCT.

HUMANS ALSO HAVE A SAYING, COMMANDER: *"IF YOU WANT SOMETHING DONE RIGHT, DO IT YOURSELF."* HOW AM I SUPPOSED TO GET ANYTHING DONE IF EVERY SPECIES IS ALLOWED TO PLAY BY ITS OWN RULES?

I MEAN, *LOOK* AT THESE IDIOTS!

THAT'S YOUR PROBLEM TO SOLVE. HUMAN LAW GOVERNS THIS PRECINCT, SO IT IS *YOUR JOB* TO MAKE THEM FOLLOW IT.

UNLESS YOU GIVE ME AN ALTERNATIVE, VORGAS REMAINS YOUR PARTNER AND YOUR RESPONSIBILITY.

I CAN'T *THINK* OF AN ALTERNATIVE!

THEN YOU DON'T *HAVE* AN ALTERNATIVE, DETECTIVE.

NOW GET BACK TO WORK AND CATCH ME SOME CRIMINALS.

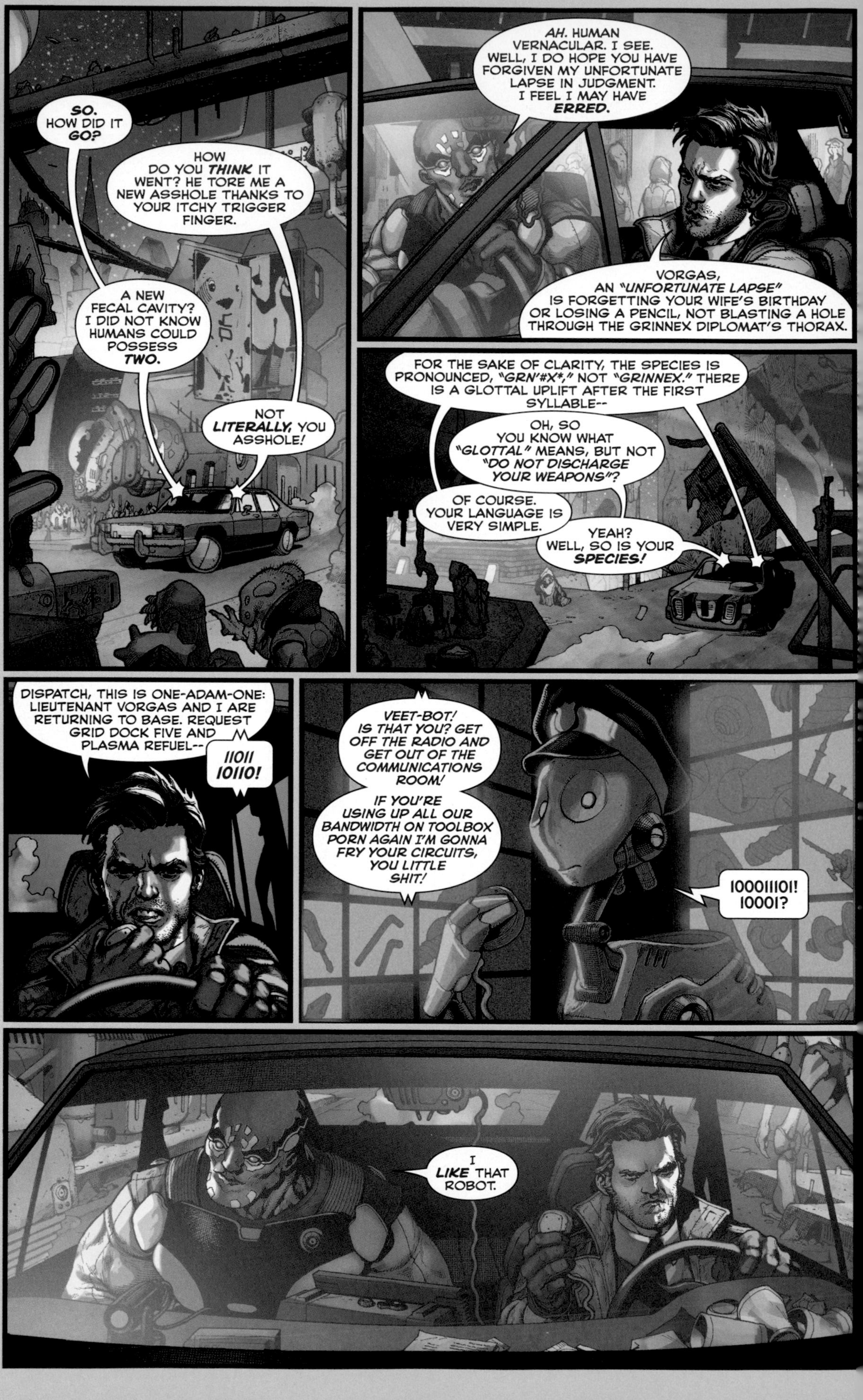
SO. HOW DID IT GO?
HOW DO YOU THINK IT WENT? HE TORE ME A NEW ASSHOLE THANKS TO YOUR ITCHY TRIGGER FINGER.
A NEW FECAL CAVITY? I DID NOT KNOW HUMANS COULD POSSESS TWO.
NOT LITERALLY, YOU ASSHOLE!
AH. HUMAN VERNACULAR. I SEE. WELL, I DO HOPE YOU HAVE FORGIVEN MY UNFORTUNATE LAPSE IN JUDGMENT. I FEEL I MAY HAVE ERRED.
VORGAS, AN "UNFORTUNATE LAPSE" IS FORGETTING YOUR WIFE'S BIRTHDAY OR LOSING A PENCIL, NOT BLASTING A HOLE THROUGH THE GRINNEX DIPLOMAT'S THORAX.
FOR THE SAKE OF CLARITY, THE SPECIES IS PRONOUNCED, "GRN'#X*," NOT "GRINNEX." THERE IS A GLOTTAL UPLIFT AFTER THE FIRST SYLLABLE--
OH, SO YOU KNOW WHAT "GLOTTAL" MEANS, BUT NOT "DO NOT DISCHARGE YOUR WEAPONS"?
OF COURSE. YOUR LANGUAGE IS VERY SIMPLE.
YEAH? WELL, SO IS YOUR SPECIES!
DISPATCH, THIS IS ONE-ADAM-ONE: LIEUTENANT VORGAS AND I ARE RETURNING TO BASE. REQUEST GRID DOCK FIVE AND PLASMA REFUEL--
11011 10110!
VEET-BOT! IS THAT YOU? GET OFF THE RADIO AND GET OUT OF THE COMMUNICATIONS ROOM!
IF YOU'RE USING UP ALL OUR BANDWIDTH ON TOOLBOX PORN AGAIN I'M GONNA FRY YOUR CIRCUITS, YOU LITTLE SHIT!
100011101! 10001?
I LIKE THAT ROBOT.

PERHAPS WE SHOULD CHANGE THE SUBJECT. I WILL NOT MENTION THE GRN'#X* INCIDENT AGAIN--
THAT'S *MENTIONING* IT!
MY APOLOGIES. I AM MERELY TRYING TO OBSERVE PROTOCOL.
YOU'RE MAKING IT *WORSE!*
PROFLAK XTRA WIDTH
[redacted] 50% OFF PURCHASE OF ADDITIONAL CLONE!
JUST... GIVE IT A REST FOR FIVE MINUTES--OKAY, VORGAS? I'M GONNA HAVE TO WORK OUT HOW TO WRITE A REPORT ON ALL OF THIS.
I SWEAR, SOMETIMES I WISH THERE WERE *TWO* OF ME--
YOO TOO! 50% OFF PURCHASE OF ADDITIONAL CLONE!
BUILD YOUR IDENTI-BUDDY TODAY!
SKREEEEEEE
YOO TOO! 50% OFF PURCHASE OF ADDITIONAL CLONE!
BUILD YOUR IDENTI-BUDDY TODAY!
WHAT? WHAT IS IT?
TREVOR?
[redacted] 50% OFF PURCHASE OF ADDITIONAL CLONE!
*WELL,* NOW.

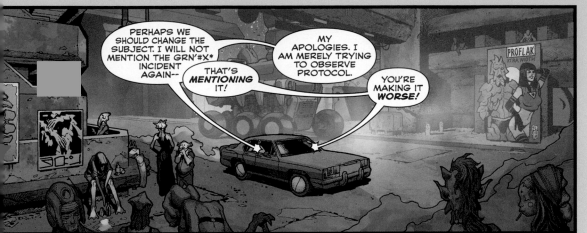

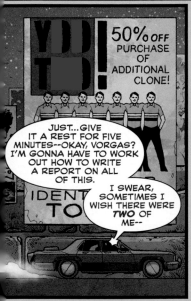

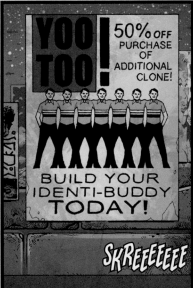

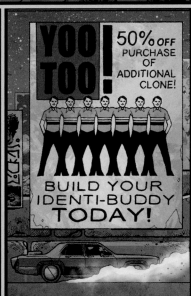

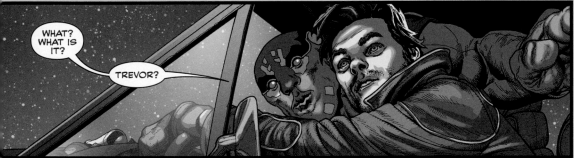

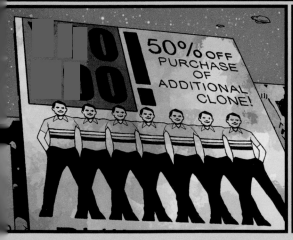

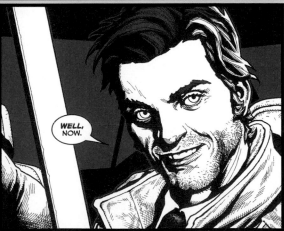

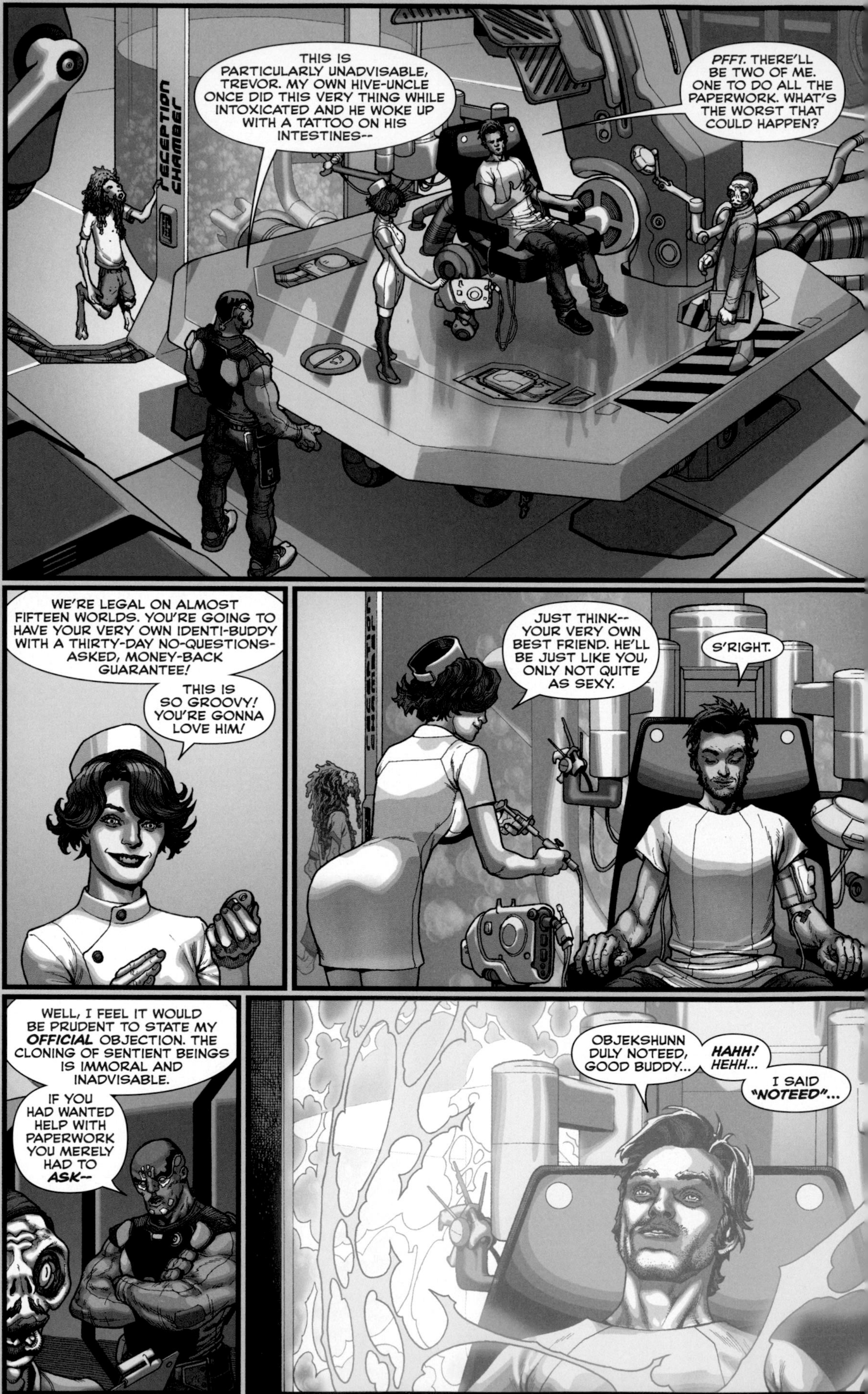
THIS IS PARTICULARLY UNADVISABLE, TREVOR. MY OWN HIVE-UNCLE ONCE DID THIS VERY THING WHILE INTOXICATED AND HE WOKE UP WITH A TATTOO ON HIS INTESTINES--
PFFT. THERE'LL BE TWO OF ME. ONE TO DO ALL THE PAPERWORK. WHAT'S THE WORST THAT COULD HAPPEN?
RECEPTION CHAMBER
WE'RE LEGAL ON ALMOST FIFTEEN WORLDS. YOU'RE GOING TO HAVE YOUR VERY OWN IDENTI-BUDDY WITH A THIRTY-DAY NO-QUESTIONS-ASKED, MONEY-BACK GUARANTEE!
THIS IS SO GROOVY! YOU'RE GONNA LOVE HIM!
JUST THINK-- YOUR VERY OWN BEST FRIEND. HE'LL BE JUST LIKE YOU, ONLY NOT QUITE AS SEXY.
S'RIGHT.
WELL, I FEEL IT WOULD BE PRUDENT TO STATE MY OFFICIAL OBJECTION. THE CLONING OF SENTIENT BEINGS IS IMMORAL AND INADVISABLE.
IF YOU HAD WANTED HELP WITH PAPERWORK YOU MERELY HAD TO ASK--
OBJEKSHUNN DULY NOTEED, GOOD BUDDY...
HAHH! HEHH...
I SAID "NOTEED"...

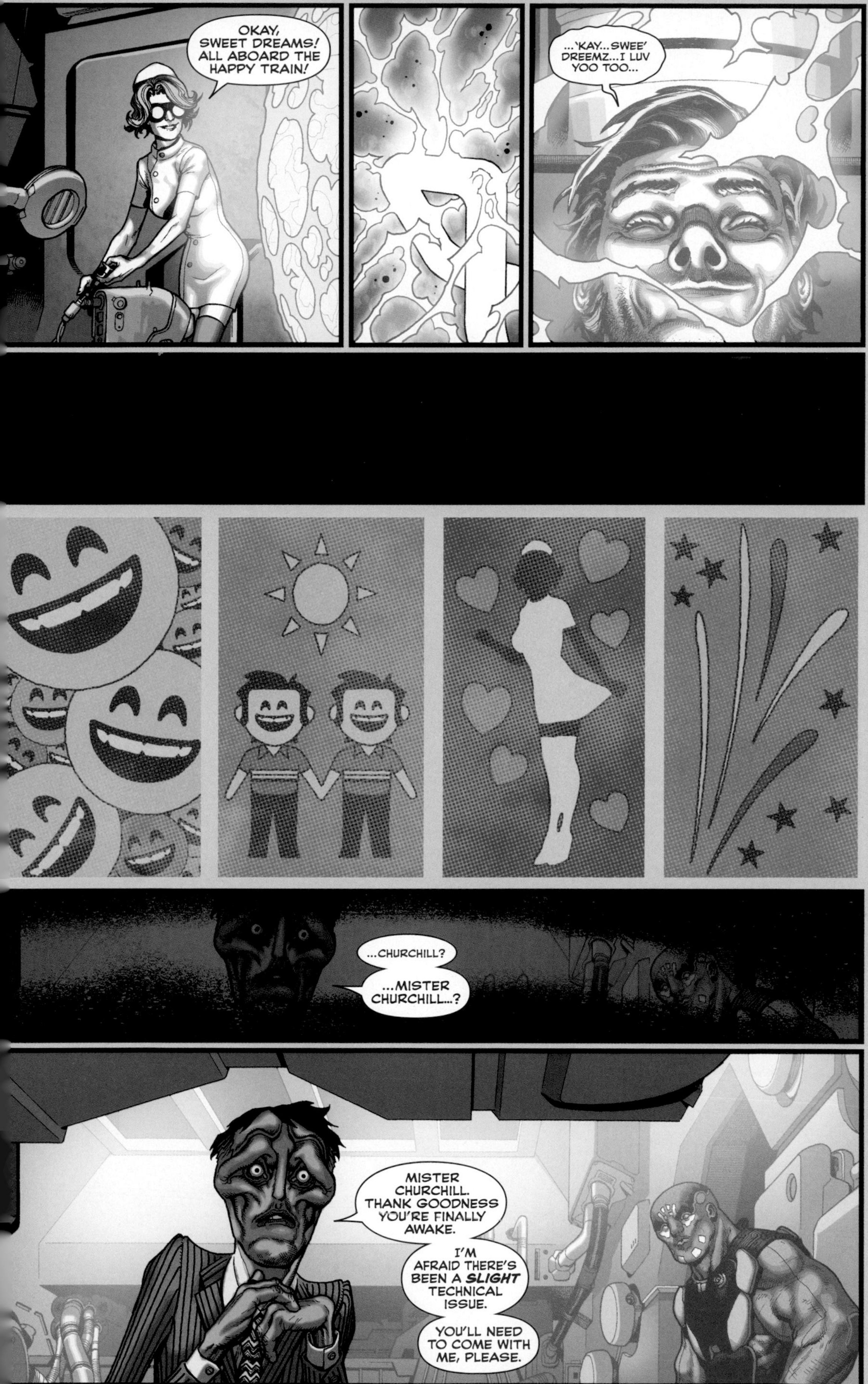
OKAY, SWEET DREAMS! ALL ABOARD THE HAPPY TRAIN!
...'KAY...SWEE' DREEMZ...I LUV YOO TOO...
...CHURCHILL?
...MISTER CHURCHILL...?
MISTER CHURCHILL. THANK GOODNESS YOU'RE FINALLY AWAKE.
I'M AFRAID THERE'S BEEN A *SLIGHT* TECHNICAL ISSUE.
YOU'LL NEED TO COME WITH ME, PLEASE.

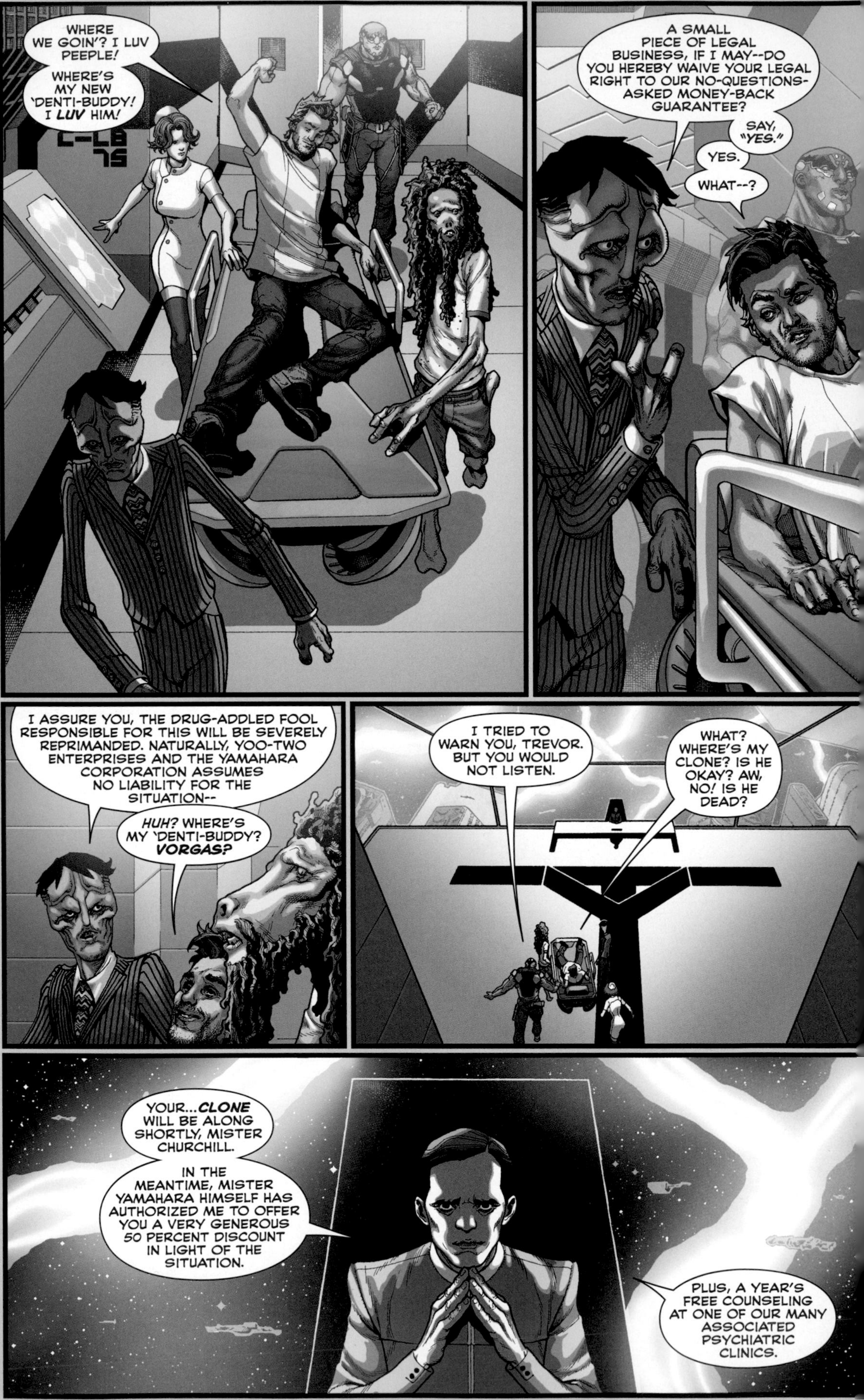
WHERE WE GOIN'? I LUV PEEPLE!
WHERE'S MY NEW 'DENTI-BUDDY! I *LUV* HIM!
C-LB 75
A SMALL PIECE OF LEGAL BUSINESS, IF I MAY--DO YOU HEREBY WAIVE YOUR LEGAL RIGHT TO OUR NO-QUESTIONS-ASKED MONEY-BACK GUARANTEE?
SAY, *"YES."*
YES.
WHAT--?
I ASSURE YOU, THE DRUG-ADDLED FOOL RESPONSIBLE FOR THIS WILL BE SEVERELY REPRIMANDED. NATURALLY, YOO-TWO ENTERPRISES AND THE YAMAHARA CORPORATION ASSUMES NO LIABILITY FOR THE SITUATION--
*HUH?* WHERE'S MY 'DENTI-BUDDY? ***VORGAS?***
I TRIED TO WARN YOU, TREVOR. BUT YOU WOULD NOT LISTEN.
WHAT? WHERE'S MY CLONE? IS HE OKAY? AW, NO! IS HE DEAD?
YOUR...***CLONE*** WILL BE ALONG SHORTLY, MISTER CHURCHILL.
IN THE MEANTIME, MISTER YAMAHARA HIMSELF HAS AUTHORIZED ME TO OFFER YOU A VERY GENEROUS 50 PERCENT DISCOUNT IN LIGHT OF THE SITUATION.
PLUS, A YEAR'S FREE COUNSELING AT ONE OF OUR MANY ASSOCIATED PSYCHIATRIC CLINICS.

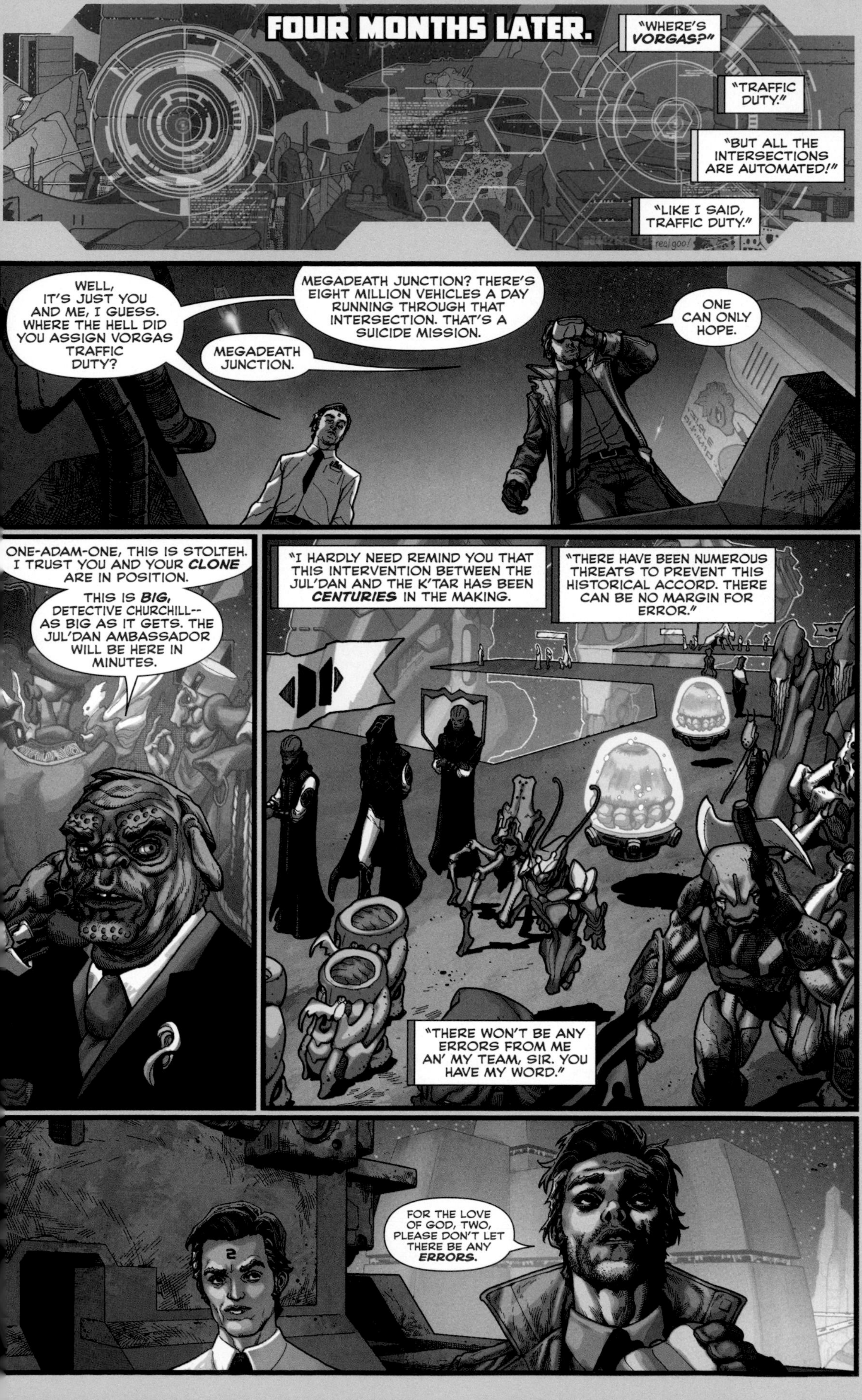
FOUR MONTHS LATER.
"WHERE'S *VORGAS?*"
"TRAFFIC DUTY."
"BUT ALL THE INTERSECTIONS ARE AUTOMATED!"
"LIKE I SAID, TRAFFIC DUTY."
WELL, IT'S JUST YOU AND ME, I GUESS. WHERE THE HELL DID YOU ASSIGN VORGAS TRAFFIC DUTY?
MEGADEATH JUNCTION.
MEGADEATH JUNCTION? THERE'S EIGHT MILLION VEHICLES A DAY RUNNING THROUGH THAT INTERSECTION. THAT'S A SUICIDE MISSION.
ONE CAN ONLY HOPE.
ONE-ADAM-ONE, THIS IS STOLTEH. I TRUST YOU AND YOUR *CLONE* ARE IN POSITION.
THIS IS *BIG,* DETECTIVE CHURCHILL-- AS BIG AS IT GETS. THE JUL'DAN AMBASSADOR WILL BE HERE IN MINUTES.
"I HARDLY NEED REMIND YOU THAT THIS INTERVENTION BETWEEN THE JUL'DAN AND THE K'TAR HAS BEEN *CENTURIES* IN THE MAKING.
"THERE HAVE BEEN NUMEROUS THREATS TO PREVENT THIS HISTORICAL ACCORD. THERE CAN BE NO MARGIN FOR ERROR."
"THERE WON'T BE ANY ERRORS FROM ME AN' MY TEAM, SIR. YOU HAVE MY WORD."
FOR THE LOVE OF GOD, TWO, PLEASE DON'T LET THERE BE ANY *ERRORS.*

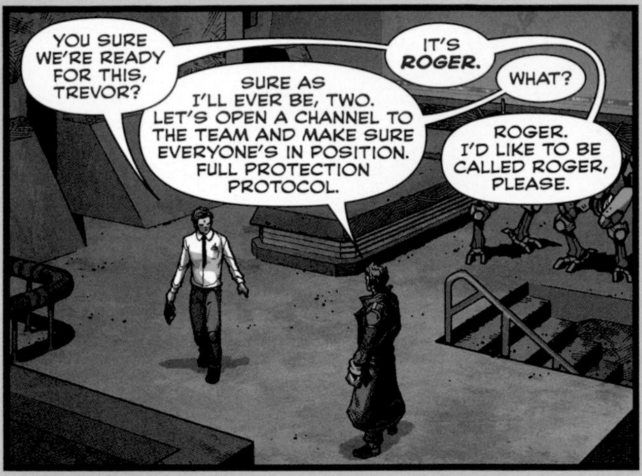
YOU SURE WE'RE READY FOR THIS, TREVOR?
SURE AS I'LL EVER BE, TWO. LET'S OPEN A CHANNEL TO THE TEAM AND MAKE SURE EVERYONE'S IN POSITION. FULL PROTECTION PROTOCOL.
IT'S ***ROGER.***
WHAT?
ROGER. I'D LIKE TO BE CALLED ROGER, PLEASE.

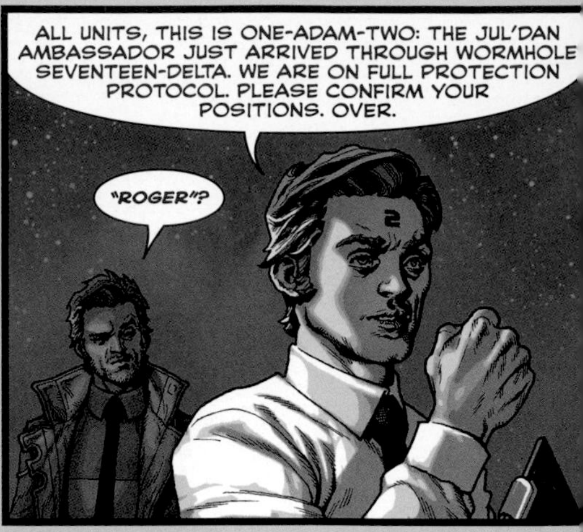
ALL UNITS, THIS IS ONE-ADAM-TWO: THE JUL'DAN AMBASSADOR JUST ARRIVED THROUGH WORMHOLE SEVENTEEN-DELTA. WE ARE ON FULL PROTECTION PROTOCOL. PLEASE CONFIRM YOUR POSITIONS. OVER.
*"ROGER"?*

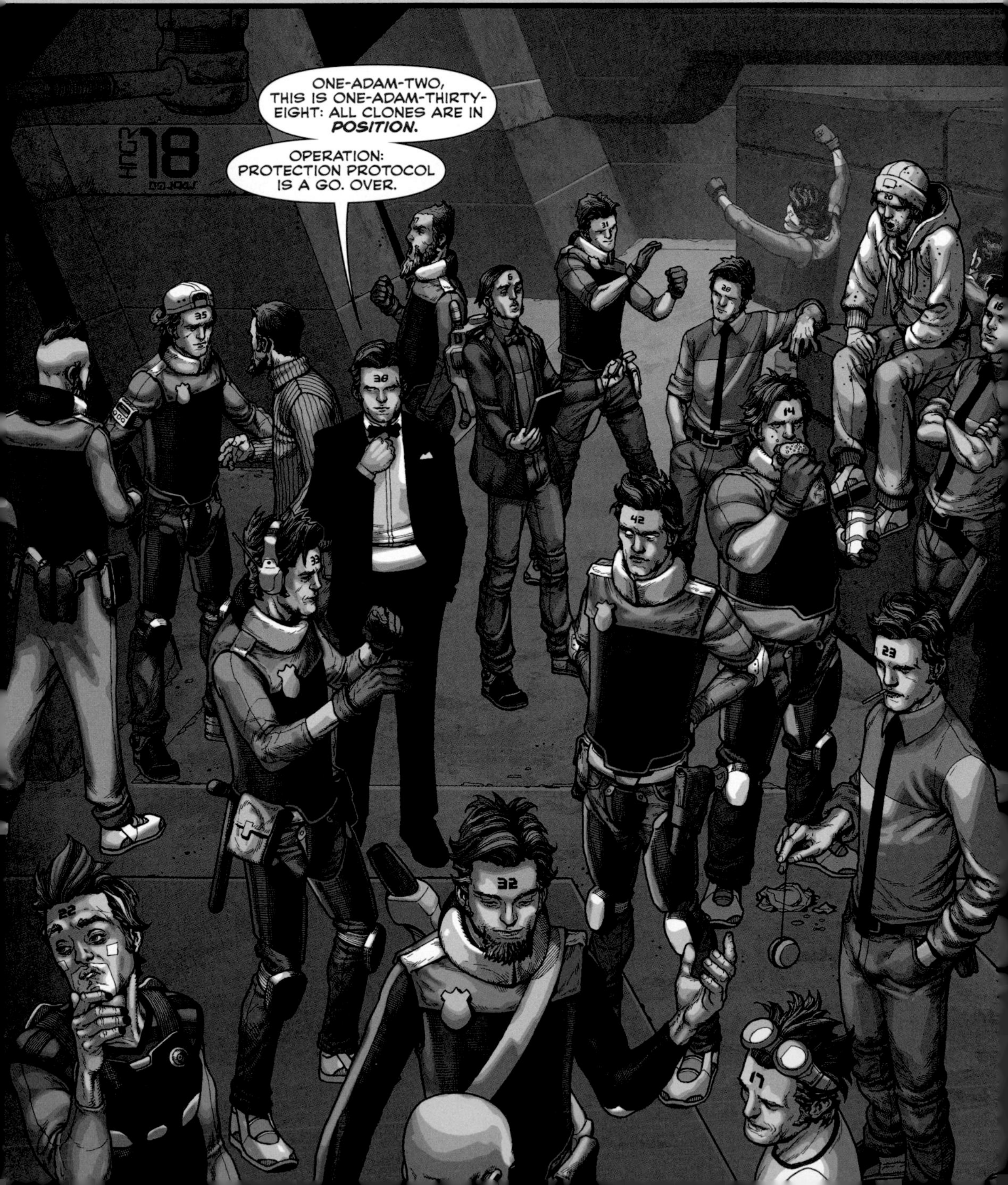
ONE-ADAM-TWO, THIS IS ONE-ADAM-THIRTY-EIGHT: ALL CLONES ARE IN ***POSITION.***
OPERATION: PROTECTION PROTOCOL IS A GO. OVER.

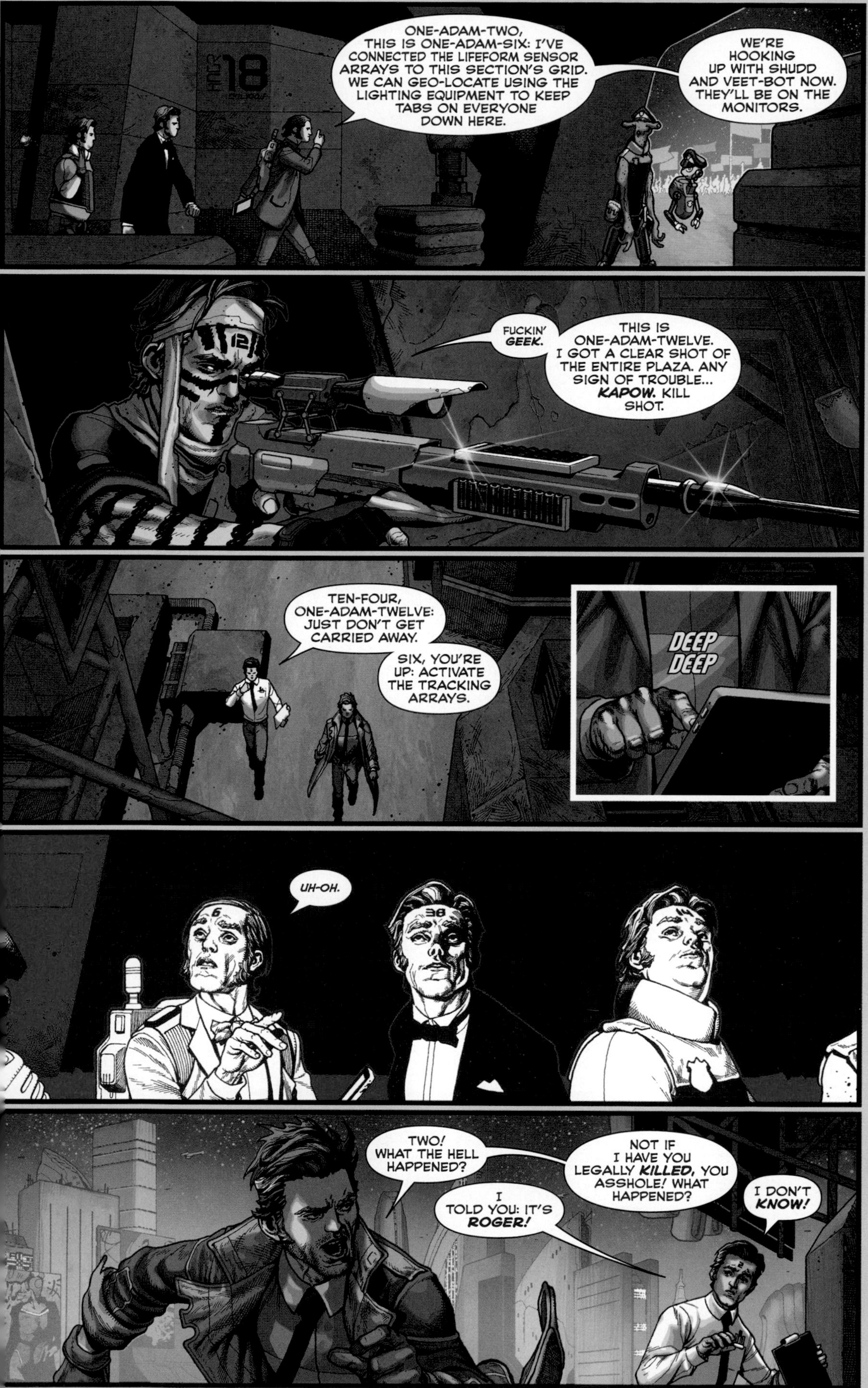
ONE-ADAM-TWO, THIS IS ONE-ADAM-SIX: I'VE CONNECTED THE LIFEFORM SENSOR ARRAYS TO THIS SECTION'S GRID. WE CAN GEO-LOCATE USING THE LIGHTING EQUIPMENT TO KEEP TABS ON EVERYONE DOWN HERE.
WE'RE HOOKING UP WITH SHUDD AND VEET-BOT NOW. THEY'LL BE ON THE MONITORS.
FUCKIN' GEEK.
THIS IS ONE-ADAM-TWELVE. I GOT A CLEAR SHOT OF THE ENTIRE PLAZA. ANY SIGN OF TROUBLE... KAPOW. KILL SHOT.
TEN-FOUR, ONE-ADAM-TWELVE: JUST DON'T GET CARRIED AWAY.
SIX, YOU'RE UP: ACTIVATE THE TRACKING ARRAYS.
DEEP DEEP
UH-OH.
TWO! WHAT THE HELL HAPPENED?
I TOLD YOU: IT'S ROGER!
NOT IF I HAVE YOU LEGALLY KILLED, YOU ASSHOLE! WHAT HAPPENED?
I DON'T KNOW!

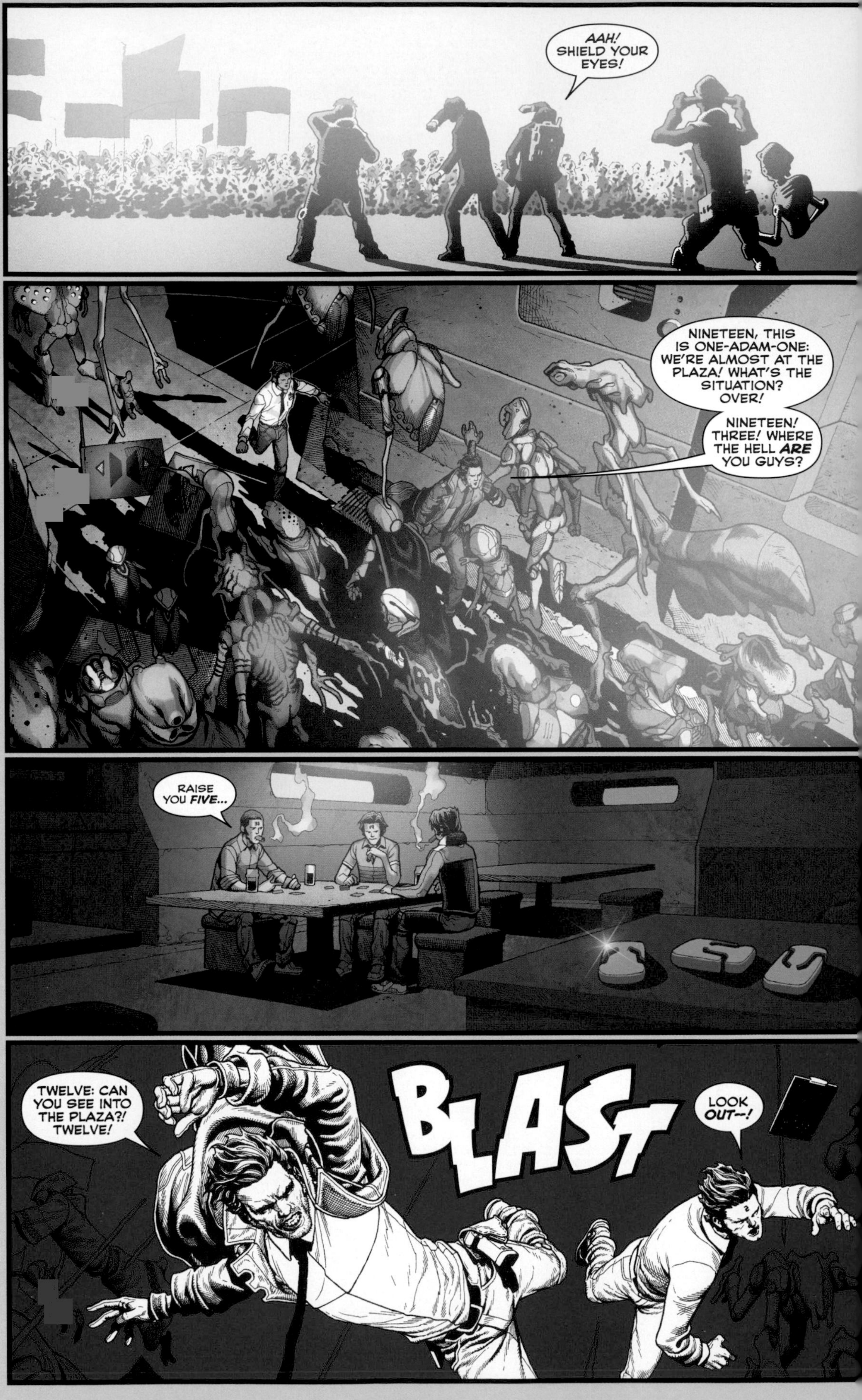
AAH! SHIELD YOUR EYES!
NINETEEN, THIS IS ONE-ADAM-ONE: WE'RE ALMOST AT THE PLAZA! WHAT'S THE SITUATION? OVER!
NINETEEN! THREE! WHERE THE HELL ARE YOU GUYS?
RAISE YOU FIVE...
TWELVE: CAN YOU SEE INTO THE PLAZA?! TWELVE!
BLAST
LOOK OUT--!

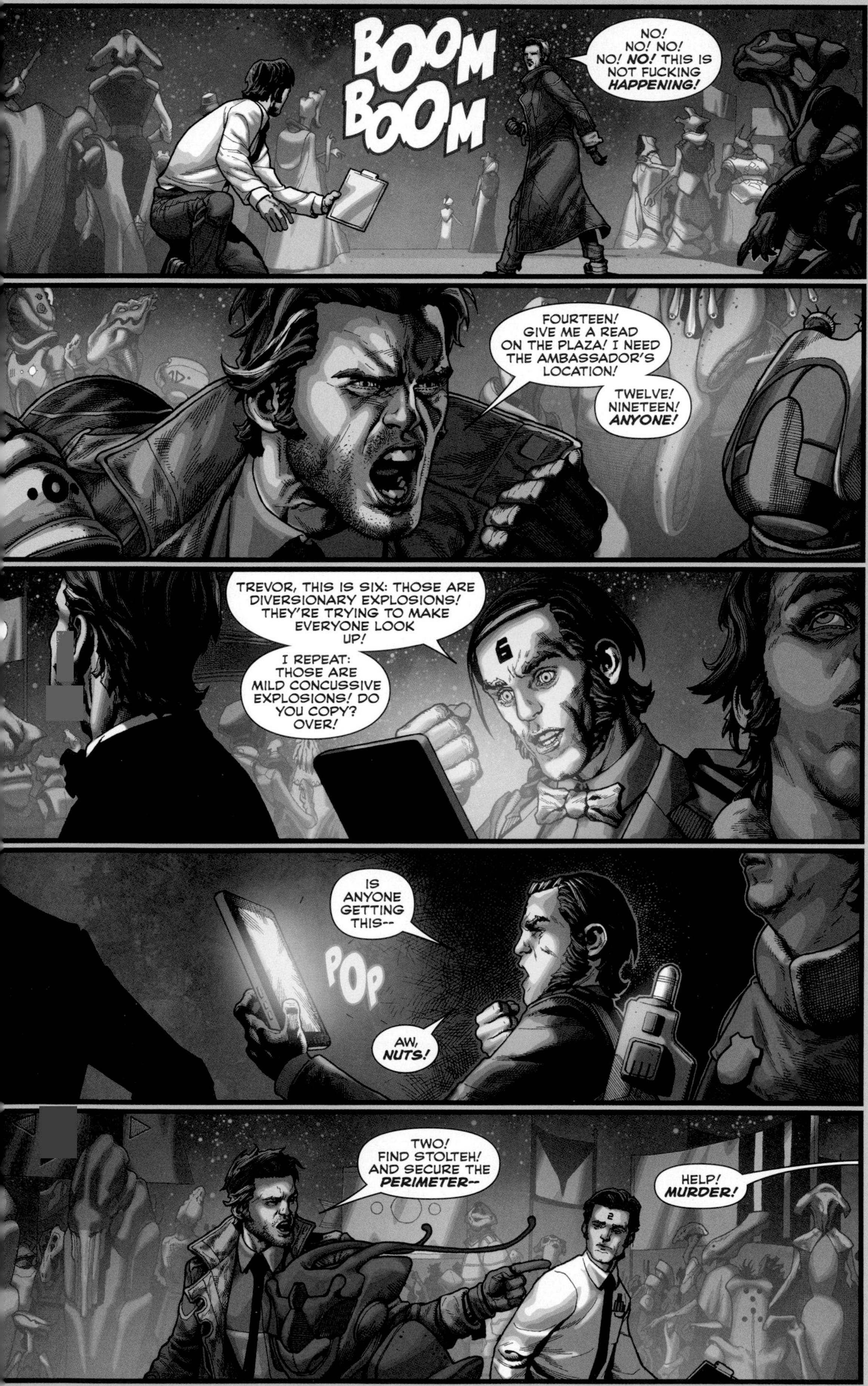
BOOM BOOM
NO! NO! NO! NO! NO! THIS IS NOT FUCKING HAPPENING!
FOURTEEN! GIVE ME A READ ON THE PLAZA! I NEED THE AMBASSADOR'S LOCATION!
TWELVE! NINETEEN! ANYONE!
TREVOR, THIS IS SIX: THOSE ARE DIVERSIONARY EXPLOSIONS! THEY'RE TRYING TO MAKE EVERYONE LOOK UP!
I REPEAT: THOSE ARE MILD CONCUSSIVE EXPLOSIONS! DO YOU COPY? OVER!
IS ANYONE GETTING THIS--
POP
AW, NUTS!
TWO! FIND STOLTEH! AND SECURE THE PERIMETER--
HELP! MURDER!

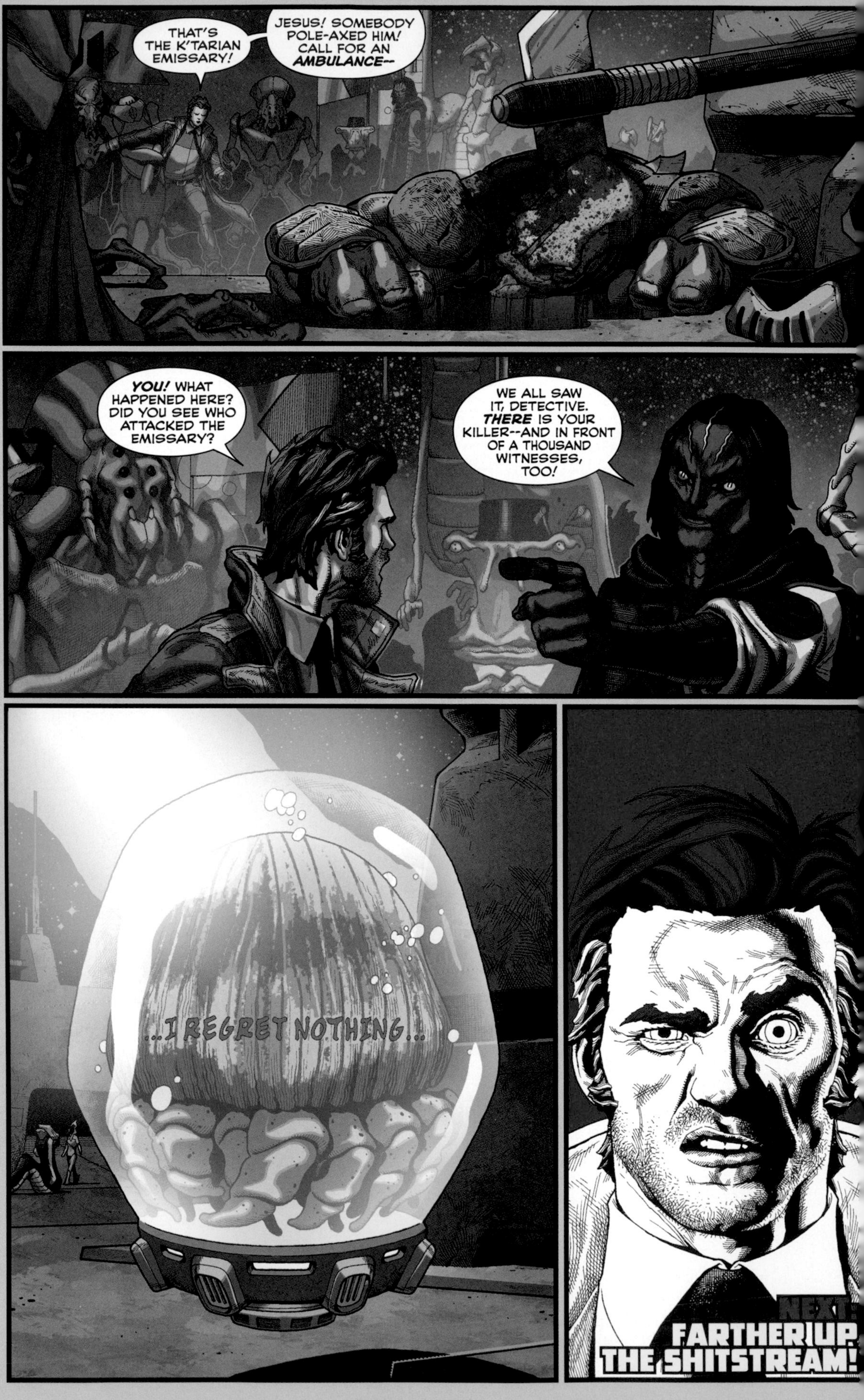
THAT'S THE K'TARIAN EMISSARY!
JESUS! SOMEBODY POLE-AXED HIM! CALL FOR AN AMBULANCE--
YOU! WHAT HAPPENED HERE? DID YOU SEE WHO ATTACKED THE EMISSARY?
WE ALL SAW IT, DETECTIVE. THERE IS YOUR KILLER--AND IN FRONT OF A THOUSAND WITNESSES, TOO!
...I REGRET NOTHING...
NEXT: FARTHER UP THE SHITSTREAM!

# 2

## "NUMBER TWO"

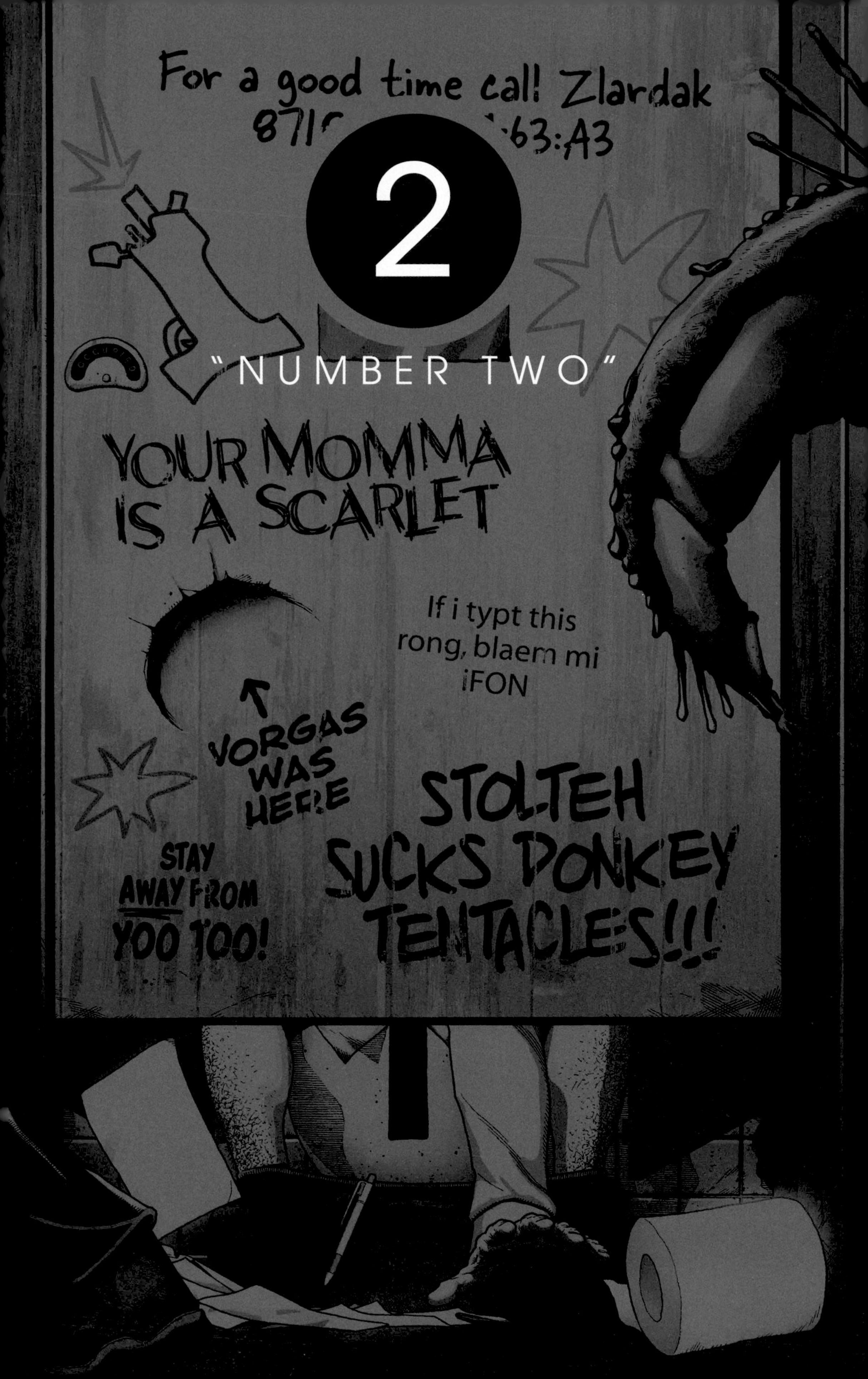
For a good time call! Zlardak
YOUR MOMMA IS A SCARLET
If i typt this rong, blaem mi iFON
VORGAS WAS HERE
STAY AWAY FROM YOO TOO!
STOLTEH SUCKS DONKEY TENTACLES!!!

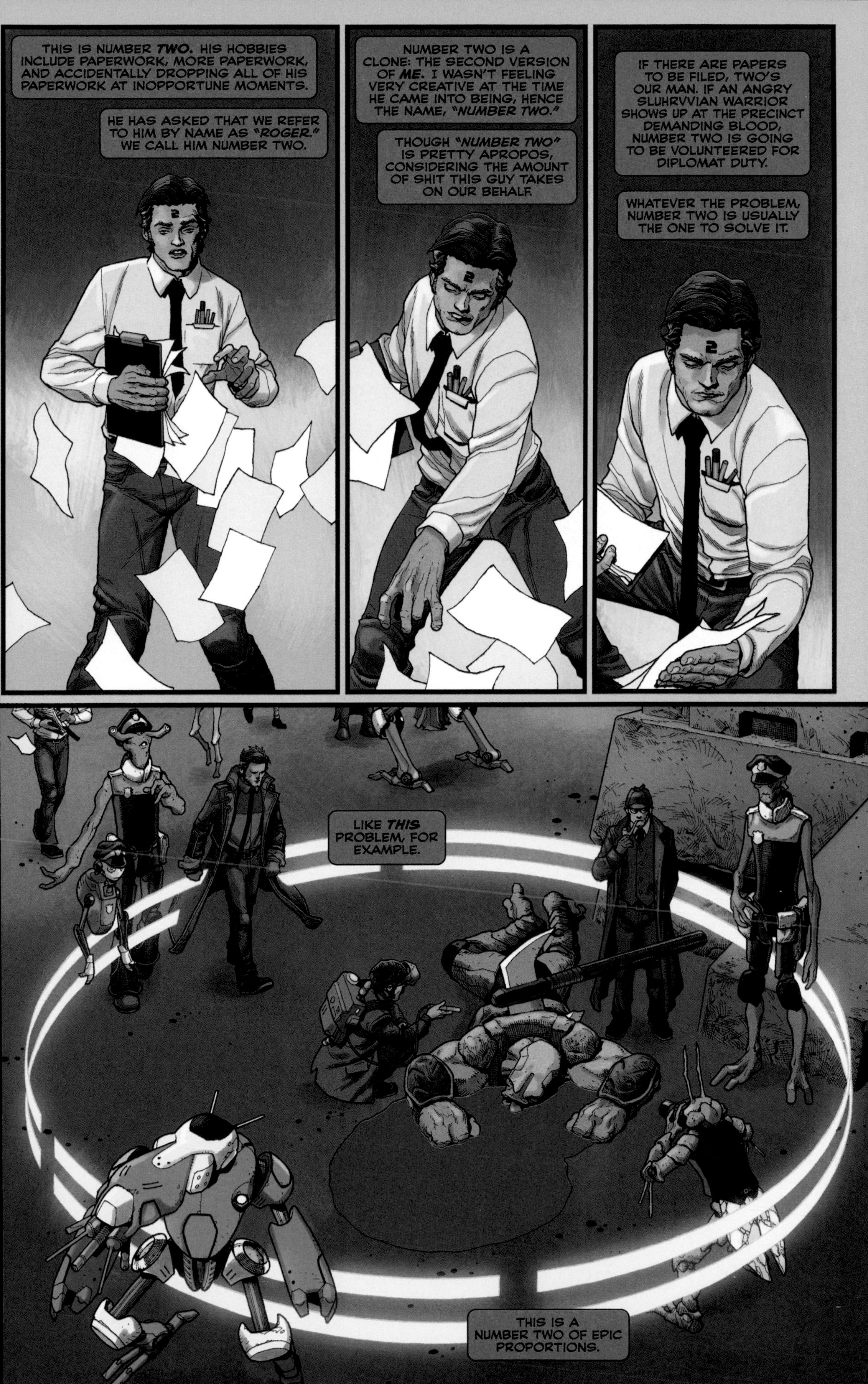
THIS IS NUMBER TWO. HIS HOBBIES INCLUDE PAPERWORK, MORE PAPERWORK, AND ACCIDENTALLY DROPPING ALL OF HIS PAPERWORK AT INOPPORTUNE MOMENTS.
HE HAS ASKED THAT WE REFER TO HIM BY NAME AS "ROGER." WE CALL HIM NUMBER TWO.
NUMBER TWO IS A CLONE: THE SECOND VERSION OF ME. I WASN'T FEELING VERY CREATIVE AT THE TIME HE CAME INTO BEING, HENCE THE NAME, "NUMBER TWO."
THOUGH "NUMBER TWO" IS PRETTY APROPOS, CONSIDERING THE AMOUNT OF SHIT THIS GUY TAKES ON OUR BEHALF.
IF THERE ARE PAPERS TO BE FILED, TWO'S OUR MAN. IF AN ANGRY SLUHRVVIAN WARRIOR SHOWS UP AT THE PRECINCT DEMANDING BLOOD, NUMBER TWO IS GOING TO BE VOLUNTEERED FOR DIPLOMAT DUTY.
WHATEVER THE PROBLEM, NUMBER TWO IS USUALLY THE ONE TO SOLVE IT.
LIKE THIS PROBLEM, FOR EXAMPLE.
THIS IS A NUMBER TWO OF EPIC PROPORTIONS.

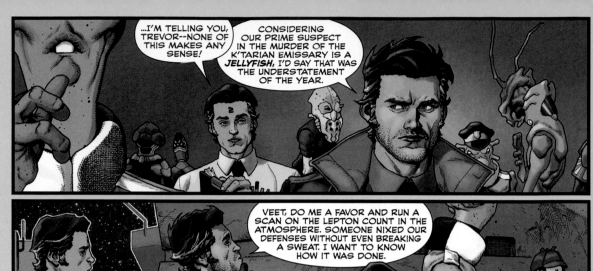

...I'M TELLING YOU, TREVOR--NONE OF THIS MAKES ANY SENSE!

CONSIDERING OUR PRIME SUSPECT IN THE MURDER OF THE K'TARIAN EMISSARY IS A *JELLYFISH*, I'D SAY THAT WAS THE UNDERSTATEMENT OF THE YEAR.

VEET, DO ME A FAVOR AND RUN A SCAN ON THE LEPTON COUNT IN THE ATMOSPHERE. SOMEONE NIXED OUR DEFENSES WITHOUT EVEN BREAKING A SWEAT. I WANT TO KNOW HOW IT WAS DONE.

100001 1001!

TREVOR, NO ONE NIXED ANYTHING! THE TECHNOLOGY DOESN'T EXIST TO DISMANTLE LEPTONIC SURVEILLANCE SYSTEMS!

THIS WAS AN INSIDE JOB! WHY WON'T ANY OF YOU *LISTEN* TO ME?

100 010010?

VEET'S GOT A POINT. TWO, CAN YOU MAKE A NOTE OF THAT?

GOT IT.

TREVOR, I THINK WE'VE STUMBLED ON SOMETHING. THE FORCE OF THE BLOW, COMBINED WITH THE ANGLE OF ATTACK SUGGESTS THE JUL'DANIAN AMBASSADOR COULD NOT HAVE BEEN THE KILLER.

RIGHT. PLUS, HE'S A JELLYFISH.

WE'RE OBLIGED TO CONSIDER ALL POSSIBILITIES.

THEY BUSTED THROUGH OUR PERIMETER. HOW THE HELL DID THEY BUST THROUGH OUR PERIMETER...?

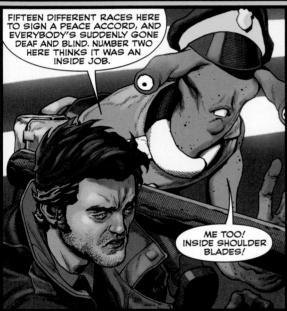

FIFTEEN DIFFERENT RACES HERE TO SIGN A PEACE ACCORD, AND EVERYBODY'S SUDDENLY GONE DEAF AND BLIND. NUMBER TWO HERE THINKS IT WAS AN INSIDE JOB.

ME TOO! INSIDE SHOULDER BLADES!

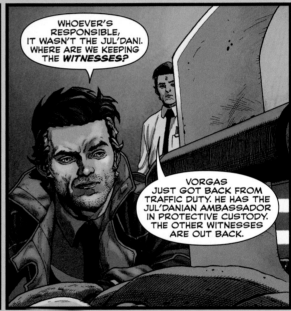

WHOEVER'S RESPONSIBLE, IT WASN'T THE JUL'DANI. WHERE ARE WE KEEPING THE *WITNESSES*?

VORGAS JUST GOT BACK FROM TRAFFIC DUTY. HE HAS THE JUL'DANIAN AMBASSADOR IN PROTECTIVE CUSTODY. THE OTHER WITNESSES ARE OUT BACK.

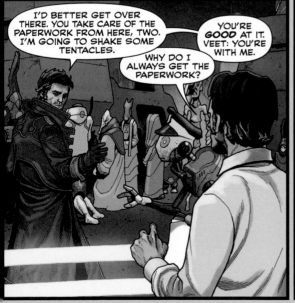

I'D BETTER GET OVER THERE. YOU TAKE CARE OF THE PAPERWORK FROM HERE, TWO. I'M GOING TO SHAKE SOME TENTACLES.

YOU'RE *GOOD* AT IT. VEET: YOU'RE WITH ME.

WHY DO I ALWAYS GET THE PAPERWORK?

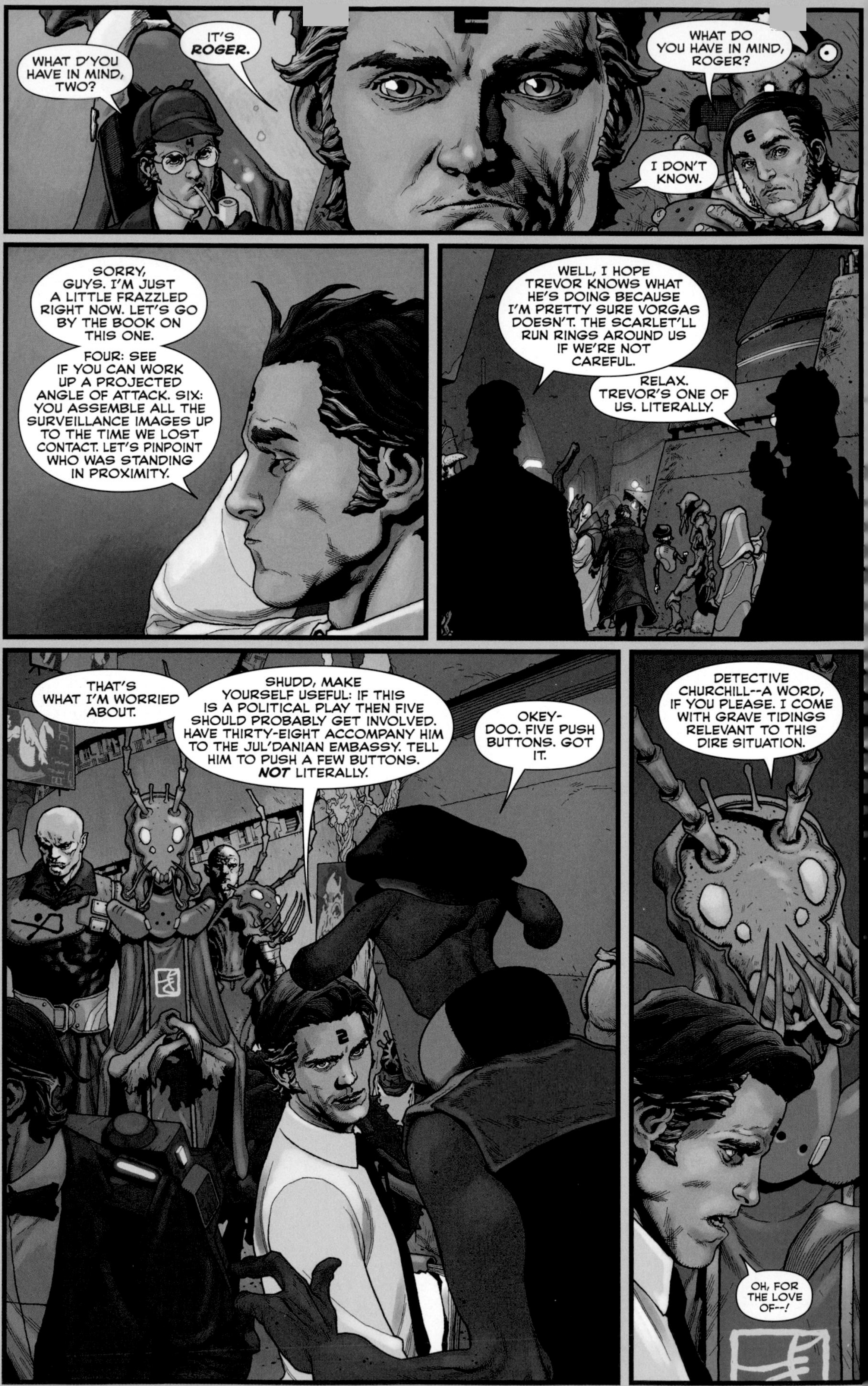
WHAT D'YOU HAVE IN MIND, TWO?
IT'S *ROGER.*
WHAT DO YOU HAVE IN MIND, ROGER?
I DON'T KNOW.
SORRY, GUYS. I'M JUST A LITTLE FRAZZLED RIGHT NOW. LET'S GO BY THE BOOK ON THIS ONE.
FOUR: SEE IF YOU CAN WORK UP A PROJECTED ANGLE OF ATTACK. SIX: YOU ASSEMBLE ALL THE SURVEILLANCE IMAGES UP TO THE TIME WE LOST CONTACT. LET'S PINPOINT WHO WAS STANDING IN PROXIMITY.
WELL, I HOPE TREVOR KNOWS WHAT HE'S DOING BECAUSE I'M PRETTY SURE VORGAS DOESN'T. THE SCARLET'LL RUN RINGS AROUND US IF WE'RE NOT CAREFUL.
RELAX. TREVOR'S ONE OF US. LITERALLY.
THAT'S WHAT I'M WORRIED ABOUT.
SHUDD, MAKE YOURSELF USEFUL: IF THIS IS A POLITICAL PLAY THEN FIVE SHOULD PROBABLY GET INVOLVED. HAVE THIRTY-EIGHT ACCOMPANY HIM TO THE JUL'DANIAN EMBASSY. TELL HIM TO PUSH A FEW BUTTONS. ***NOT*** LITERALLY.
OKEY-DOO. FIVE PUSH BUTTONS. GOT IT.
DETECTIVE CHURCHILL--A WORD, IF YOU PLEASE. I COME WITH GRAVE TIDINGS RELEVANT TO THIS DIRE SITUATION.
OH, FOR THE LOVE OF--!

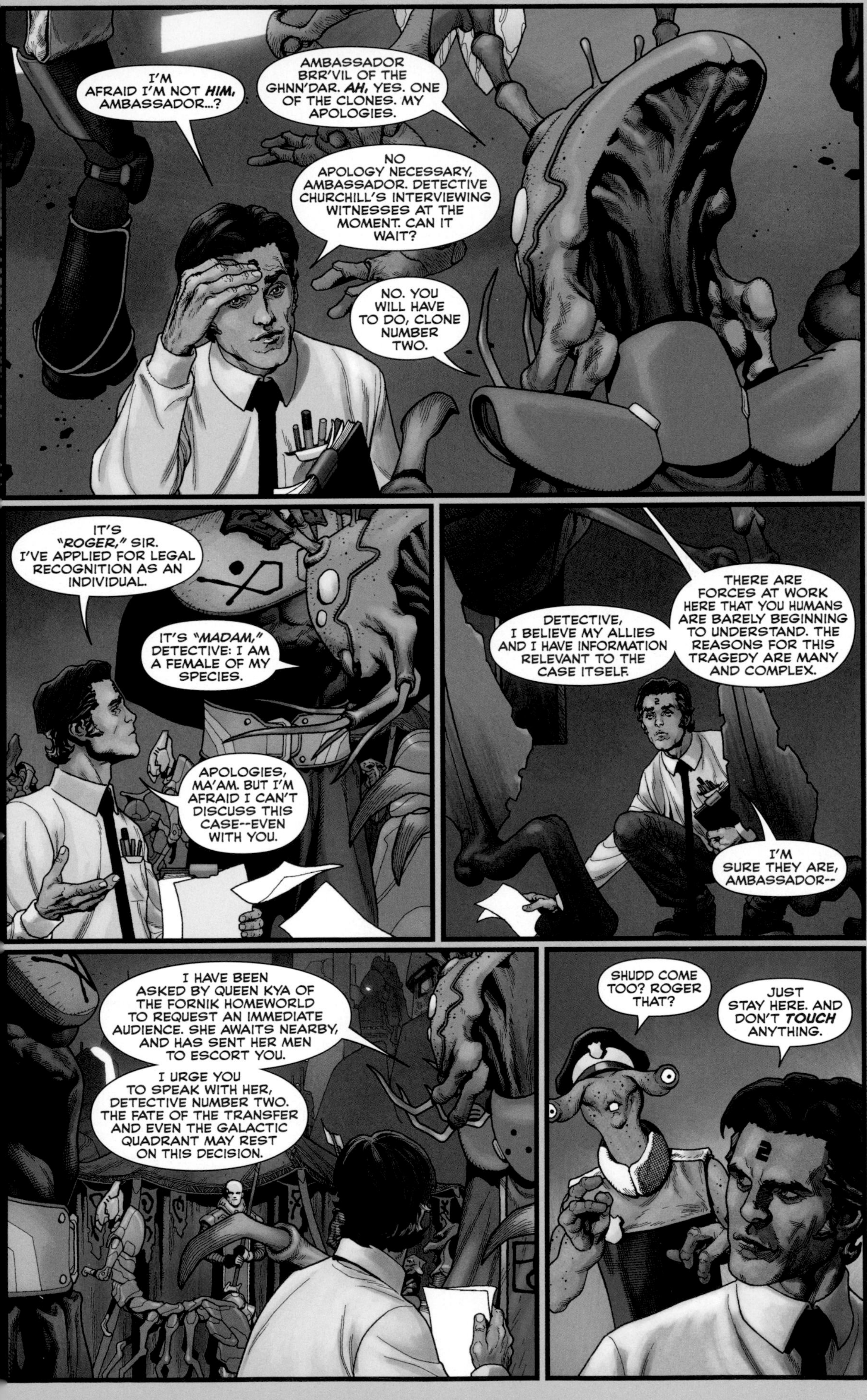
I'M AFRAID I'M NOT *HIM*, AMBASSADOR...?
AMBASSADOR BRR'VIL OF THE GHNN'DAR. *AH,* YES. ONE OF THE CLONES. MY APOLOGIES.
NO APOLOGY NECESSARY, AMBASSADOR. DETECTIVE CHURCHILL'S INTERVIEWING WITNESSES AT THE MOMENT. CAN IT WAIT?
NO. YOU WILL HAVE TO DO, CLONE NUMBER TWO.
IT'S "*ROGER,*" SIR. I'VE APPLIED FOR LEGAL RECOGNITION AS AN INDIVIDUAL.
IT'S "*MADAM,*" DETECTIVE: I AM A FEMALE OF MY SPECIES.
APOLOGIES, MA'AM. BUT I'M AFRAID I CAN'T DISCUSS THIS CASE--EVEN WITH YOU.
DETECTIVE, I BELIEVE MY ALLIES AND I HAVE INFORMATION RELEVANT TO THE CASE ITSELF.
THERE ARE FORCES AT WORK HERE THAT YOU HUMANS ARE BARELY BEGINNING TO UNDERSTAND. THE REASONS FOR THIS TRAGEDY ARE MANY AND COMPLEX.
I'M SURE THEY ARE, AMBASSADOR--
I HAVE BEEN ASKED BY QUEEN KYA OF THE FORNIK HOMEWORLD TO REQUEST AN IMMEDIATE AUDIENCE. SHE AWAITS NEARBY, AND HAS SENT HER MEN TO ESCORT YOU.
I URGE YOU TO SPEAK WITH HER, DETECTIVE NUMBER TWO. THE FATE OF THE TRANSFER AND EVEN THE GALACTIC QUADRANT MAY REST ON THIS DECISION.
SHUDD COME TOO? ROGER THAT?
JUST STAY HERE. AND DON'T *TOUCH* ANYTHING.

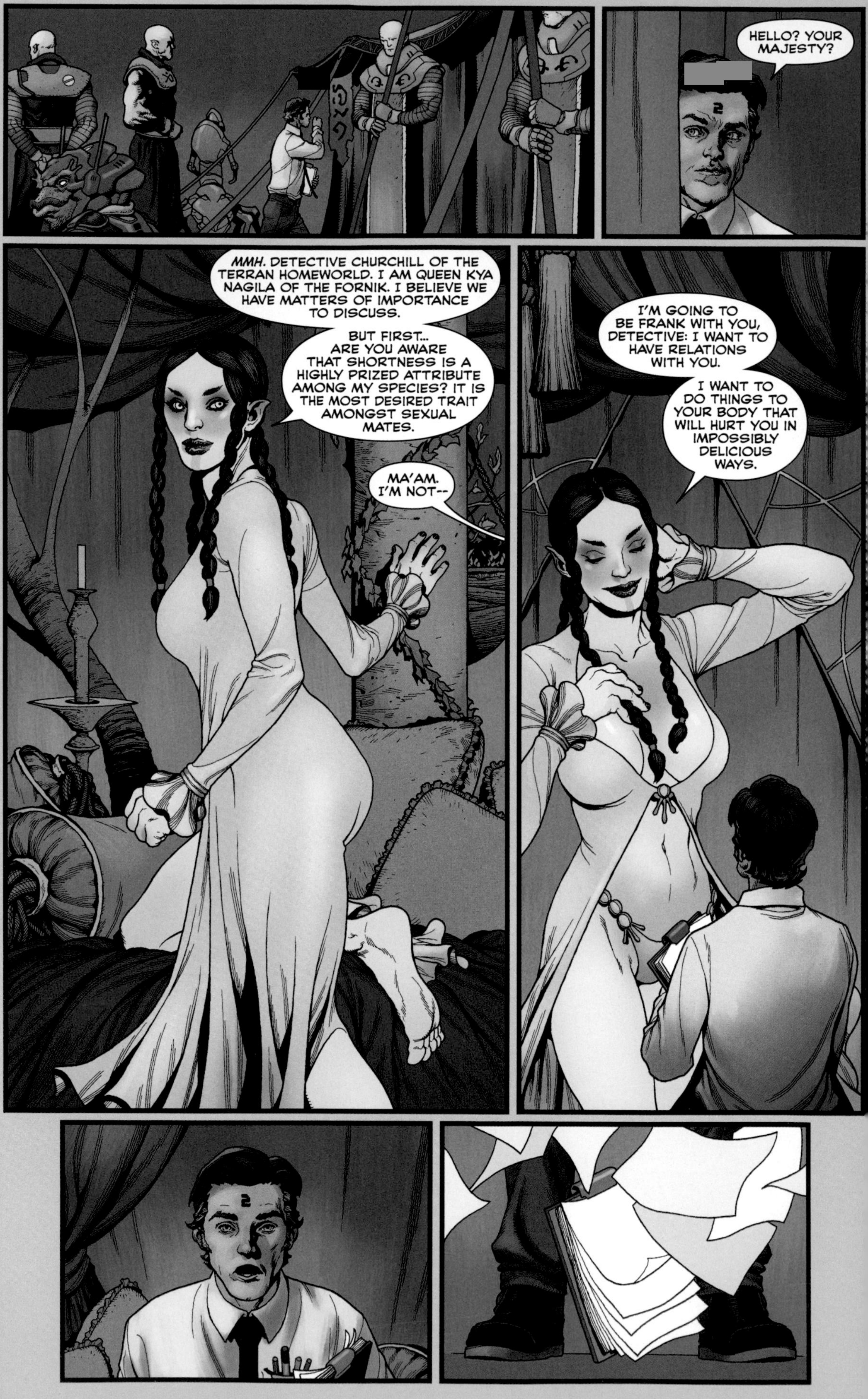
HELLO? YOUR MAJESTY?
MMH. DETECTIVE CHURCHILL OF THE TERRAN HOMEWORLD. I AM QUEEN KYA NAGILA OF THE FORNIK. I BELIEVE WE HAVE MATTERS OF IMPORTANCE TO DISCUSS.
BUT FIRST... ARE YOU AWARE THAT SHORTNESS IS A HIGHLY PRIZED ATTRIBUTE AMONG MY SPECIES? IT IS THE MOST DESIRED TRAIT AMONGST SEXUAL MATES.
MA'AM. I'M NOT--
I'M GOING TO BE FRANK WITH YOU, DETECTIVE: I WANT TO HAVE RELATIONS WITH YOU.
I WANT TO DO THINGS TO YOUR BODY THAT WILL HURT YOU IN IMPOSSIBLY DELICIOUS WAYS.

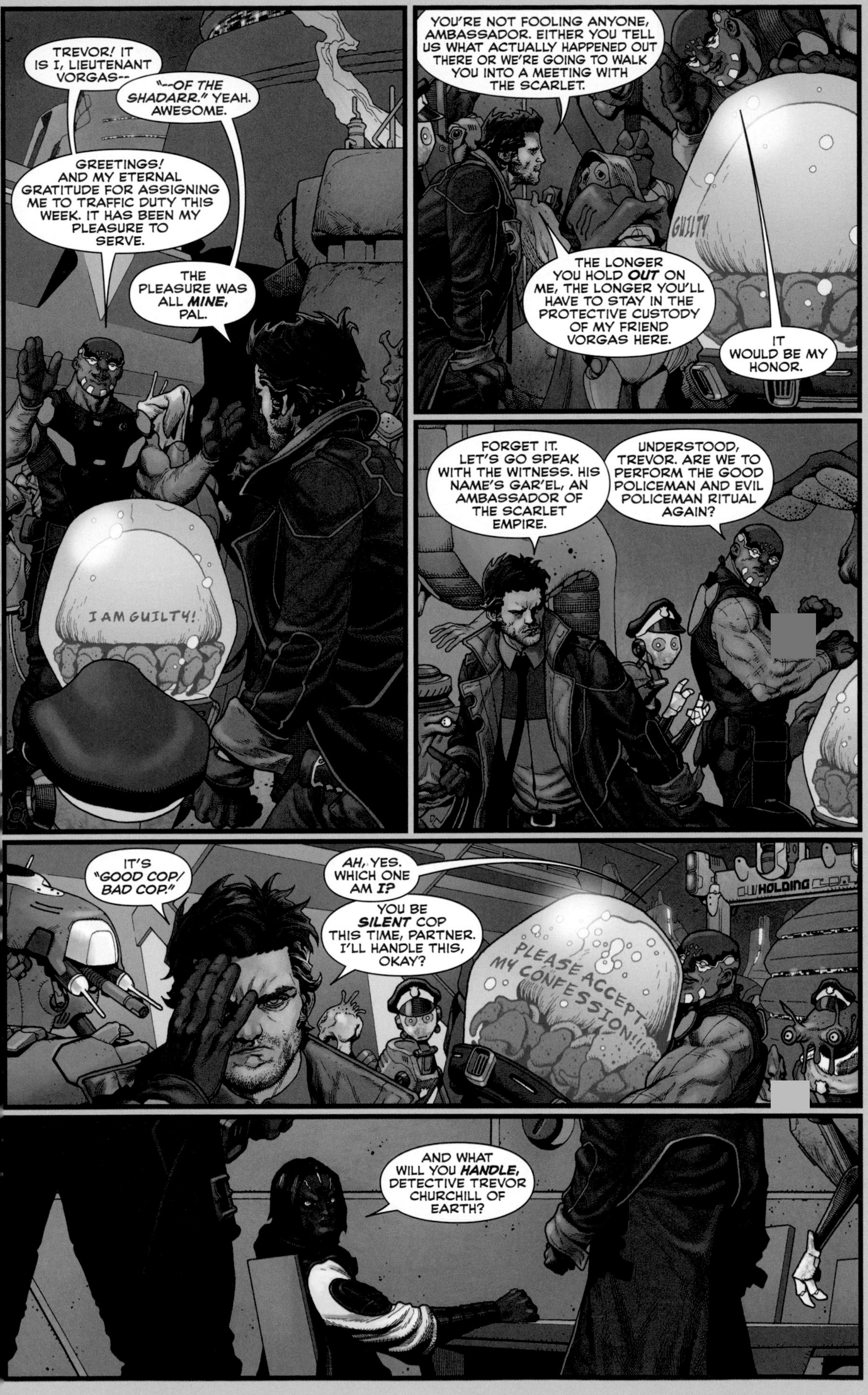
TREVOR! IT IS I, LIEUTENANT VORGAS--
"--OF THE SHADARR." YEAH. AWESOME.
GREETINGS! AND MY ETERNAL GRATITUDE FOR ASSIGNING ME TO TRAFFIC DUTY THIS WEEK. IT HAS BEEN MY PLEASURE TO SERVE.
THE PLEASURE WAS ALL MINE, PAL.
I AM GUILTY!
YOU'RE NOT FOOLING ANYONE, AMBASSADOR. EITHER YOU TELL US WHAT ACTUALLY HAPPENED OUT THERE OR WE'RE GOING TO WALK YOU INTO A MEETING WITH THE SCARLET.
GUILTY
THE LONGER YOU HOLD OUT ON ME, THE LONGER YOU'LL HAVE TO STAY IN THE PROTECTIVE CUSTODY OF MY FRIEND VORGAS HERE.
IT WOULD BE MY HONOR.
FORGET IT. LET'S GO SPEAK WITH THE WITNESS. HIS NAME'S GAR'EL, AN AMBASSADOR OF THE SCARLET EMPIRE.
UNDERSTOOD, TREVOR. ARE WE TO PERFORM THE GOOD POLICEMAN AND EVIL POLICEMAN RITUAL AGAIN?
IT'S "GOOD COP/ BAD COP."
AH, YES. WHICH ONE AM I?
YOU BE SILENT COP THIS TIME, PARTNER. I'LL HANDLE THIS, OKAY?
HOLDING
PLEASE ACCEPT MY CONFESSION!!!
AND WHAT WILL YOU HANDLE, DETECTIVE TREVOR CHURCHILL OF EARTH?

I'D LIKE TO KNOW WHY I HAVE BEEN DETAINED FOR THE LAST FOUR HOURS, DETECTIVE.

SORRY, AMBASSADOR GAR'EL. POLICE PROCEDURE. IT GETS A BIT TEDIOUS WHEN WE'RE TRYING TO CLEAN UP AFTER A MURDER.

AND YET YOU HAVE YOUR SUSPECT IN HAND, DETECTIVE.

NOT *YET*, SIR.

I ASSURE YOU, DETECTIVE, THE JUL'DAN IS GUILTY. HIS COWARDLY ATTACK ON THE K'TARIAN EMISSARY HAPPENED IN FRONT OF MORE THAN TWENTY WITNESSES.

THAT THE SCARLET WAS PAID OFF OR *THREATENED*, SIR. YOU'LL HAVE TO DO BETTER THAN THAT.

PLEASE TAKE ME TO JAIL!

I'M SURE YOU THINK YOU KNOW WHAT YOU'RE DOING HERE, DETECTIVE CHURCHILL. BUT THE REALITY IS YOU HAVE LITTLE GRASP OF THE TECHNICALITIES.

I DRAW YOUR ATTENTION TO THE COLLOQUIUM TREATY OF 37773-4, PARAGRAPH 8-A, SECOND CLAUSE.

WHAT ABOUT IT?

"THE CONSTITUTION AND GOVERNING LAWS OF EACH MEMBER ENTITY OF THE TRANSFER SHALL DICTATE--

IOOIOI!!

**KLUNK**

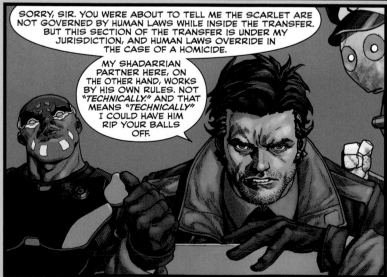

SORRY, SIR. YOU WERE ABOUT TO TELL ME THE SCARLET ARE NOT GOVERNED BY HUMAN LAWS WHILE INSIDE THE TRANSFER. BUT THIS SECTION OF THE TRANSFER IS UNDER MY JURISDICTION, AND HUMAN LAWS OVERRIDE IN THE CASE OF A HOMICIDE.

MY SHADARRIAN PARTNER HERE, ON THE OTHER HAND, WORKS BY HIS OWN RULES. NOT *"TECHNICALLY"* AND THAT MEANS *"TECHNICALLY"* I COULD HAVE HIM RIP YOUR BALLS OFF.

QUITE.

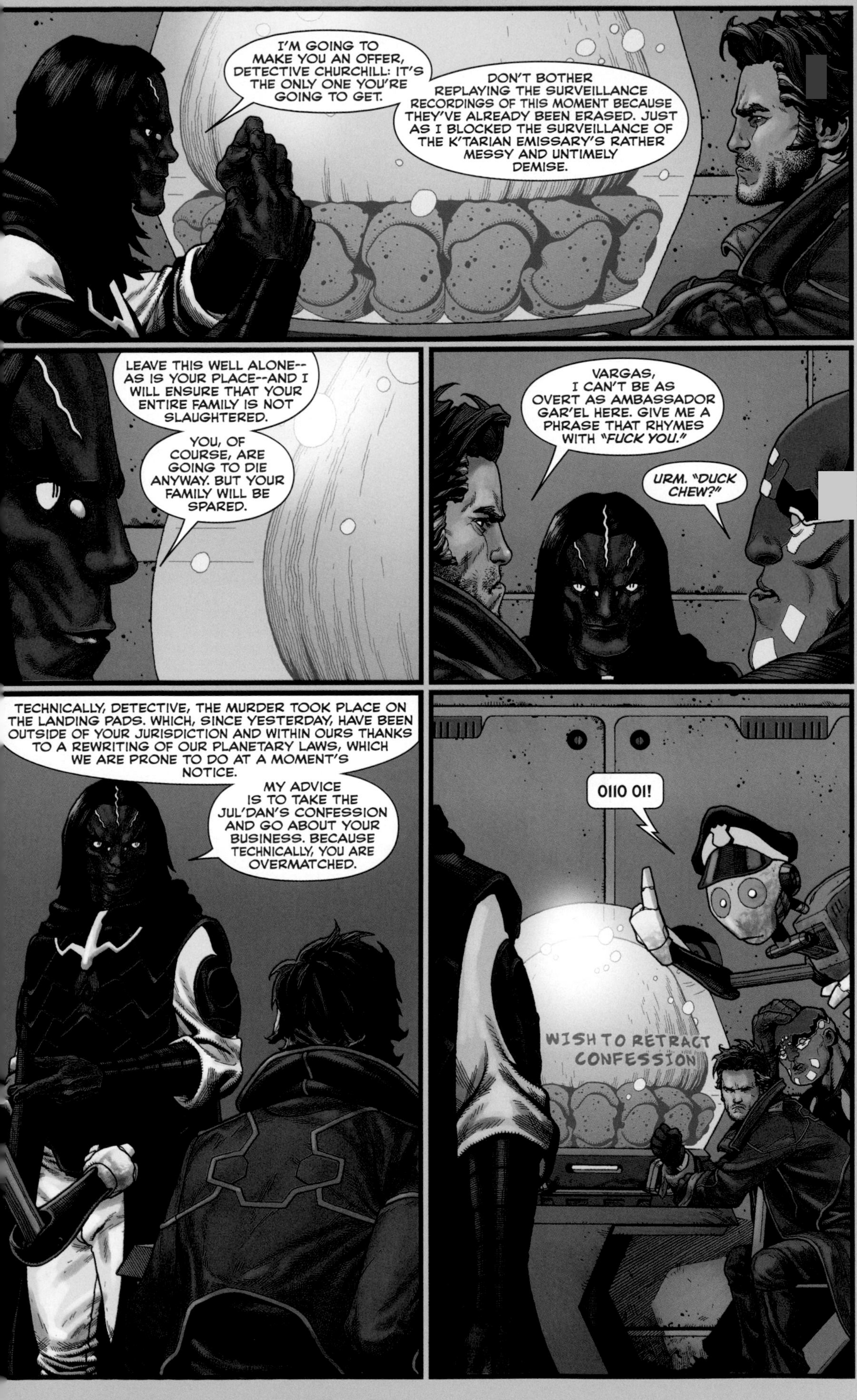
I'M GOING TO MAKE YOU AN OFFER, DETECTIVE CHURCHILL: IT'S THE ONLY ONE YOU'RE GOING TO GET.
DON'T BOTHER REPLAYING THE SURVEILLANCE RECORDINGS OF THIS MOMENT BECAUSE THEY'VE ALREADY BEEN ERASED. JUST AS I BLOCKED THE SURVEILLANCE OF THE K'TARIAN EMISSARY'S RATHER MESSY AND UNTIMELY DEMISE.
LEAVE THIS WELL ALONE--AS IS YOUR PLACE--AND I WILL ENSURE THAT YOUR ENTIRE FAMILY IS NOT SLAUGHTERED.
YOU, OF COURSE, ARE GOING TO DIE ANYWAY. BUT YOUR FAMILY WILL BE SPARED.
VARGAS, I CAN'T BE AS OVERT AS AMBASSADOR GAR'EL HERE. GIVE ME A PHRASE THAT RHYMES WITH *"FUCK YOU."*
*URM. "DUCK CHEW?"*
TECHNICALLY, DETECTIVE, THE MURDER TOOK PLACE ON THE LANDING PADS. WHICH, SINCE YESTERDAY, HAVE BEEN OUTSIDE OF YOUR JURISDICTION AND WITHIN OURS THANKS TO A REWRITING OF OUR PLANETARY LAWS, WHICH WE ARE PRONE TO DO AT A MOMENT'S NOTICE.
MY ADVICE IS TO TAKE THE JUL'DAN'S CONFESSION AND GO ABOUT YOUR BUSINESS. BECAUSE TECHNICALLY, YOU ARE OVERMATCHED.
0110 01!
WISH TO RETRACT CONFESSION

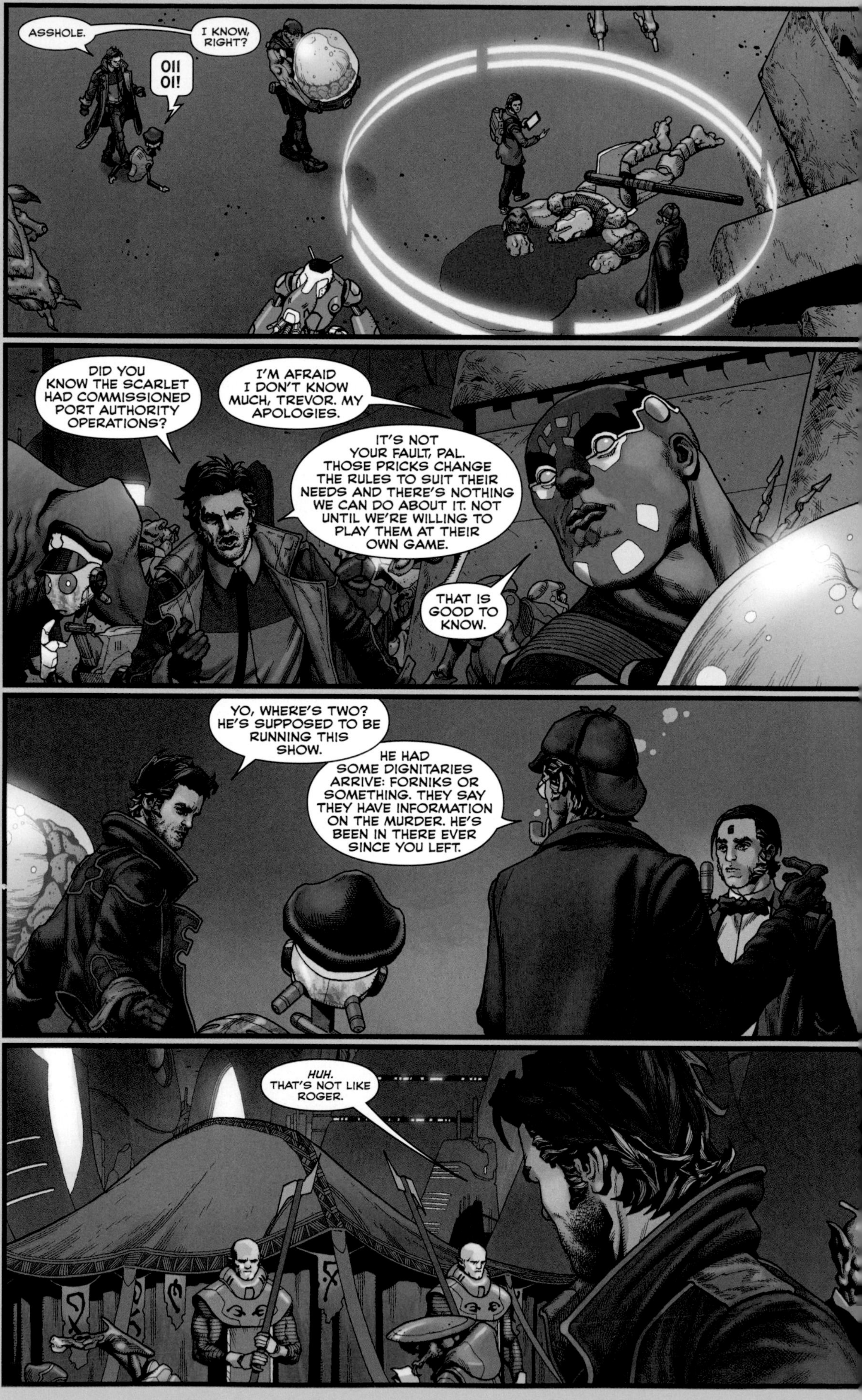
ASSHOLE.
I KNOW, RIGHT?
OI! OI!
DID YOU KNOW THE SCARLET HAD COMMISSIONED PORT AUTHORITY OPERATIONS?
I'M AFRAID I DON'T KNOW MUCH, TREVOR. MY APOLOGIES.
IT'S NOT YOUR FAULT, PAL. THOSE PRICKS CHANGE THE RULES TO SUIT THEIR NEEDS AND THERE'S NOTHING WE CAN DO ABOUT IT. NOT UNTIL WE'RE WILLING TO PLAY THEM AT THEIR OWN GAME.
THAT IS GOOD TO KNOW.
YO, WHERE'S TWO? HE'S SUPPOSED TO BE RUNNING THIS SHOW.
HE HAD SOME DIGNITARIES ARRIVE: FORNIKS OR SOMETHING. THEY SAY THEY HAVE INFORMATION ON THE MURDER. HE'S BEEN IN THERE EVER SINCE YOU LEFT.
*HUH.* THAT'S NOT LIKE ROGER.

OKAY, WE GOTTA PROBLEM ON OUR HANDS: IF THE SCARLET ARE INVOLVED, ALL OF THE RULES ARE SUBJECT TO CHANGE. WHERE'S FIVE?

TWO SENT HIM TO THE JUL'DAN EMBASSY.

GOOD. SEND THIRTY-EIGHT WITH HIM.

TWO ALREADY DID THAT.

RIGHT. GOOD AGAIN.

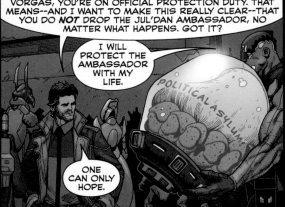

VORGAS, YOU'RE ON OFFICIAL PROTECTION DUTY. THAT MEANS--AND I WANT TO MAKE THIS REALLY CLEAR--THAT YOU DO *NOT* DROP THE JUL'DAN AMBASSADOR, NO MATTER WHAT HAPPENS. GOT IT?

I WILL PROTECT THE AMBASSADOR WITH MY LIFE.

POLITICAL ASYLUM

ONE CAN ONLY HOPE.

AMBASSADOR, IT WAS A NICE TRY--AND I'M SURE YOU HAVE YOUR REASONS FOR THIS--BUT I'M GOING TO ASSUME YOU WERE COERCED BY THE SCARLET INTO YOUR CONFESSION.

I'M HOLDING YOU AS A MATERIAL WITNESS IN PROTECTIVE CUSTODY UNTIL SUCH TIME AS THE SITUATION CLEARS.

FOUR, YOU'RE RUNNING THE SHOW UNTIL TWO GETS BACK--

AW! WHY CAN'T WE CALL *THREE*?

I THINK YOU KNOW THE ANSWER TO THAT.

WELL, WHERE ARE *YOU* GOING?

I'M GOING TO VISIT WITH SOME FRIENDS OF MINE!

YOU *GOT* THAT, ASSHOLES?

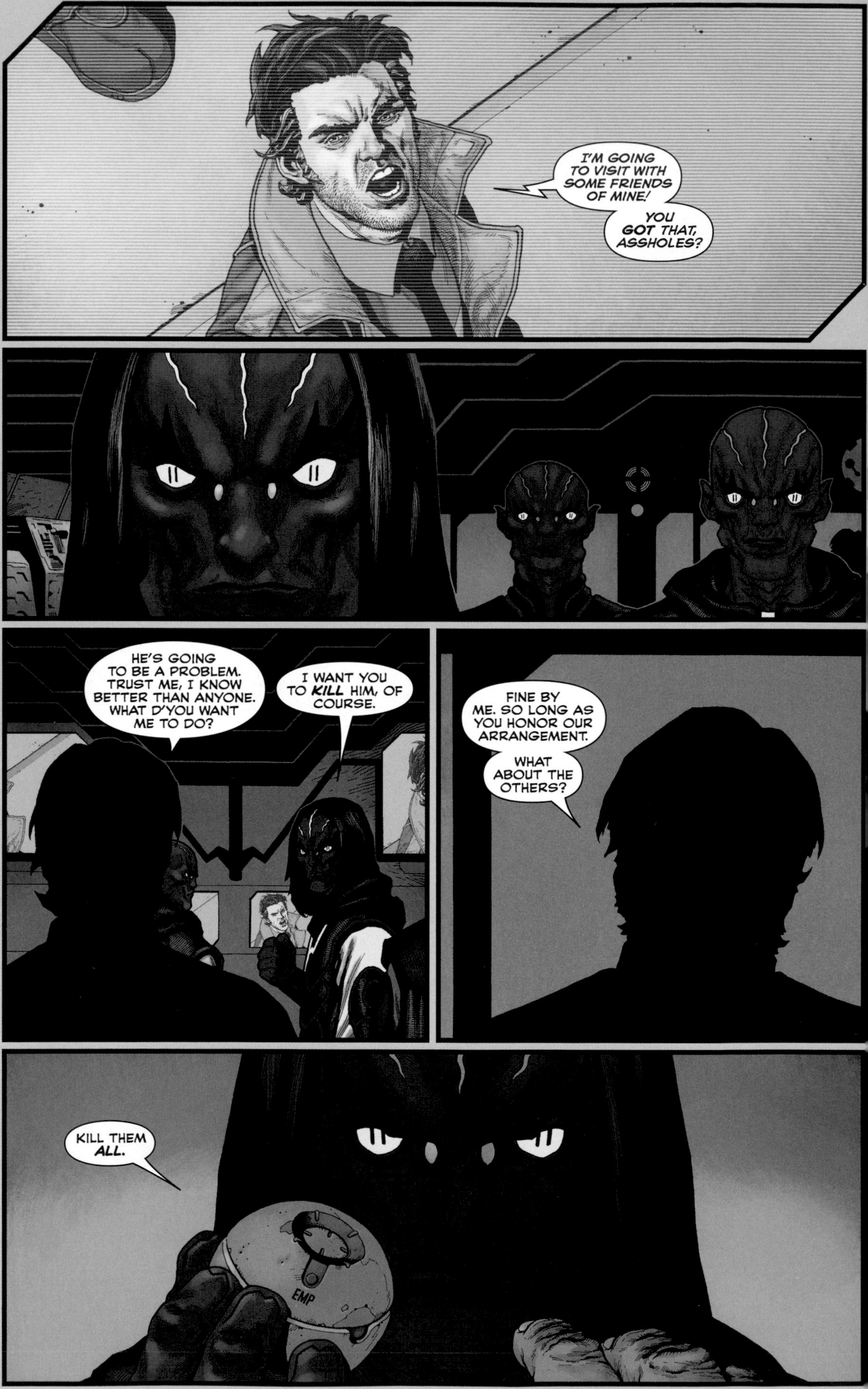
I'M GOING TO VISIT WITH SOME FRIENDS OF MINE!
YOU GOT THAT, ASSHOLES?
HE'S GOING TO BE A PROBLEM. TRUST ME, I KNOW BETTER THAN ANYONE. WHAT D'YOU WANT ME TO DO?
I WANT YOU TO KILL HIM, OF COURSE.
FINE BY ME. SO LONG AS YOU HONOR OUR ARRANGEMENT.
WHAT ABOUT THE OTHERS?
KILL THEM ALL.
EMP

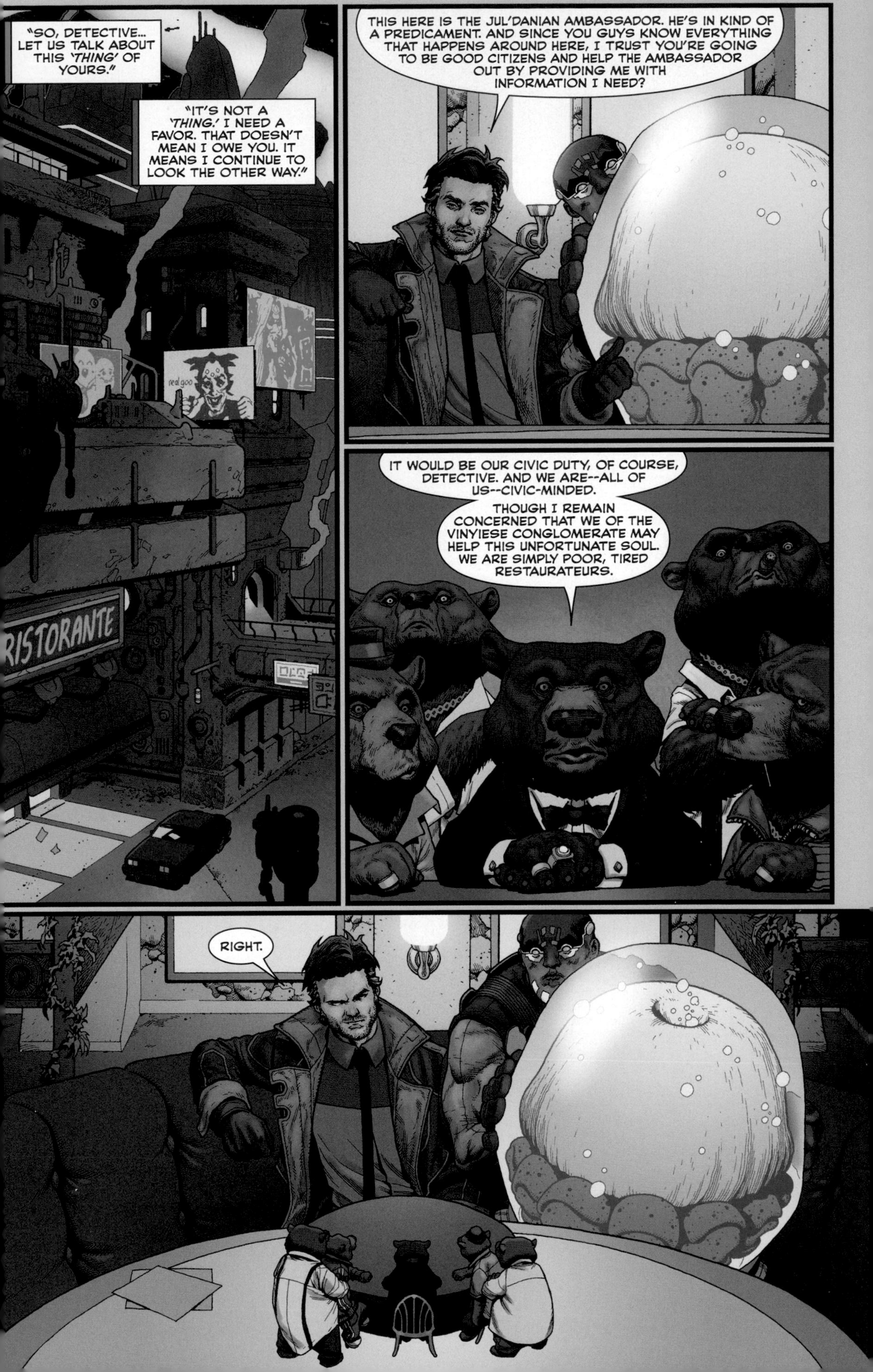
"SO, DETECTIVE... LET US TALK ABOUT THIS 'THING' OF YOURS."
"IT'S NOT A 'THING.' I NEED A FAVOR. THAT DOESN'T MEAN I OWE YOU. IT MEANS I CONTINUE TO LOOK THE OTHER WAY."
real goo
RISTORANTE
THIS HERE IS THE JUL'DANIAN AMBASSADOR. HE'S IN KIND OF A PREDICAMENT. AND SINCE YOU GUYS KNOW EVERYTHING THAT HAPPENS AROUND HERE, I TRUST YOU'RE GOING TO BE GOOD CITIZENS AND HELP THE AMBASSADOR OUT BY PROVIDING ME WITH INFORMATION I NEED?
IT WOULD BE OUR CIVIC DUTY, OF COURSE, DETECTIVE. AND WE ARE--ALL OF US--CIVIC-MINDED.
THOUGH I REMAIN CONCERNED THAT WE OF THE VINYIESE CONGLOMERATE MAY HELP THIS UNFORTUNATE SOUL. WE ARE SIMPLY POOR, TIRED RESTAURATEURS.
RIGHT.

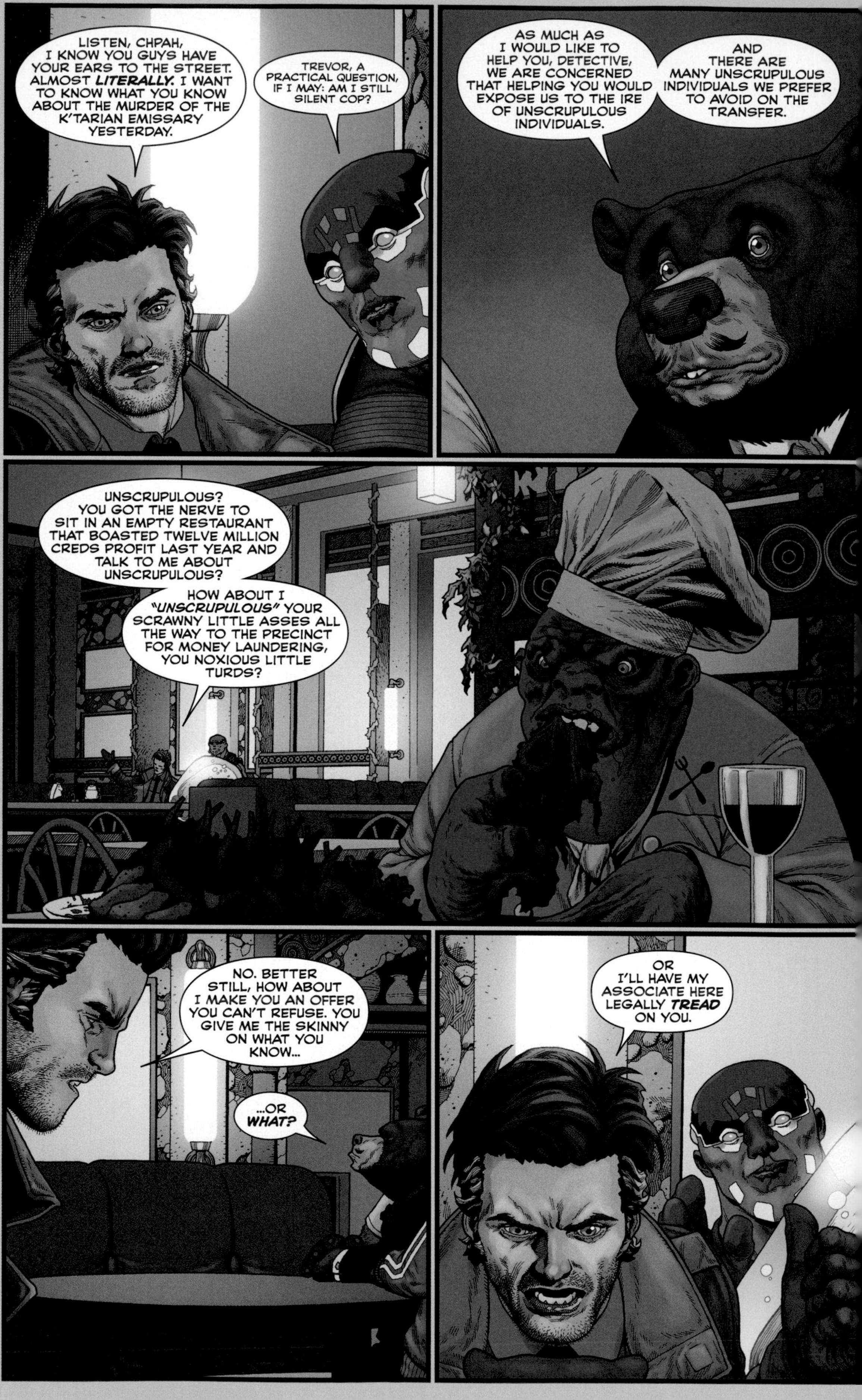
LISTEN, CHPAH, I KNOW YOU GUYS HAVE YOUR EARS TO THE STREET. ALMOST *LITERALLY.* I WANT TO KNOW WHAT YOU KNOW ABOUT THE MURDER OF THE K'TARIAN EMISSARY YESTERDAY.
TREVOR, A PRACTICAL QUESTION, IF I MAY: AM I STILL SILENT COP?
AS MUCH AS I WOULD LIKE TO HELP YOU, DETECTIVE, WE ARE CONCERNED THAT HELPING YOU WOULD EXPOSE US TO THE IRE OF UNSCRUPULOUS INDIVIDUALS.
AND THERE ARE MANY UNSCRUPULOUS INDIVIDUALS WE PREFER TO AVOID ON THE TRANSFER.
UNSCRUPULOUS? YOU GOT THE NERVE TO SIT IN AN EMPTY RESTAURANT THAT BOASTED TWELVE MILLION CREDS PROFIT LAST YEAR AND TALK TO ME ABOUT UNSCRUPULOUS?
HOW ABOUT I *"UNSCRUPULOUS"* YOUR SCRAWNY LITTLE ASSES ALL THE WAY TO THE PRECINCT FOR MONEY LAUNDERING, YOU NOXIOUS LITTLE TURDS?
NO. BETTER STILL, HOW ABOUT I MAKE YOU AN OFFER YOU CAN'T REFUSE. YOU GIVE ME THE SKINNY ON WHAT YOU KNOW...
...OR *WHAT?*
OR I'LL HAVE MY ASSOCIATE HERE LEGALLY *TREAD* ON YOU.

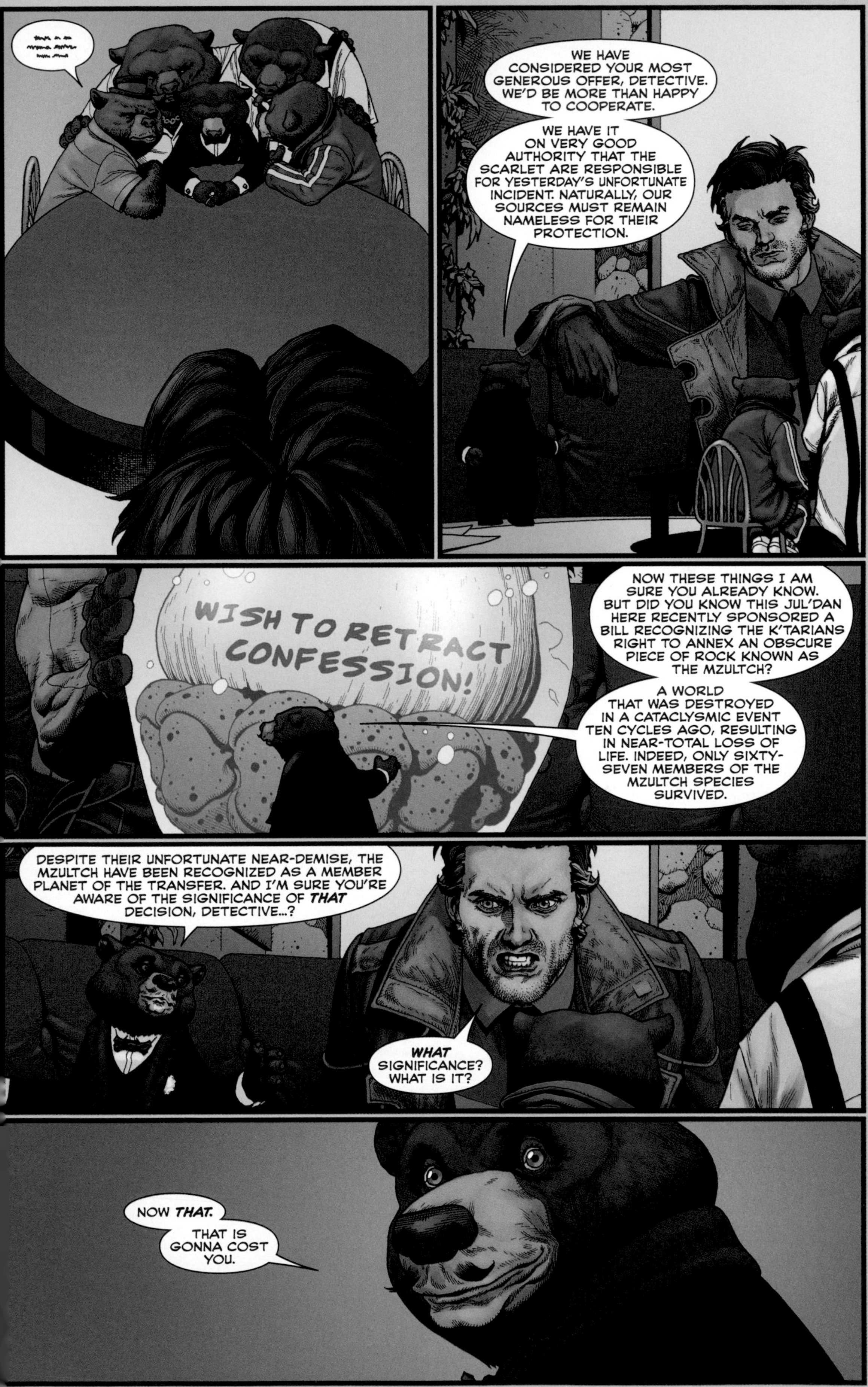
WE HAVE CONSIDERED YOUR MOST GENEROUS OFFER, DETECTIVE. WE'D BE MORE THAN HAPPY TO COOPERATE.
WE HAVE IT ON VERY GOOD AUTHORITY THAT THE SCARLET ARE RESPONSIBLE FOR YESTERDAY'S UNFORTUNATE INCIDENT. NATURALLY, OUR SOURCES MUST REMAIN NAMELESS FOR THEIR PROTECTION.
WISH TO RETRACT CONFESSION!
NOW THESE THINGS I AM SURE YOU ALREADY KNOW. BUT DID YOU KNOW THIS JUL'DAN HERE RECENTLY SPONSORED A BILL RECOGNIZING THE K'TARIANS RIGHT TO ANNEX AN OBSCURE PIECE OF ROCK KNOWN AS THE MZULTCH?
A WORLD THAT WAS DESTROYED IN A CATACLYSMIC EVENT TEN CYCLES AGO, RESULTING IN NEAR-TOTAL LOSS OF LIFE. INDEED, ONLY SIXTY-SEVEN MEMBERS OF THE MZULTCH SPECIES SURVIVED.
DESPITE THEIR UNFORTUNATE NEAR-DEMISE, THE MZULTCH HAVE BEEN RECOGNIZED AS A MEMBER PLANET OF THE TRANSFER. AND I'M SURE YOU'RE AWARE OF THE SIGNIFICANCE OF *THAT* DECISION, DETECTIVE...?
*WHAT* SIGNIFICANCE? WHAT IS IT?
NOW *THAT.*
THAT IS GONNA COST YOU.

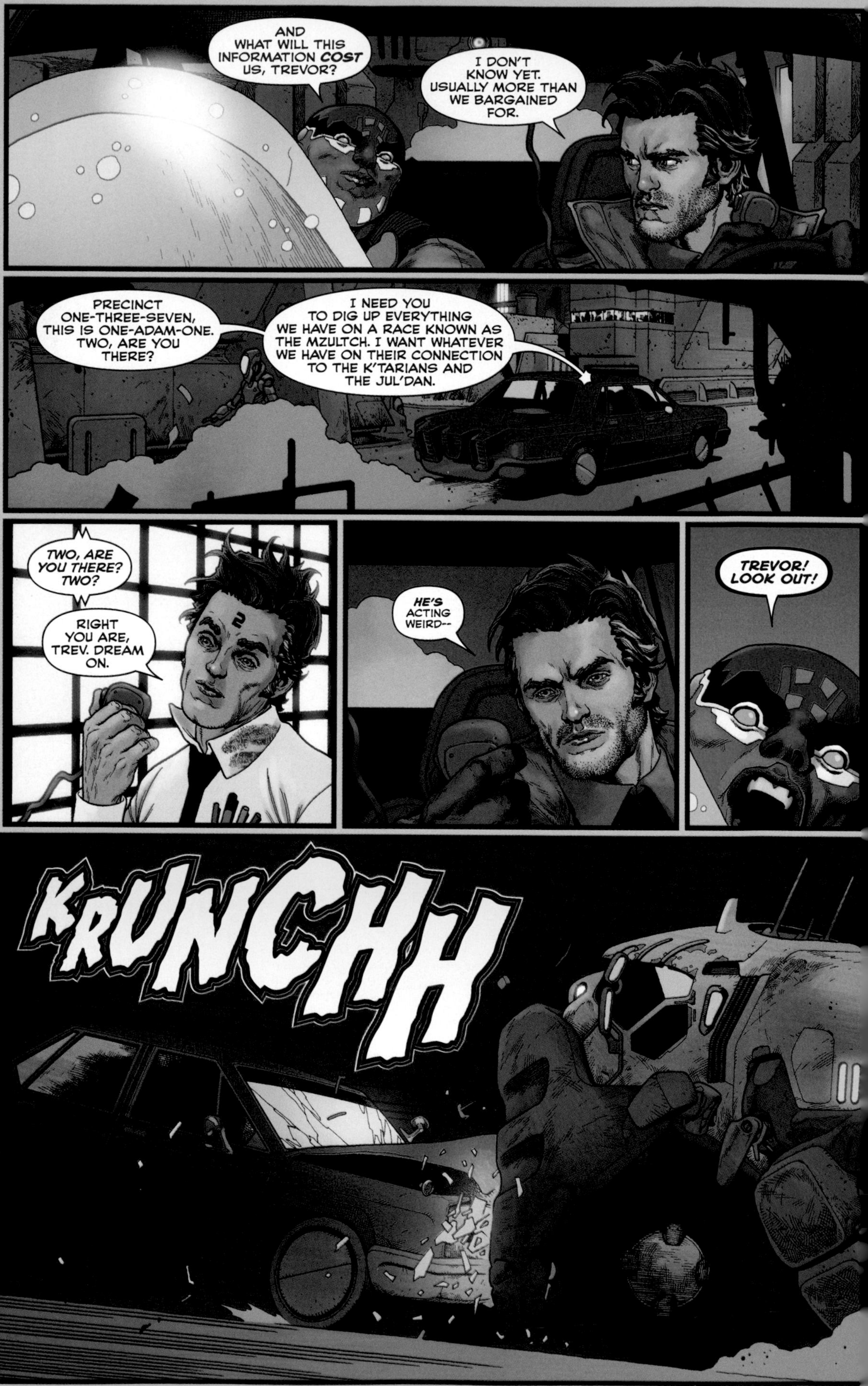
AND WHAT WILL THIS INFORMATION COST US, TREVOR?
I DON'T KNOW YET. USUALLY MORE THAN WE BARGAINED FOR.
PRECINCT ONE-THREE-SEVEN, THIS IS ONE-ADAM-ONE. TWO, ARE YOU THERE?
I NEED YOU TO DIG UP EVERYTHING WE HAVE ON A RACE KNOWN AS THE MZULTCH. I WANT WHATEVER WE HAVE ON THEIR CONNECTION TO THE K'TARIANS AND THE JUL'DAN.
TWO, ARE YOU THERE? TWO?
RIGHT YOU ARE, TREV. DREAM ON.
HE'S ACTING WEIRD--
TREVOR! LOOK OUT!
KRUNCHH

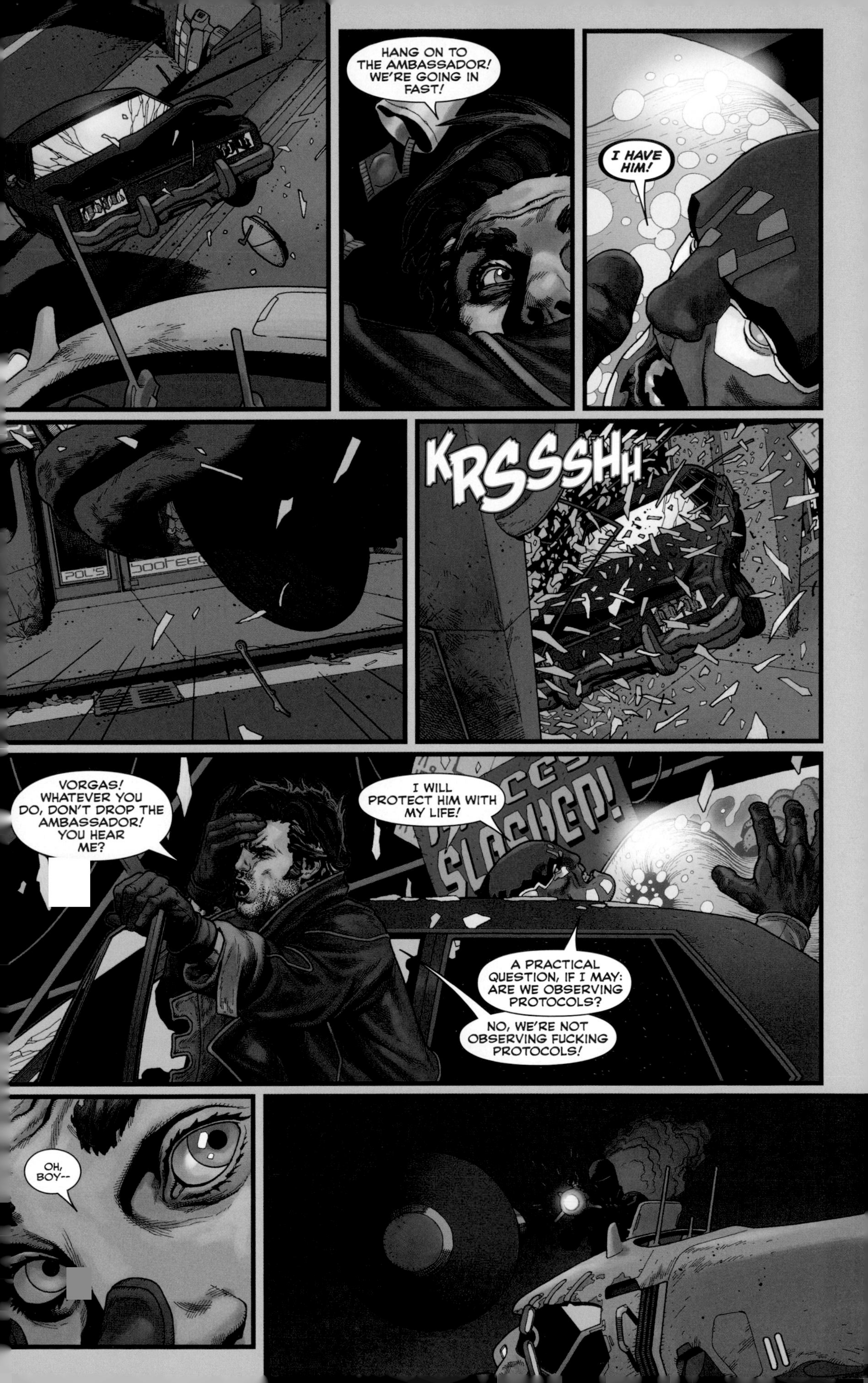
HANG ON TO THE AMBASSADOR! WE'RE GOING IN FAST!
I HAVE HIM!
KRSSSHH
VORGAS! WHATEVER YOU DO, DON'T DROP THE AMBASSADOR! YOU HEAR ME?
I WILL PROTECT HIM WITH MY LIFE!
A PRACTICAL QUESTION, IF I MAY: ARE WE OBSERVING PROTOCOLS?
NO, WE'RE NOT OBSERVING FUCKING PROTOCOLS!
OH, BOY--

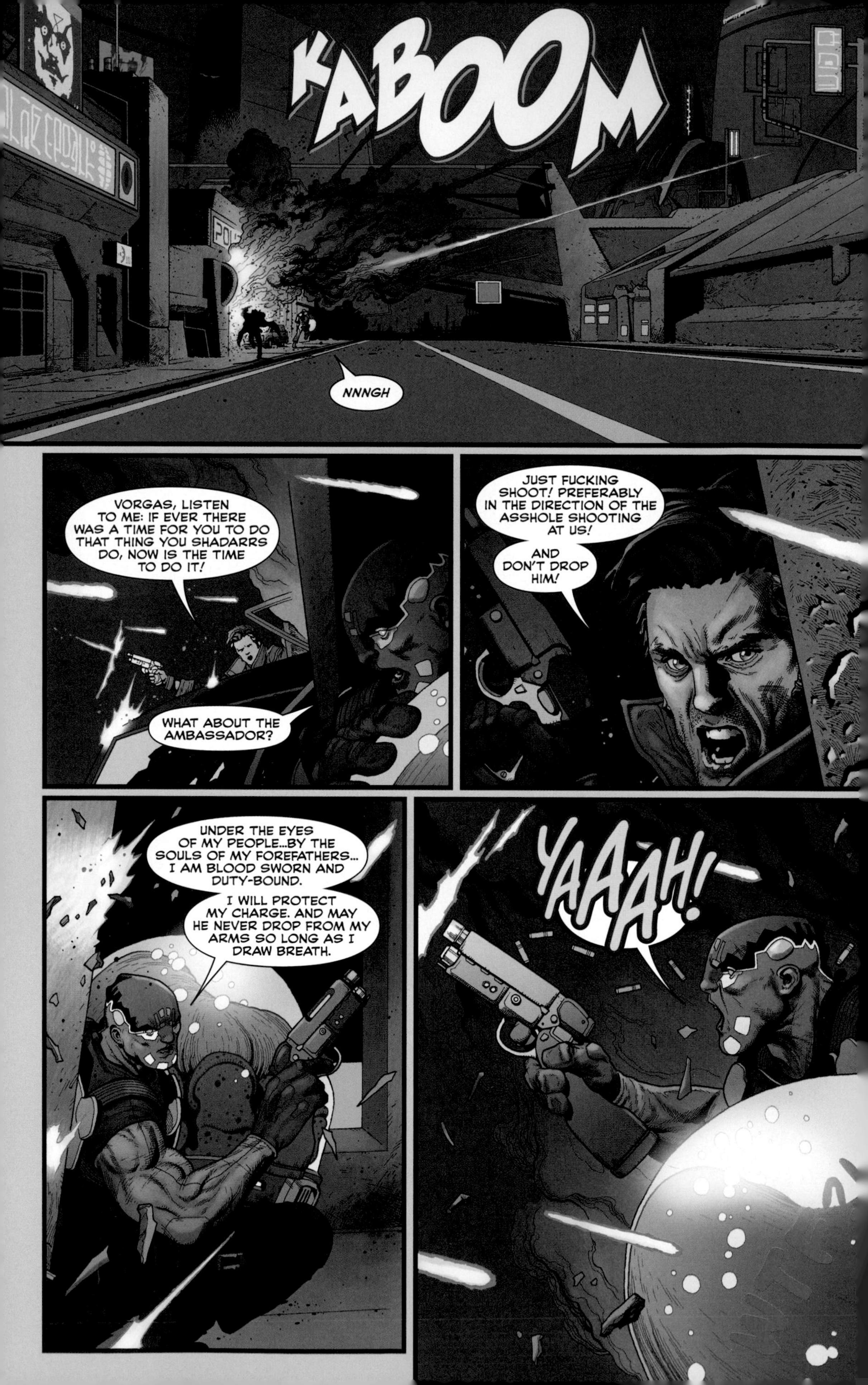
KABOOM
NNNGH
VORGAS, LISTEN TO ME: IF EVER THERE WAS A TIME FOR YOU TO DO THAT THING YOU SHADARRS DO, NOW IS THE TIME TO DO IT!
WHAT ABOUT THE AMBASSADOR?
JUST FUCKING SHOOT! PREFERABLY IN THE DIRECTION OF THE ASSHOLE SHOOTING AT US!
AND DON'T DROP HIM!
UNDER THE EYES OF MY PEOPLE...BY THE SOULS OF MY FOREFATHERS... I AM BLOOD SWORN AND DUTY-BOUND.
I WILL PROTECT MY CHARGE. AND MAY HE NEVER DROP FROM MY ARMS SO LONG AS I DRAW BREATH.
YAAAAH!

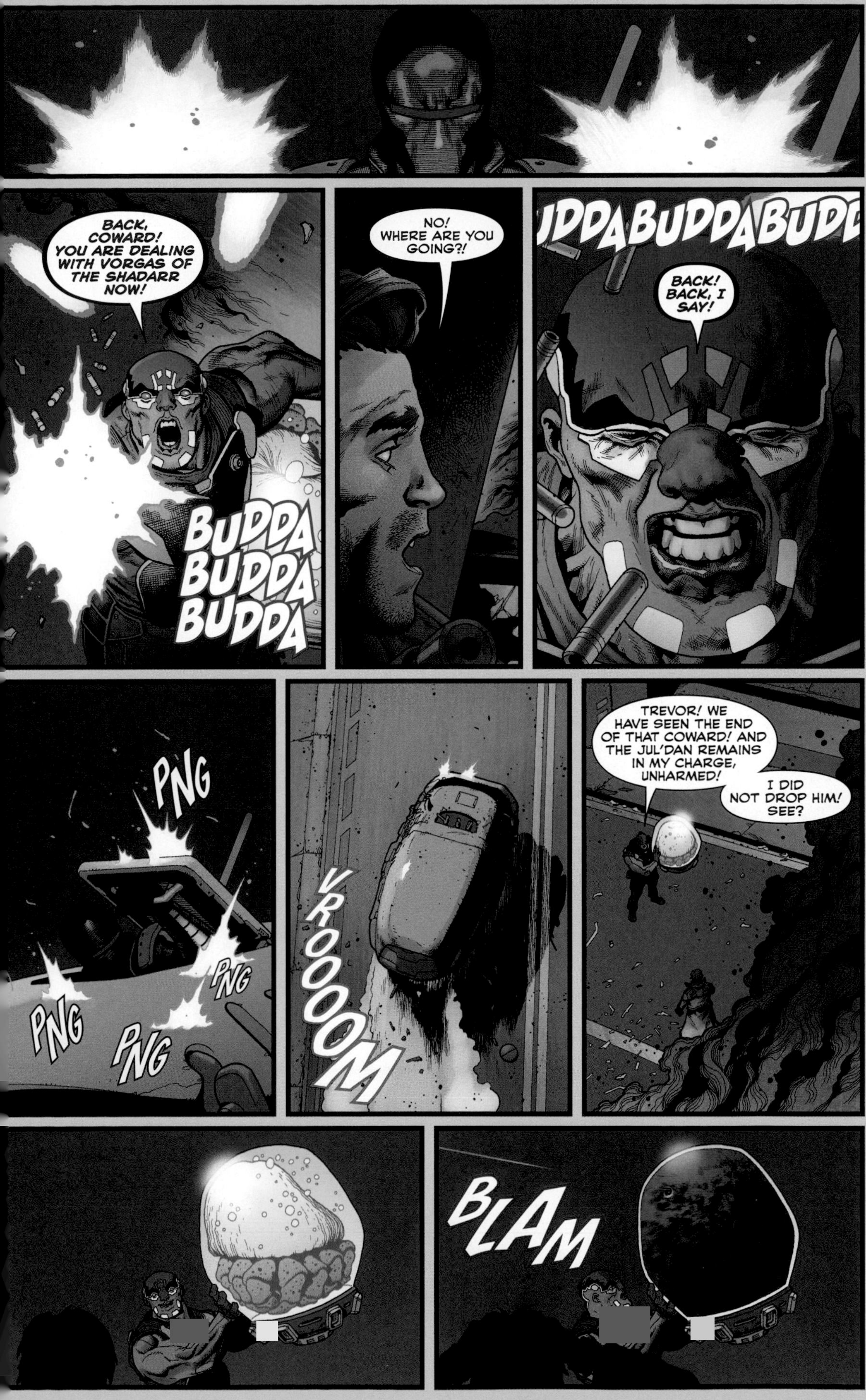
BACK, COWARD! YOU ARE DEALING WITH VORGAS OF THE SHADARR NOW!
BUDDA BUDDA BUDDA
NO! WHERE ARE YOU GOING?!
UDDABUDDABUDD
BACK! BACK, I SAY!
PNG
PNG
PNG
PNG
VROOOOOM
TREVOR! WE HAVE SEEN THE END OF THAT COWARD! AND THE JUL'DAN REMAINS IN MY CHARGE, UNHARMED!
I DID NOT DROP HIM! SEE?
BLAM

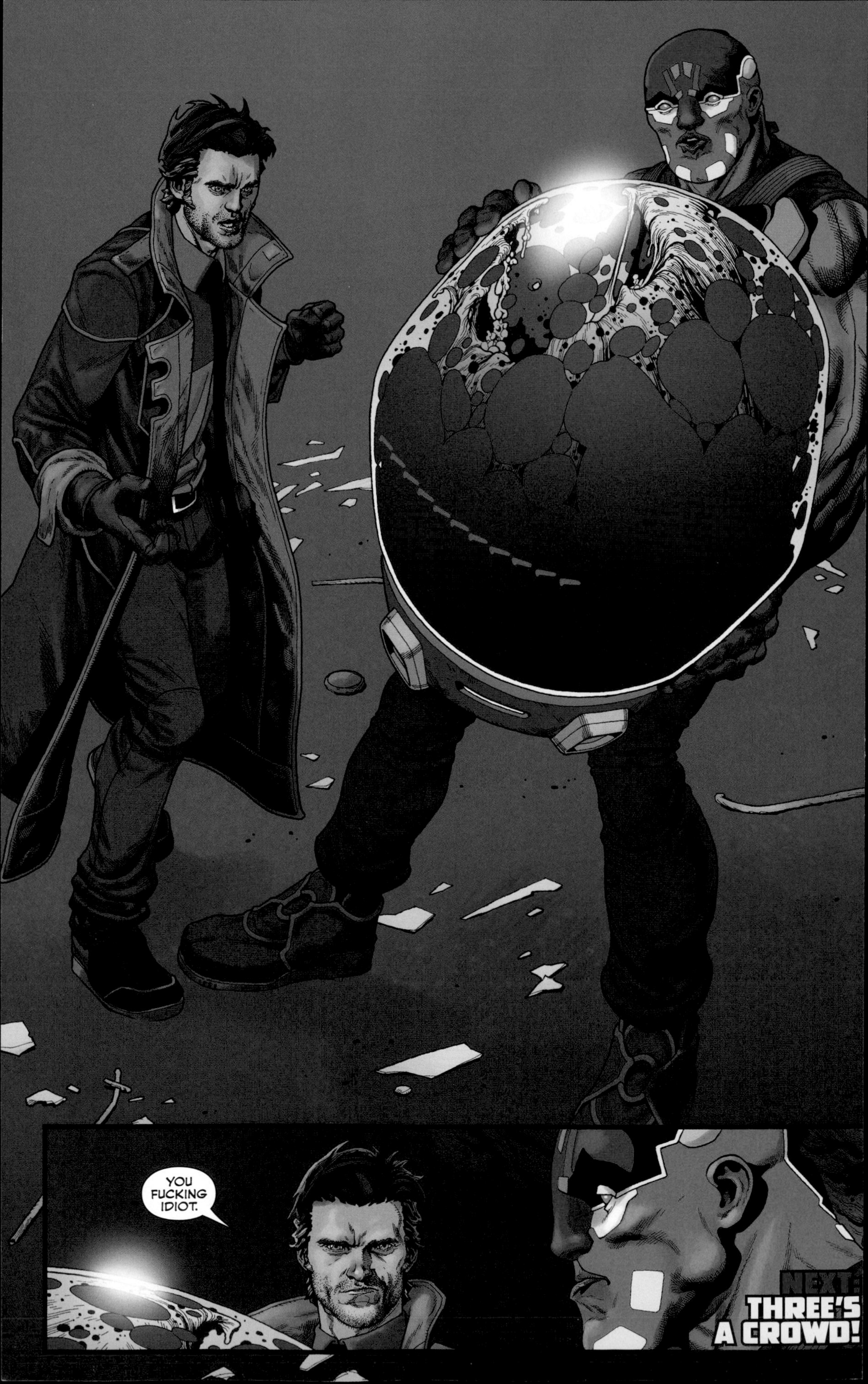
YOU FUCKING IDIOT.
NEXT:
THREE'S A CROWD!

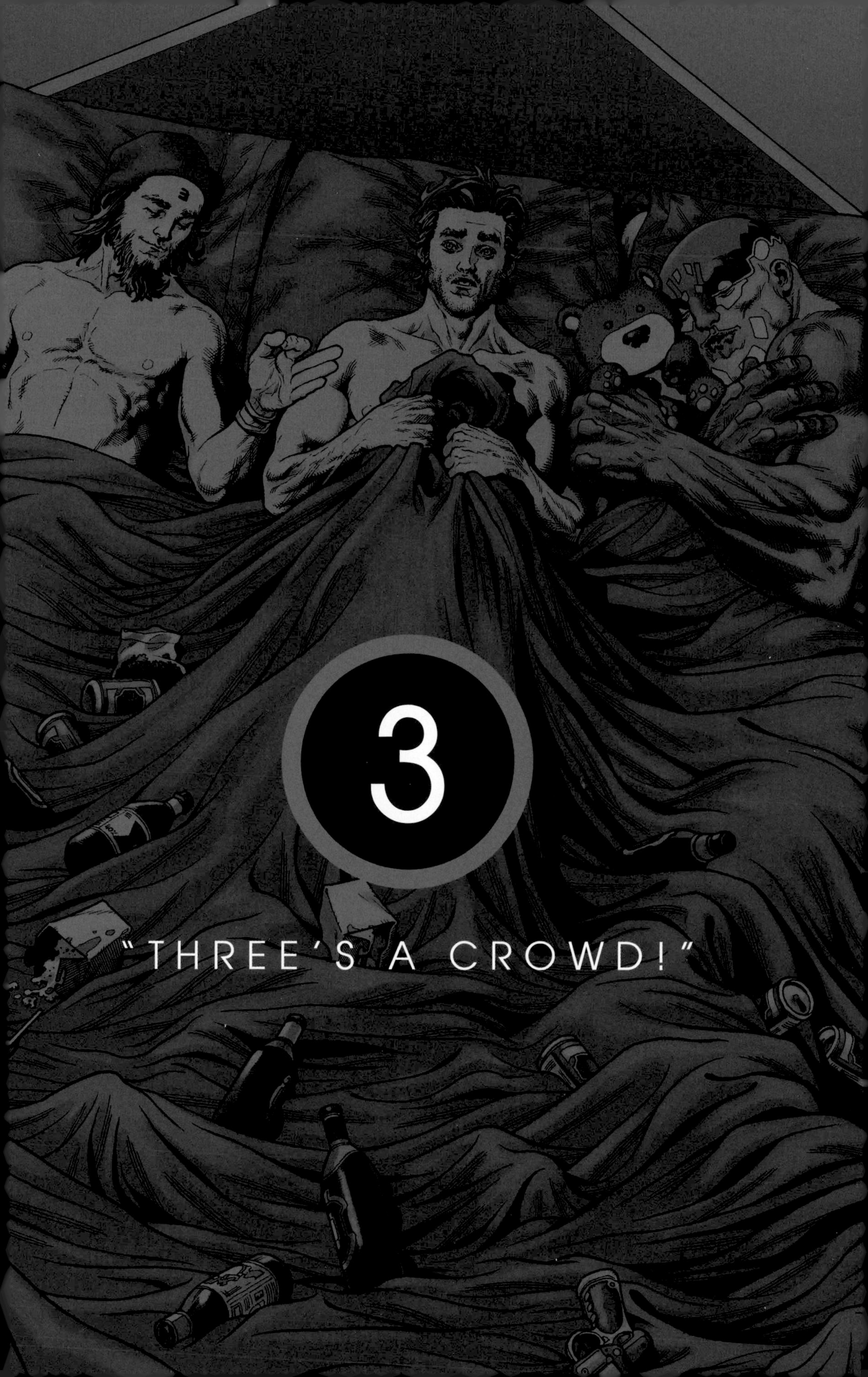
3
"THREE'S A CROWD!"

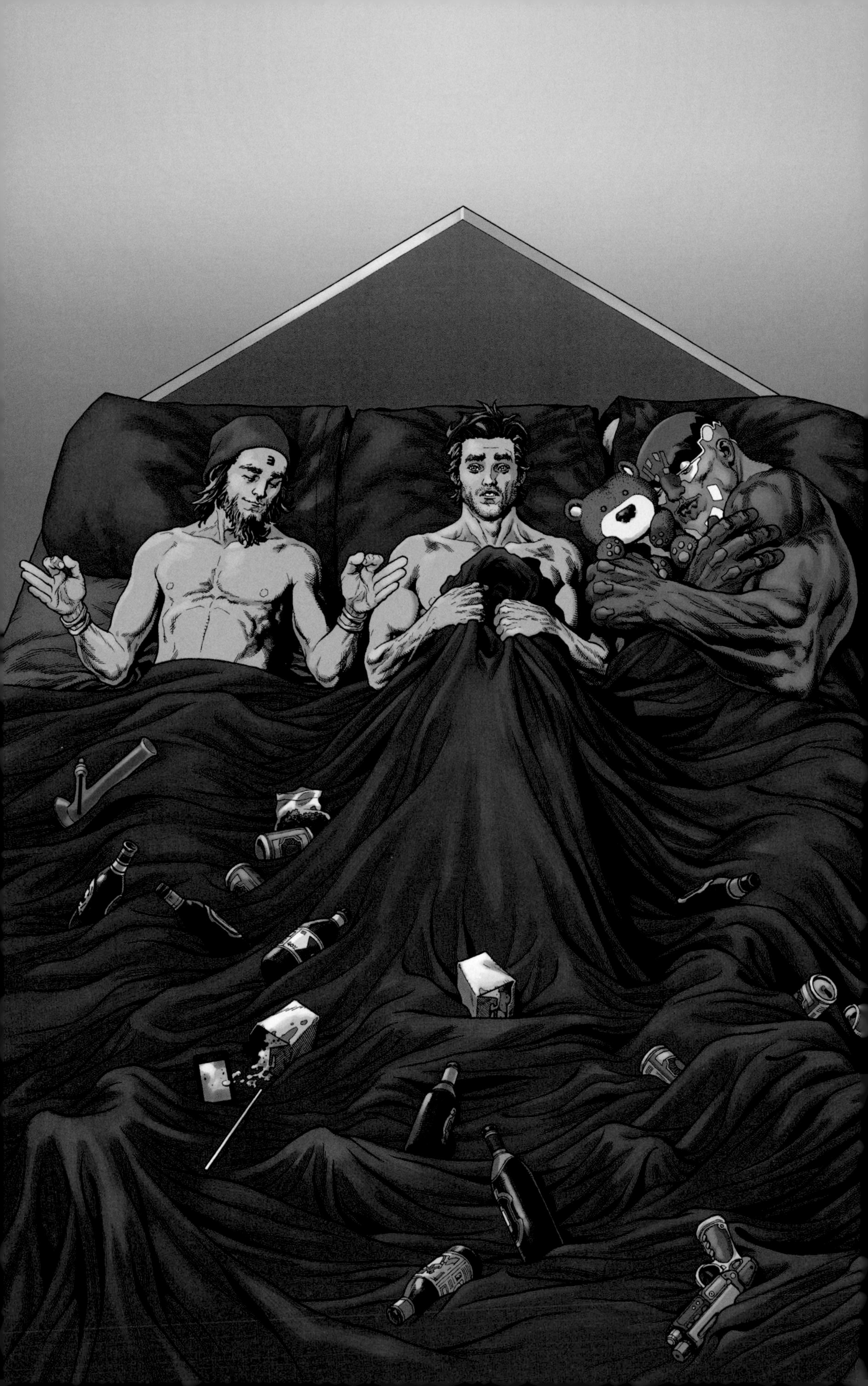

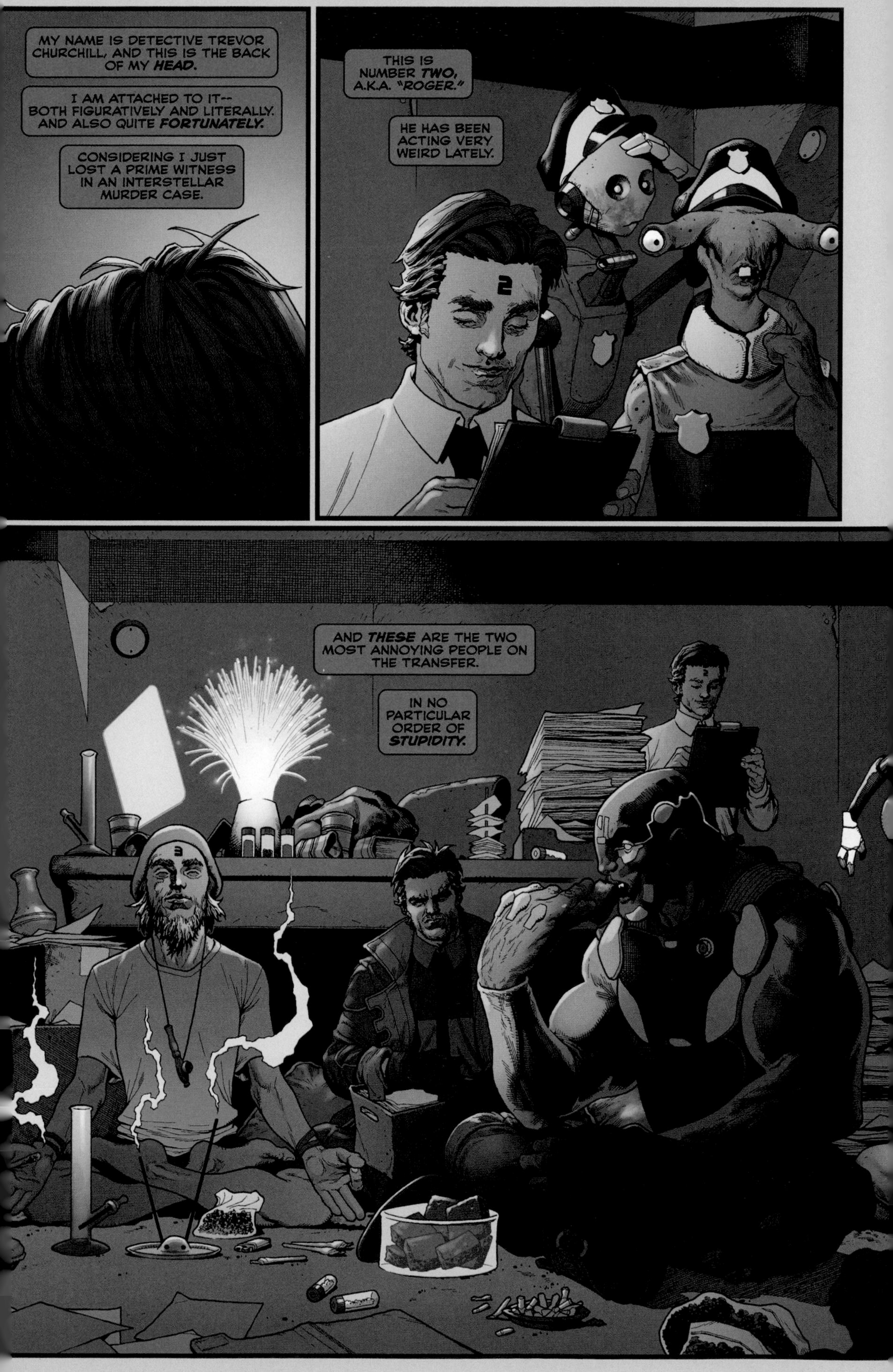
MY NAME IS DETECTIVE TREVOR CHURCHILL, AND THIS IS THE BACK OF MY *HEAD*.
I AM ATTACHED TO IT-- BOTH FIGURATIVELY AND LITERALLY. AND ALSO QUITE *FORTUNATELY*.
CONSIDERING I JUST LOST A PRIME WITNESS IN AN INTERSTELLAR MURDER CASE.
THIS IS NUMBER *TWO*, A.K.A. *"ROGER."*
HE HAS BEEN ACTING VERY WEIRD LATELY.
AND *THESE* ARE THE TWO MOST ANNOYING PEOPLE ON THE TRANSFER.
IN NO PARTICULAR ORDER OF *STUPIDITY*.

...ALL I'M ASKING IS THAT YOU *WORK* WITH ME HERE, THREE.

*THREE?*

MAN, YOU ARE, LIKE, COMPLETE *DULLSVILLE*, TREVOR.

LIGHTEN *UP.* THE BEAUTIFUL PEOPLE ARE TRYING TO ESTABLISH HARMONIC *RESONANCE.*

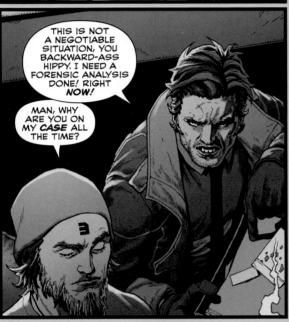

THIS IS NOT A NEGOTIABLE SITUATION, YOU BACKWARD-ASS HIPPY. I NEED A FORENSIC ANALYSIS DONE! RIGHT *NOW!*

MAN, WHY ARE YOU ON MY *CASE* ALL THE TIME?

I'M NOT "ON YOUR CASE"! IT'S YOUR *JOB!* YOU WERE GENETICALLY PROGRAMMED TO BE MY FORENSICS EXPERT!

HEY, I DIDN'T ASK THEM TO CLONE ME FROM A TOTAL *SQUARE!*

AND I DIDN'T ASK THEM TO CLONE ME INTO A *BEATNIK!* NOW ARE YOU GOING TO DO THIS JOB OR NOT?

VORGAS, WHAT THE HELL ARE YOU EATING? DO YOU HAVE ANY IDEA WHAT'S IN THOSE BROWNIES?

WELL, THEY'RE ABOUT TO REVEAL THEIR SECRET INGREDIENT.

NO...*MPHH...* BUT THEY ARE MOST *DELIGHTFUL.*

REPORT. MY DESK. END OF DAY.

OWW! HEY!

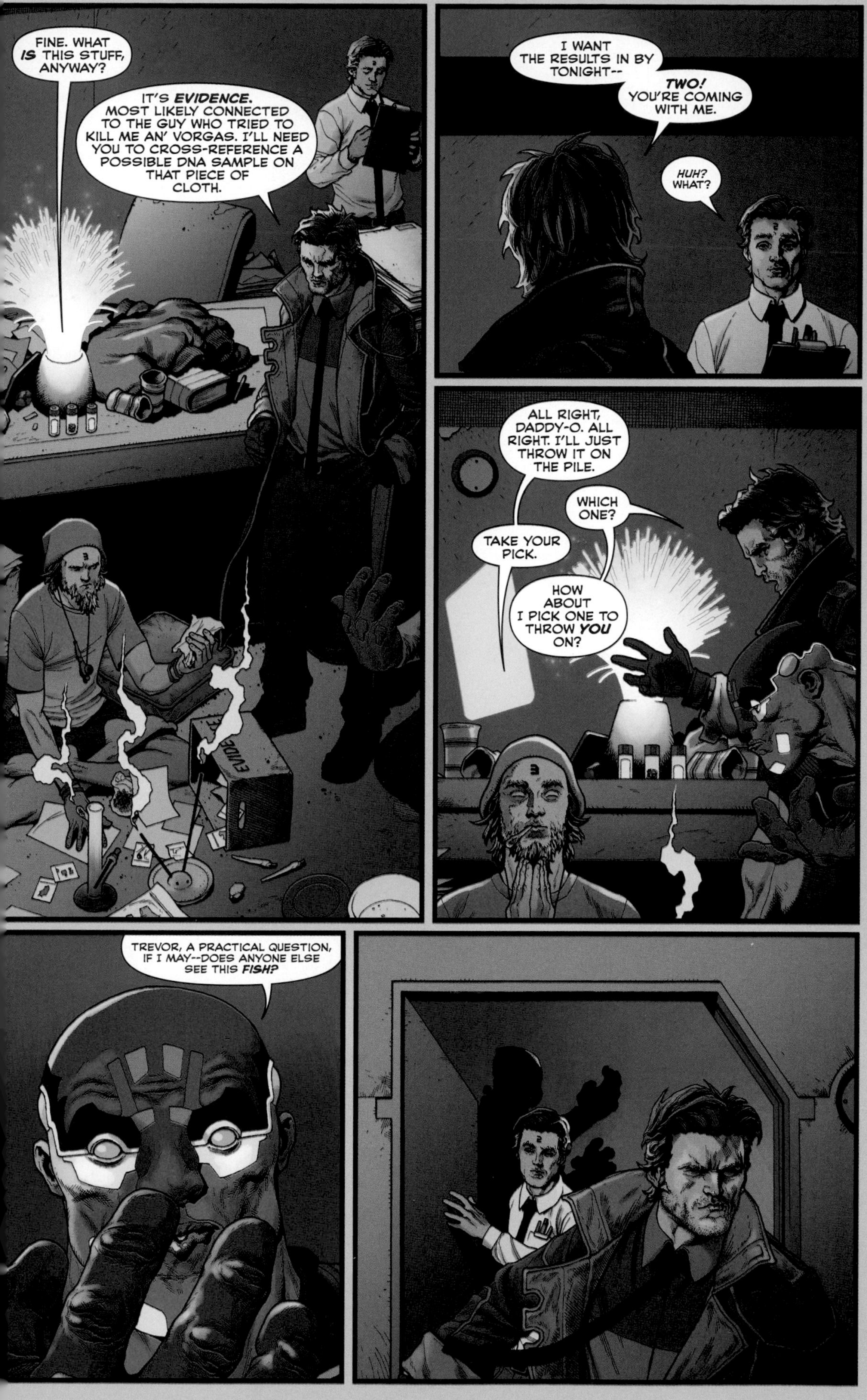

FINE. WHAT *IS* THIS STUFF, ANYWAY?
IT'S ***EVIDENCE.*** MOST LIKELY CONNECTED TO THE GUY WHO TRIED TO KILL ME AN' VORGAS. I'LL NEED YOU TO CROSS-REFERENCE A POSSIBLE DNA SAMPLE ON THAT PIECE OF CLOTH.
EVIDE
I WANT THE RESULTS IN BY TONIGHT--
***TWO!*** YOU'RE COMING WITH ME.
*HUH? WHAT?*
ALL RIGHT, DADDY-O. ALL RIGHT. I'LL JUST THROW IT ON THE PILE.
WHICH ONE?
TAKE YOUR PICK.
HOW ABOUT I PICK ONE TO THROW ***YOU*** ON?
TREVOR, A PRACTICAL QUESTION, IF I MAY--DOES ANYONE ELSE SEE THIS ***FISH?***

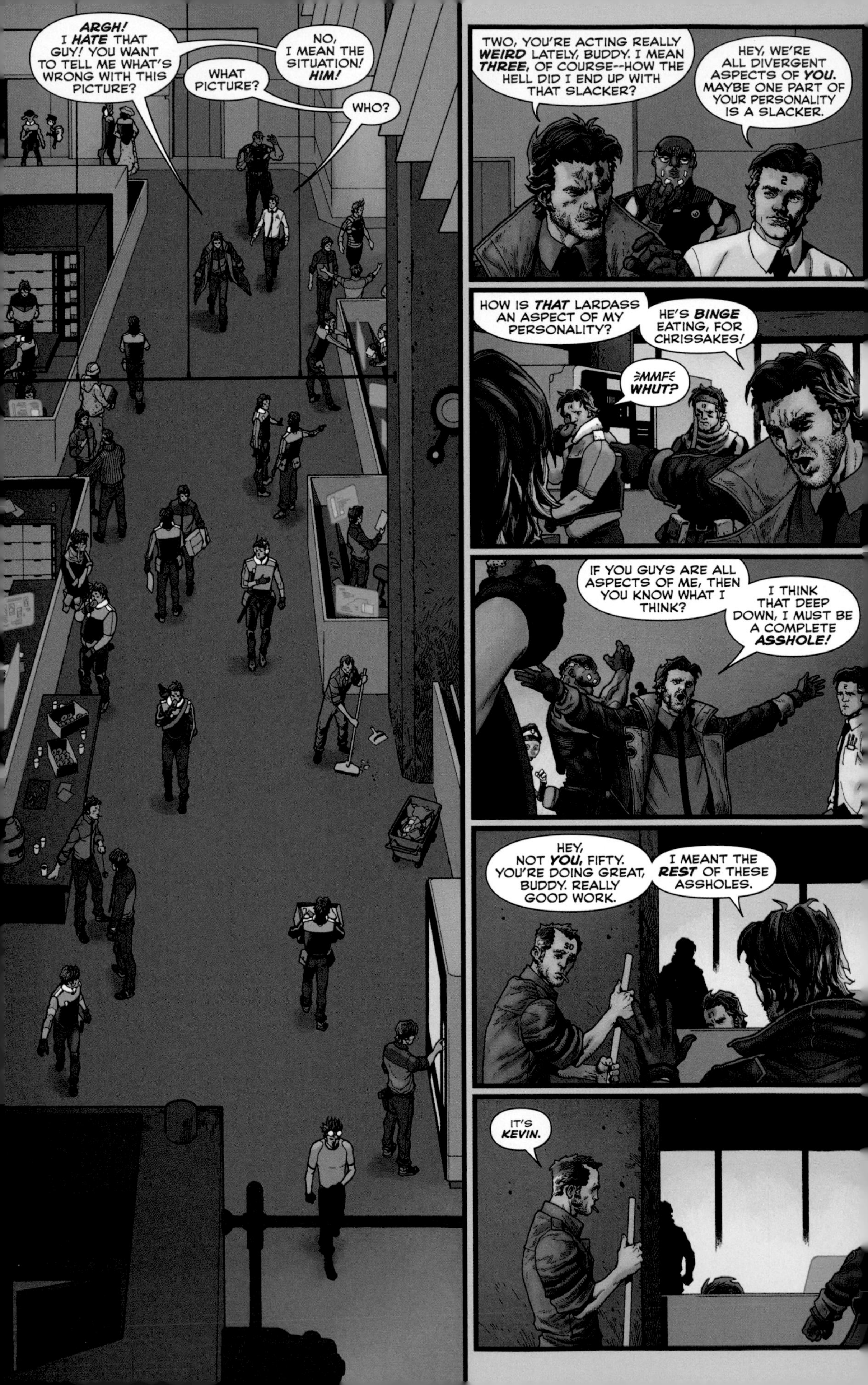
ARGH! I HATE THAT GUY! YOU WANT TO TELL ME WHAT'S WRONG WITH THIS PICTURE?
WHAT PICTURE?
NO, I MEAN THE SITUATION! HIM!
WHO?
TWO, YOU'RE ACTING REALLY WEIRD LATELY, BUDDY. I MEAN THREE, OF COURSE--HOW THE HELL DID I END UP WITH THAT SLACKER?
HEY, WE'RE ALL DIVERGENT ASPECTS OF YOU. MAYBE ONE PART OF YOUR PERSONALITY IS A SLACKER.
HOW IS THAT LARDASS AN ASPECT OF MY PERSONALITY?
HE'S BINGE EATING, FOR CHRISSAKES!
MMF WHUT?
IF YOU GUYS ARE ALL ASPECTS OF ME, THEN YOU KNOW WHAT I THINK?
I THINK THAT DEEP DOWN, I MUST BE A COMPLETE ASSHOLE!
HEY, NOT YOU, FIFTY. YOU'RE DOING GREAT, BUDDY. REALLY GOOD WORK.
I MEANT THE REST OF THESE ASSHOLES.
IT'S KEVIN.

WE GOTTA TAKE **STOCK**, TWO. WHAT'VE WE GOT?

ALL RIGHT, LET'S SEE...THREE'S ON FORENSICS. FIVE AND THIRTY-EIGHT ARE OVER AT THE JUL'DAN EMBASSY.

SIX AND FORTY-EIGHT ARE ON SURVEILLANCE. NINETEEN PULLED US A LEAD ON SOME ACTIVITY OVER AT THE SCARLET CONSULATE.

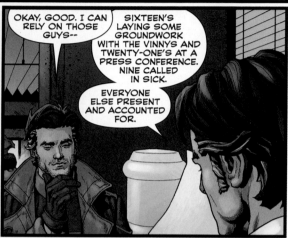

OKAY, GOOD. I CAN RELY ON THOSE GUYS--

SIXTEEN'S LAYING SOME GROUNDWORK WITH THE VINNYS AND TWENTY-ONE'S AT A PRESS CONFERENCE. NINE CALLED IN SICK.

EVERYONE ELSE PRESENT AND ACCOUNTED FOR.

ALL RIGHT, ALL RIGHT...NOW WE'RE **GETTING** SOMEWHERE. WHAT ABOUT ME? WHAT'S ON THE AGENDA?

WE HAVE A FOLLOW-UP MEETING WITH QUEEN KYA AND AMBASSADOR BRR'VIL AND, *UH*...YEAH...

UH, YEAH, **WHAT?**

NOTHING. THERE WAS JUST KIND OF A MIX-UP LAST TIME.

WHAT **KIND** OF MIX-UP?

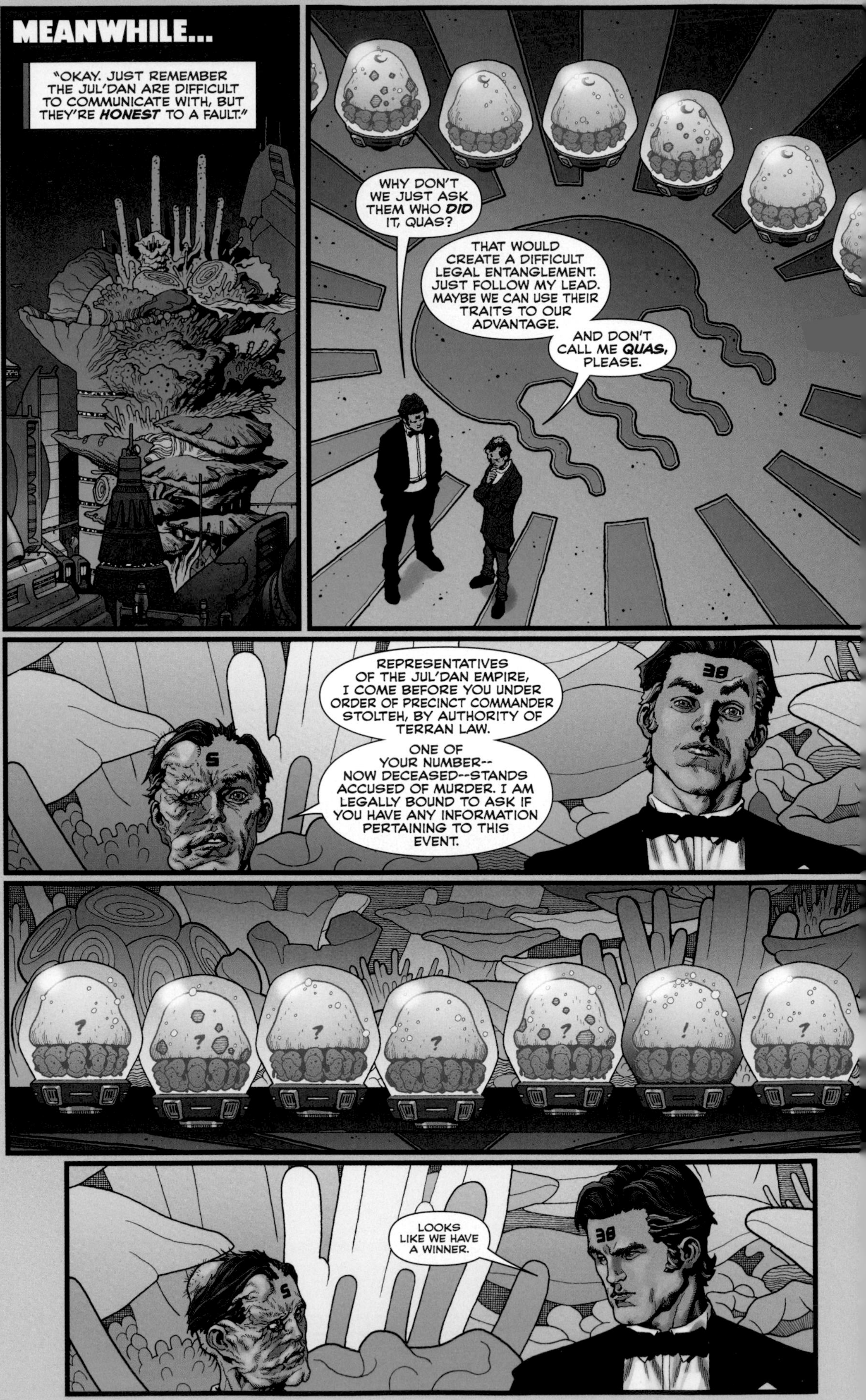
MEANWHILE...
"OKAY. JUST REMEMBER THE JUL'DAN ARE DIFFICULT TO COMMUNICATE WITH, BUT THEY'RE HONEST TO A FAULT."
WHY DON'T WE JUST ASK THEM WHO DID IT, QUAS?
THAT WOULD CREATE A DIFFICULT LEGAL ENTANGLEMENT. JUST FOLLOW MY LEAD. MAYBE WE CAN USE THEIR TRAITS TO OUR ADVANTAGE.
AND DON'T CALL ME QUAS, PLEASE.
REPRESENTATIVES OF THE JUL'DAN EMPIRE, I COME BEFORE YOU UNDER ORDER OF PRECINCT COMMANDER STOLTEH, BY AUTHORITY OF TERRAN LAW.
ONE OF YOUR NUMBER-- NOW DECEASED--STANDS ACCUSED OF MURDER. I AM LEGALLY BOUND TO ASK IF YOU HAVE ANY INFORMATION PERTAINING TO THIS EVENT.
?
?
?
?
?
!
?
LOOKS LIKE WE HAVE A WINNER.

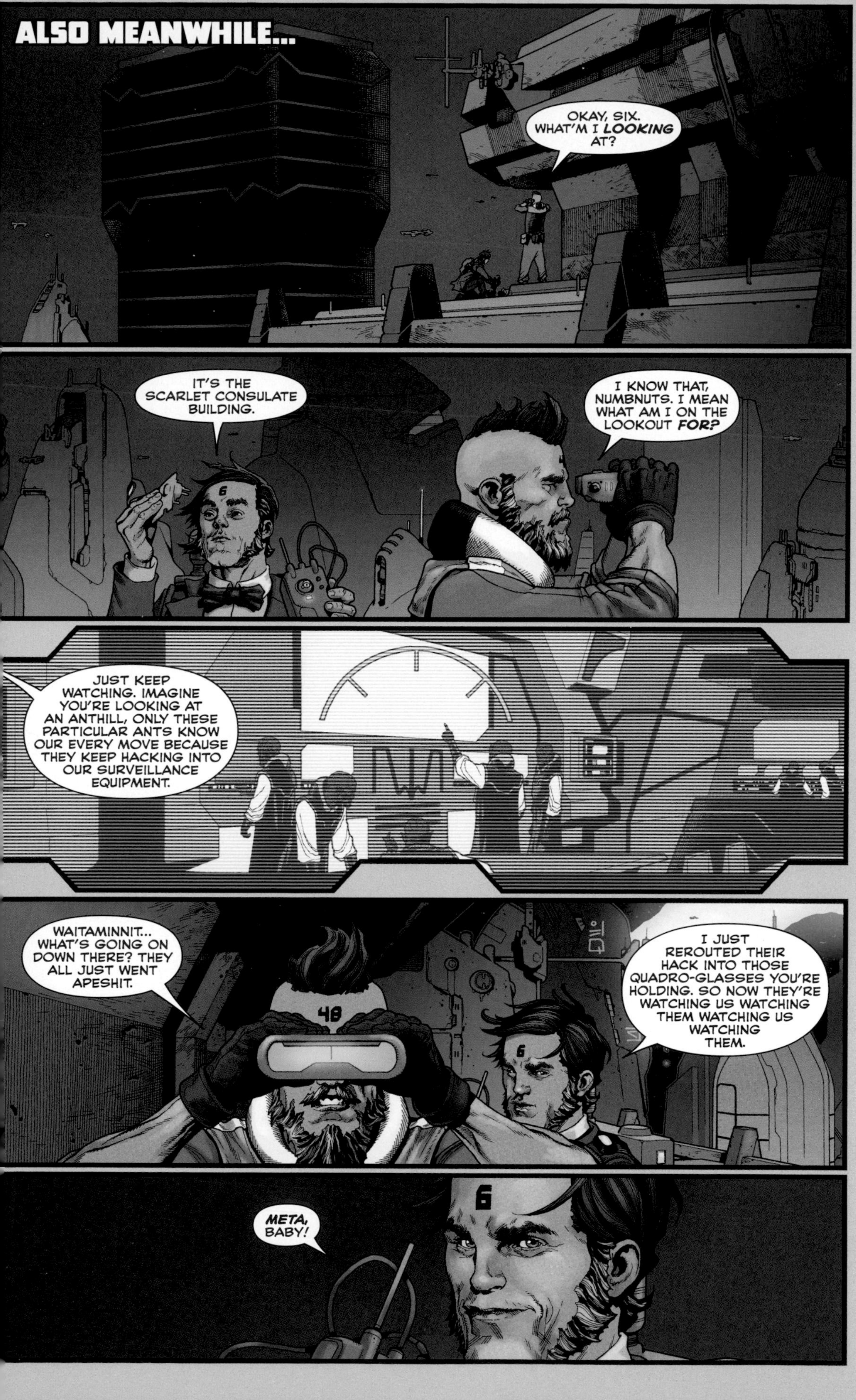
ALSO MEANWHILE...
OKAY, SIX. WHAT'M I LOOKING AT?
IT'S THE SCARLET CONSULATE BUILDING.
I KNOW THAT, NUMBNUTS. I MEAN WHAT AM I ON THE LOOKOUT FOR?
JUST KEEP WATCHING. IMAGINE YOU'RE LOOKING AT AN ANTHILL, ONLY THESE PARTICULAR ANTS KNOW OUR EVERY MOVE BECAUSE THEY KEEP HACKING INTO OUR SURVEILLANCE EQUIPMENT.
WAITAMINNIT... WHAT'S GOING ON DOWN THERE? THEY ALL JUST WENT APESHIT.
I JUST REROUTED THEIR HACK INTO THOSE QUADRO-GLASSES YOU'RE HOLDING. SO NOW THEY'RE WATCHING US WATCHING THEM WATCHING US WATCHING THEM.
META, BABY!

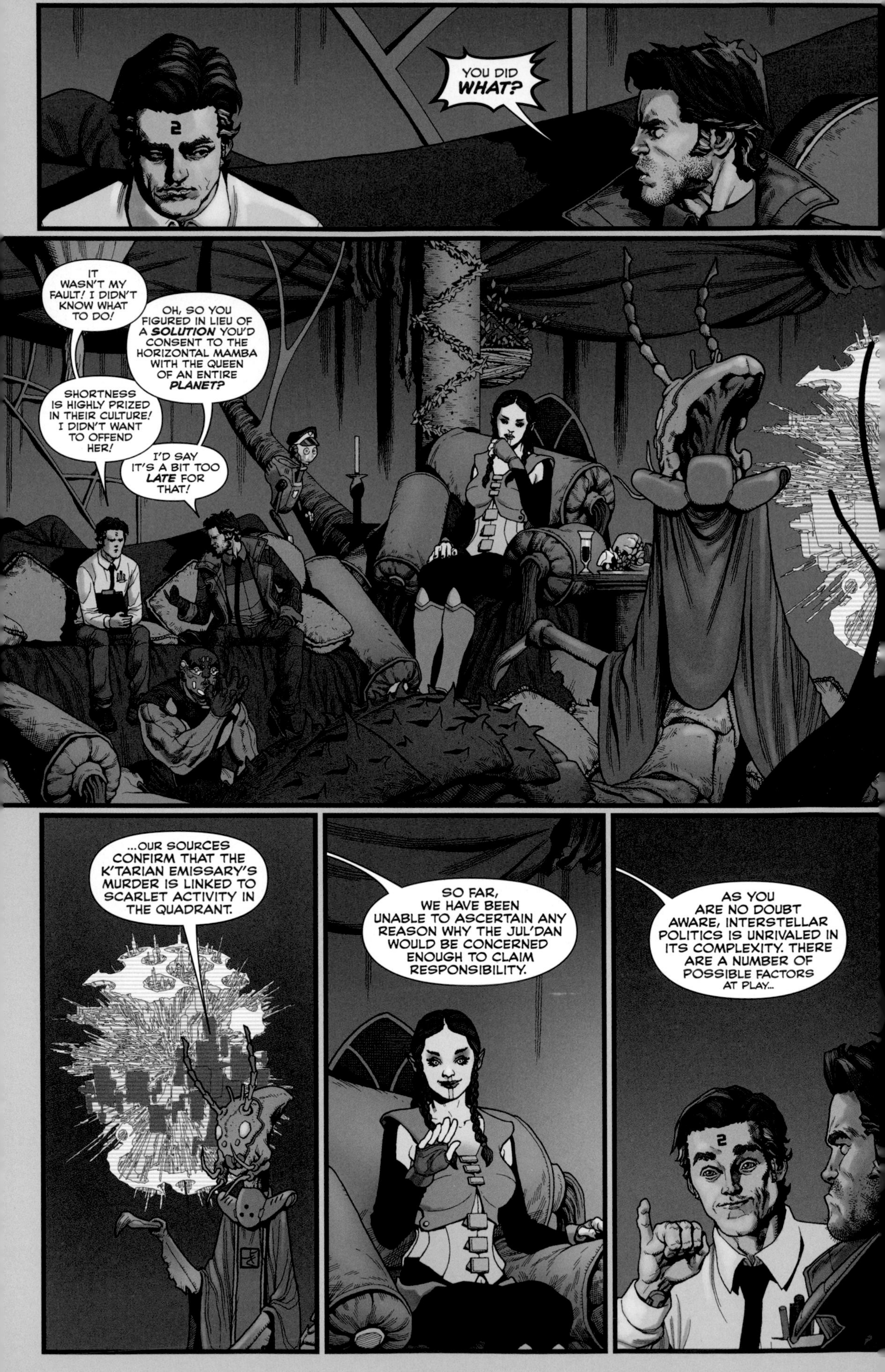
YOU DID WHAT?
IT WASN'T MY FAULT! I DIDN'T KNOW WHAT TO DO!
OH, SO YOU FIGURED IN LIEU OF A SOLUTION YOU'D CONSENT TO THE HORIZONTAL MAMBA WITH THE QUEEN OF AN ENTIRE PLANET?
SHORTNESS IS HIGHLY PRIZED IN THEIR CULTURE! I DIDN'T WANT TO OFFEND HER!
I'D SAY IT'S A BIT TOO LATE FOR THAT!
...OUR SOURCES CONFIRM THAT THE K'TARIAN EMISSARY'S MURDER IS LINKED TO SCARLET ACTIVITY IN THE QUADRANT.
SO FAR, WE HAVE BEEN UNABLE TO ASCERTAIN ANY REASON WHY THE JUL'DAN WOULD BE CONCERNED ENOUGH TO CLAIM RESPONSIBILITY.
AS YOU ARE NO DOUBT AWARE, INTERSTELLAR POLITICS IS UNRIVALED IN ITS COMPLEXITY. THERE ARE A NUMBER OF POSSIBLE FACTORS AT PLAY...

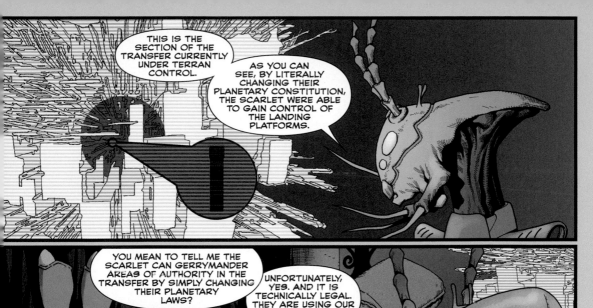

THIS IS THE SECTION OF THE TRANSFER CURRENTLY UNDER TERRAN CONTROL.

AS YOU CAN SEE, BY LITERALLY CHANGING THEIR PLANETARY CONSTITUTION, THE SCARLET WERE ABLE TO GAIN CONTROL OF THE LANDING PLATFORMS.

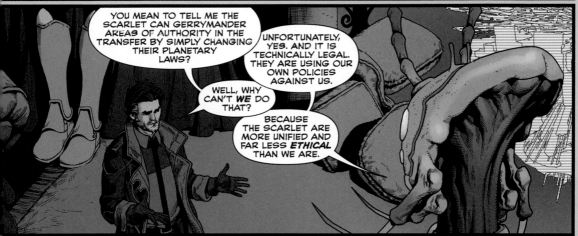

YOU MEAN TO TELL ME THE SCARLET CAN GERRYMANDER AREAS OF AUTHORITY IN THE TRANSFER BY SIMPLY CHANGING THEIR PLANETARY LAWS?

UNFORTUNATELY, YES. AND IT IS TECHNICALLY LEGAL. THEY ARE USING OUR OWN POLICIES AGAINST US.

WELL, WHY CAN'T *WE* DO THAT?

BECAUSE THE SCARLET ARE MORE UNIFIED AND FAR LESS *ETHICAL* THAN WE ARE.

SOURCE TELLS ME THIS HAS SOMETHING TO DO WITH A SPACE ROCK CALLED *MZULTCH*. YOU EVER HEARD OF IT?

WHAT? *THE* MZULTCH? ARE YOU SURE?

HOW MANY MZULTCHES ARE THERE?

JUST *ONE*, DETECTIVE CHURCHILL--AND SIXTY-SEVEN SURVIVORS WHO HAVE APPLIED FOR FULL PLANETARY STATUS.

AND NOW I FEAR I UNDERSTAND THE NATURE OF THE SCARLET'S INVOLVEMENT--THEY ARE TRYING TO GAIN ACCESS TO THE MACHINE INTERFACTION SECTION OF THE TRANSFER.

I DIDN'T HEAR THAT.

OF *COURSE* YOU DID!

OR THAT! NO MACHINES!

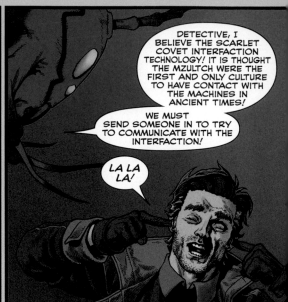

DETECTIVE, I BELIEVE THE SCARLET COVET INTERFACTION TECHNOLOGY! IT IS THOUGHT THE MZULTCH WERE THE FIRST AND ONLY CULTURE TO HAVE CONTACT WITH THE MACHINES IN ANCIENT TIMES!

WE MUST SEND SOMEONE IN TO TRY TO COMMUNICATE WITH THE INTERFACTION!

LA LA LA!

WAITAMINNIT... NO ONE'S EVER GONE IN THE MACHINE SECTION AND COME BACK OUT. CAN WE SEND *VORGAS?*

NOT UNLESS WE WANT TO START A THERMONUCLEAR WAR.

WELL, WHO'VE WE GOT?

LET'S SEE...WHAT ABOUT THIRTY-EIGHT?

TOO VALUABLE.

ELEVEN?

IDIOT.

*TWELVE!*

AMBASSADOR BRR'VIL...YOUR ROYAL HIGHNESS...WE'LL NEED A LITTLE TIME TO SET THIS UP.

I BELIEVE WE MAY HAVE A SUITABLE CANDIDATE TO TRY TO MAKE CONTACT WITH THE MACHINE INTERFACTION.

ATTABOY, DETECTIVE!

SLAP

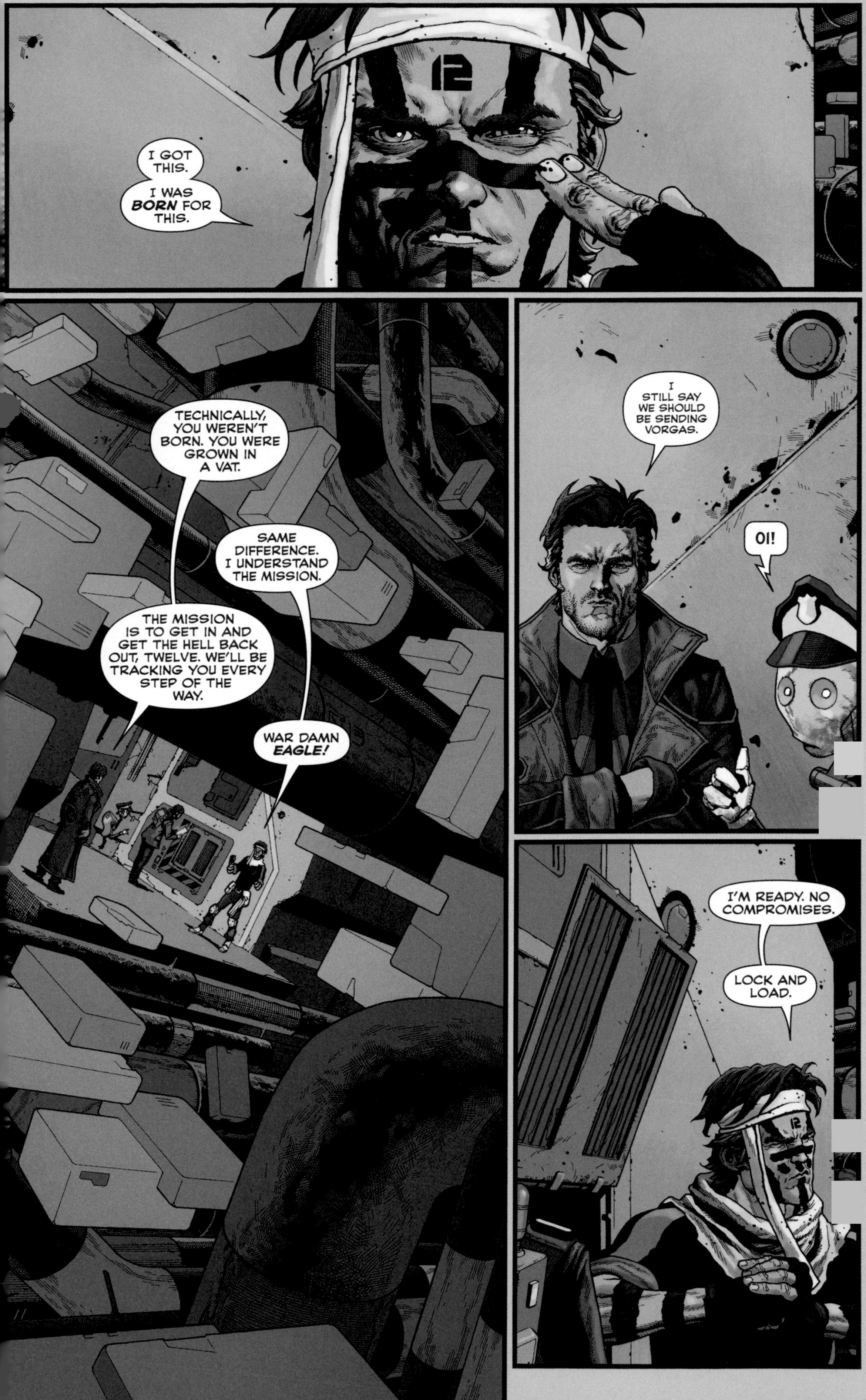
I GOT THIS.
I WAS **BORN** FOR THIS.
TECHNICALLY, YOU WEREN'T BORN. YOU WERE GROWN IN A VAT.
SAME DIFFERENCE. I UNDERSTAND THE MISSION.
THE MISSION IS TO GET IN AND GET THE HELL BACK OUT, TWELVE. WE'LL BE TRACKING YOU EVERY STEP OF THE WAY.
WAR DAMN ***EAGLE!***
I STILL SAY WE SHOULD BE SENDING VORGAS.
OI!
I'M READY. NO COMPROMISES.
LOCK AND LOAD.

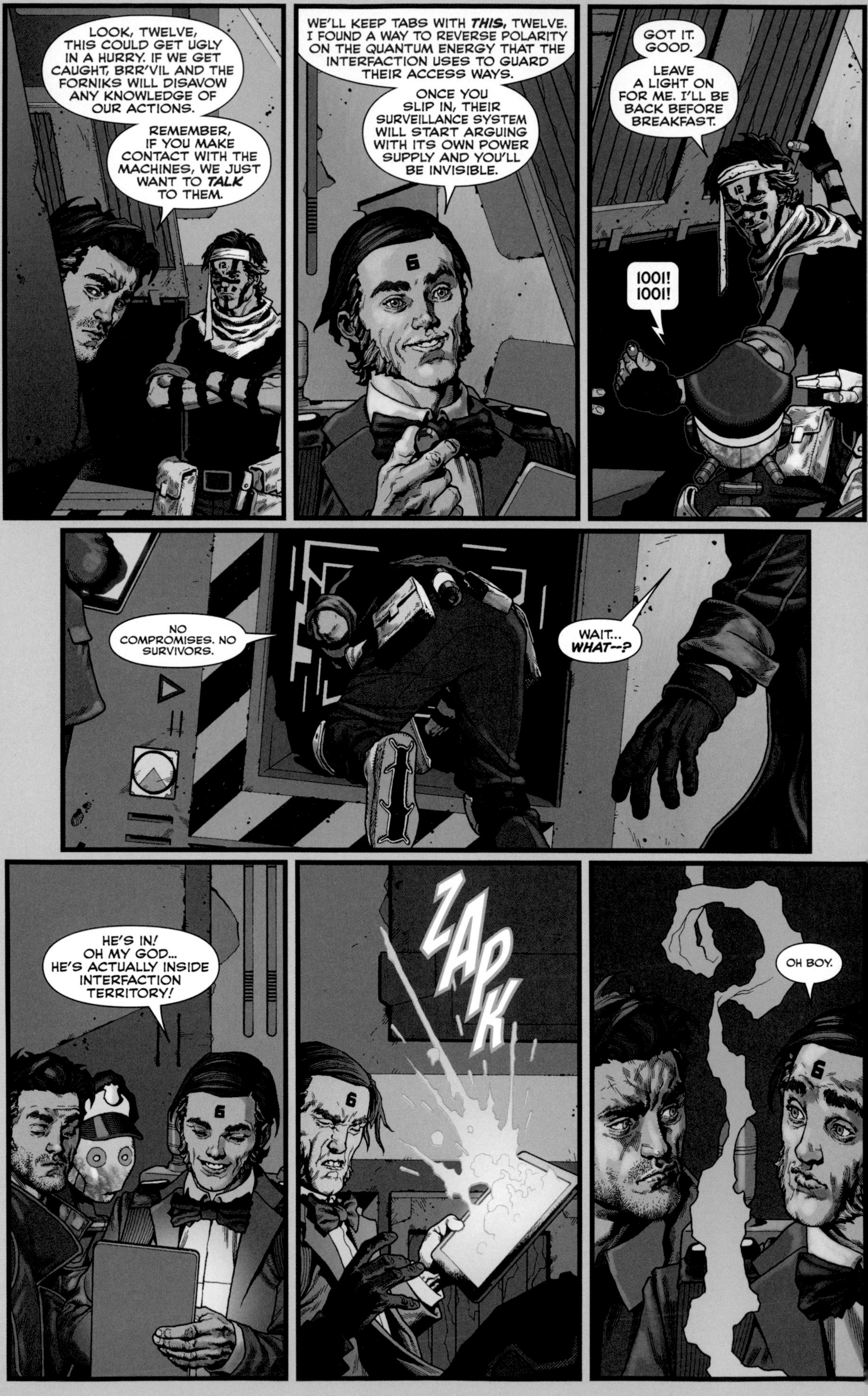
LOOK, TWELVE, THIS COULD GET UGLY IN A HURRY. IF WE GET CAUGHT, BRR'VIL AND THE FORNIKS WILL DISAVOW ANY KNOWLEDGE OF OUR ACTIONS.
REMEMBER, IF YOU MAKE CONTACT WITH THE MACHINES, WE JUST WANT TO *TALK* TO THEM.
WE'LL KEEP TABS WITH *THIS,* TWELVE. I FOUND A WAY TO REVERSE POLARITY ON THE QUANTUM ENERGY THAT THE INTERFACTION USES TO GUARD THEIR ACCESS WAYS.
ONCE YOU SLIP IN, THEIR SURVEILLANCE SYSTEM WILL START ARGUING WITH ITS OWN POWER SUPPLY AND YOU'LL BE INVISIBLE.
GOT IT. GOOD.
LEAVE A LIGHT ON FOR ME. I'LL BE BACK BEFORE BREAKFAST.
1001! 1001!
NO COMPROMISES. NO SURVIVORS.
WAIT... *WHAT--?*
HE'S IN! OH MY GOD... HE'S ACTUALLY INSIDE INTERFACTION TERRITORY!
ZAPK
OH BOY.

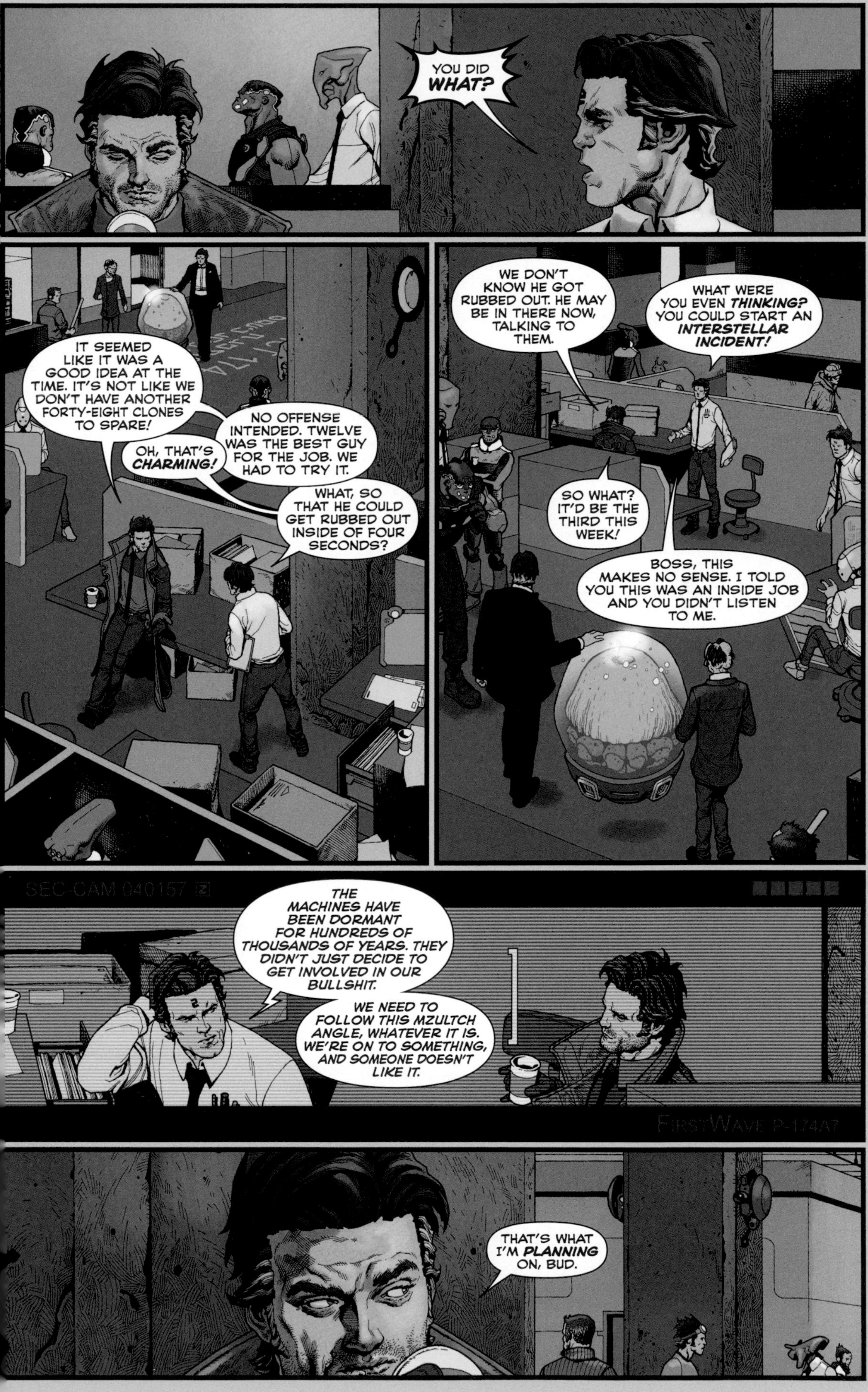
YOU DID WHAT?
IT SEEMED LIKE IT WAS A GOOD IDEA AT THE TIME. IT'S NOT LIKE WE DON'T HAVE ANOTHER FORTY-EIGHT CLONES TO SPARE!
NO OFFENSE INTENDED. TWELVE WAS THE BEST GUY FOR THE JOB. WE HAD TO TRY IT.
OH, THAT'S CHARMING!
WHAT, SO THAT HE COULD GET RUBBED OUT INSIDE OF FOUR SECONDS?
WE DON'T KNOW HE GOT RUBBED OUT. HE MAY BE IN THERE NOW, TALKING TO THEM.
WHAT WERE YOU EVEN THINKING? YOU COULD START AN INTERSTELLAR INCIDENT!
SO WHAT? IT'D BE THE THIRD THIS WEEK!
BOSS, THIS MAKES NO SENSE. I TOLD YOU THIS WAS AN INSIDE JOB AND YOU DIDN'T LISTEN TO ME.
SEC-CAM 040157
THE MACHINES HAVE BEEN DORMANT FOR HUNDREDS OF THOUSANDS OF YEARS. THEY DIDN'T JUST DECIDE TO GET INVOLVED IN OUR BULLSHIT.
WE NEED TO FOLLOW THIS MZULTCH ANGLE, WHATEVER IT IS. WE'RE ON TO SOMETHING, AND SOMEONE DOESN'T LIKE IT.
FIRSTWAVE P-174A7
THAT'S WHAT I'M PLANNING ON, BUD.

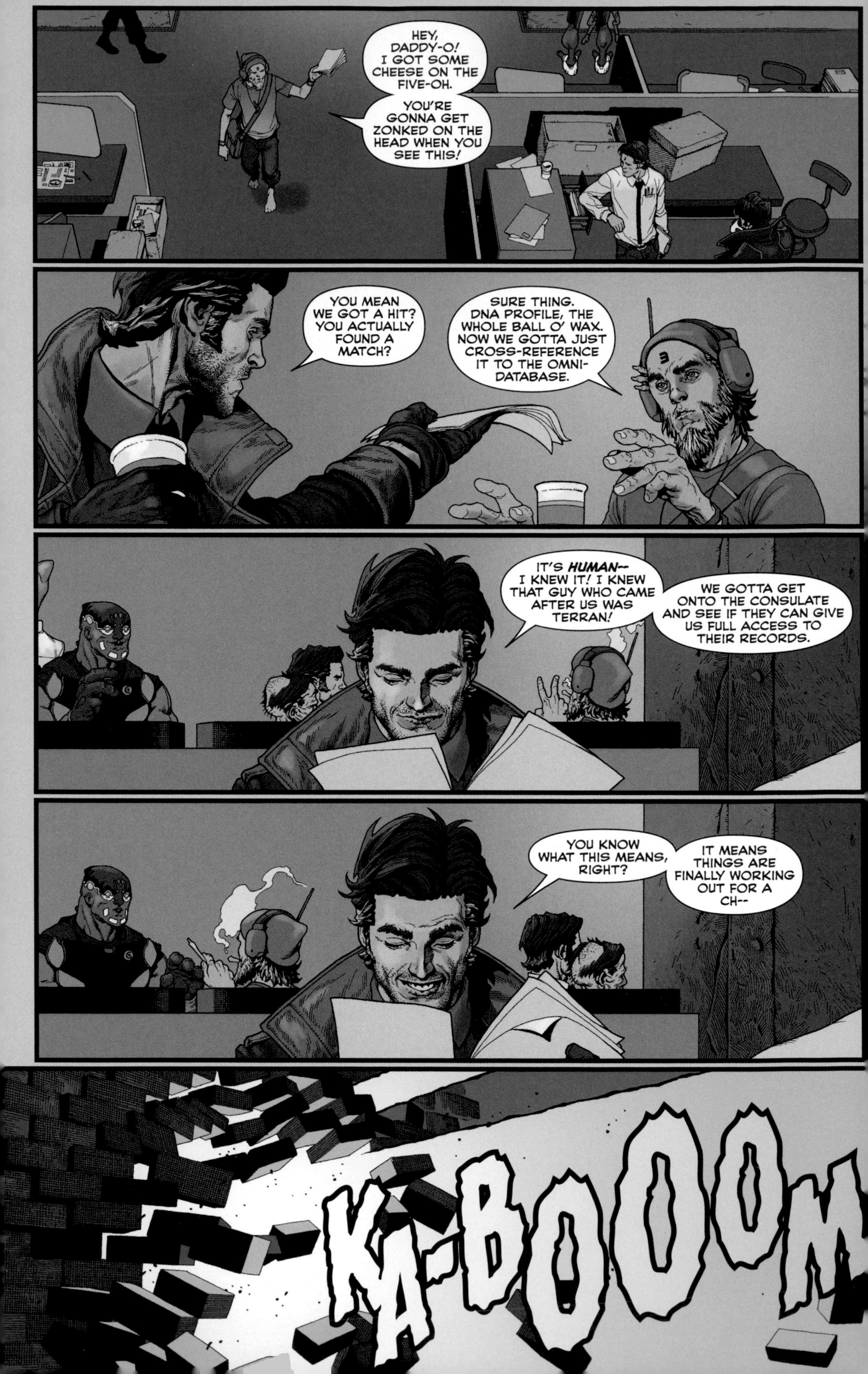
HEY, DADDY-O! I GOT SOME CHEESE ON THE FIVE-OH.
YOU'RE GONNA GET ZONKED ON THE HEAD WHEN YOU SEE THIS!
YOU MEAN WE GOT A HIT? YOU ACTUALLY FOUND A MATCH?
SURE THING. DNA PROFILE, THE WHOLE BALL O' WAX. NOW WE GOTTA JUST CROSS-REFERENCE IT TO THE OMNI-DATABASE.
IT'S HUMAN-- I KNEW IT! I KNEW THAT GUY WHO CAME AFTER US WAS TERRAN!
WE GOTTA GET ONTO THE CONSULATE AND SEE IF THEY CAN GIVE US FULL ACCESS TO THEIR RECORDS.
YOU KNOW WHAT THIS MEANS, RIGHT?
IT MEANS THINGS ARE FINALLY WORKING OUT FOR A CH--
KA-BOOOM

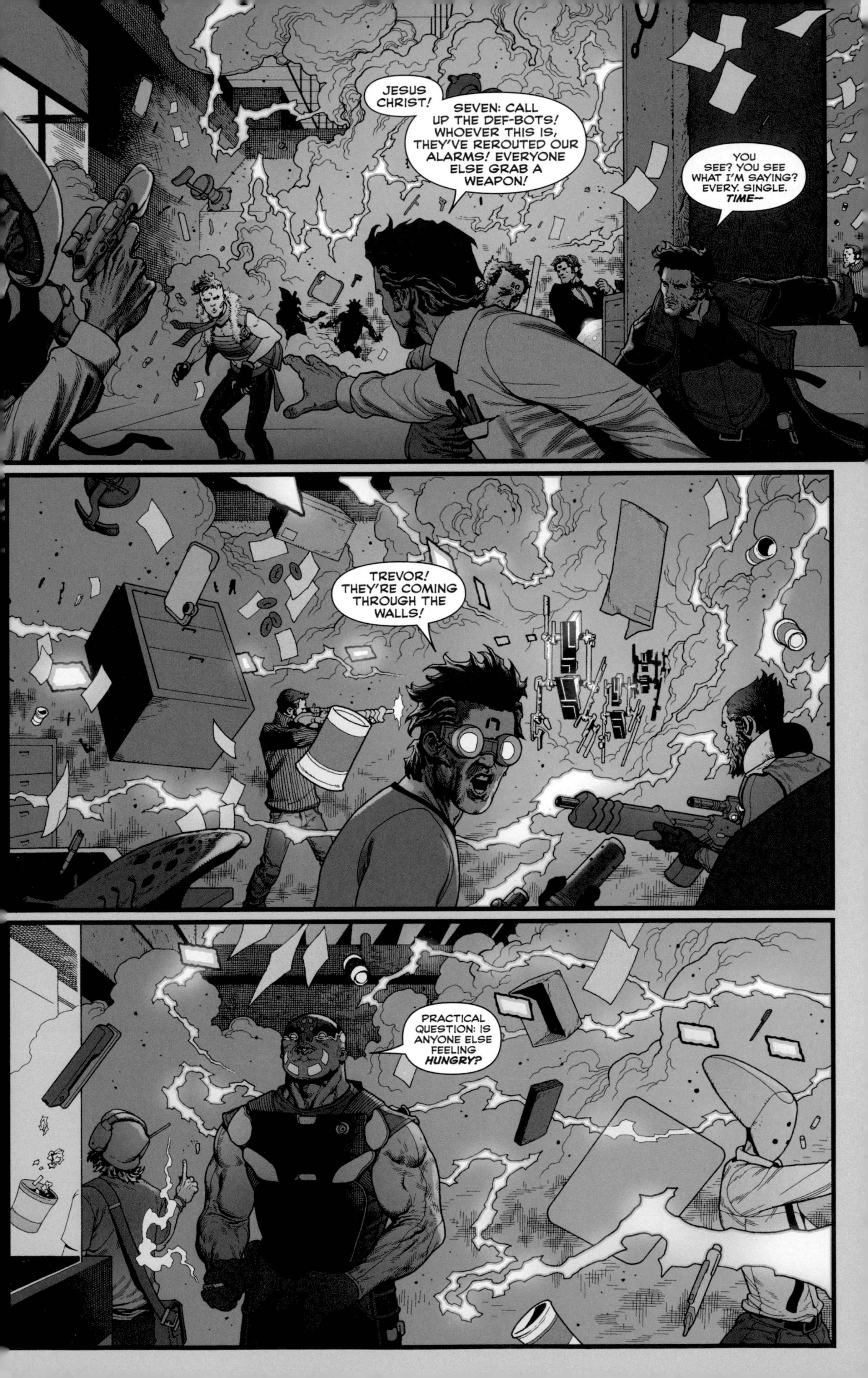
JESUS CHRIST!
SEVEN: CALL UP THE DEF-BOTS! WHOEVER THIS IS, THEY'VE REROUTED OUR ALARMS! EVERYONE ELSE GRAB A WEAPON!
YOU SEE? YOU SEE WHAT I'M SAYING? EVERY. SINGLE. TIME--
TREVOR! THEY'RE COMING THROUGH THE WALLS!
PRACTICAL QUESTION: IS ANYONE ELSE FEELING HUNGRY?

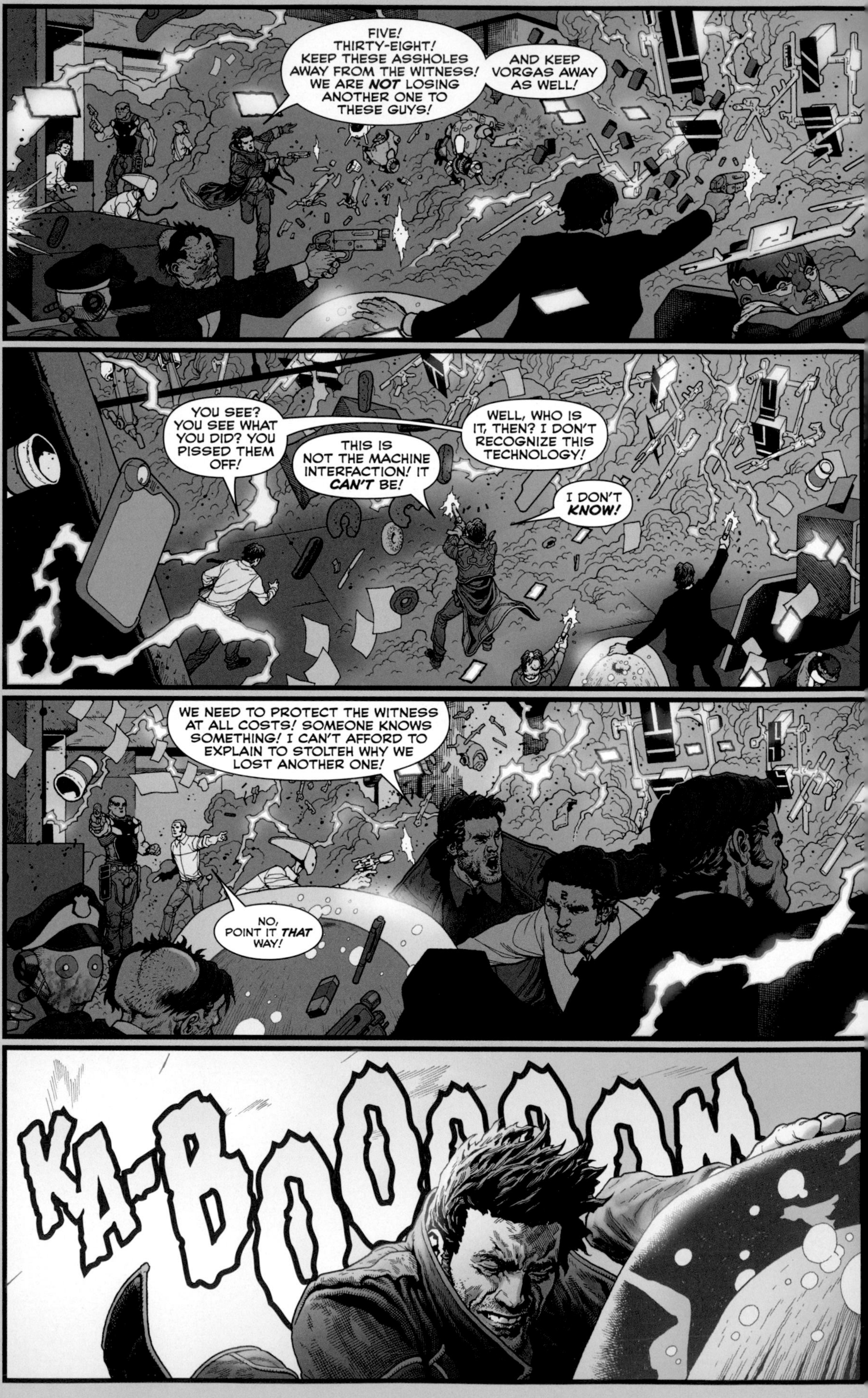
FIVE! THIRTY-EIGHT! KEEP THESE ASSHOLES AWAY FROM THE WITNESS! WE ARE NOT LOSING ANOTHER ONE TO THESE GUYS!
AND KEEP VORGAS AWAY AS WELL!
YOU SEE? YOU SEE WHAT YOU DID? YOU PISSED THEM OFF!
THIS IS NOT THE MACHINE INTERFACTION! IT CAN'T BE!
WELL, WHO IS IT, THEN? I DON'T RECOGNIZE THIS TECHNOLOGY!
I DON'T KNOW!
WE NEED TO PROTECT THE WITNESS AT ALL COSTS! SOMEONE KNOWS SOMETHING! I CAN'T AFFORD TO EXPLAIN TO STOLTEH WHY WE LOST ANOTHER ONE!
NO, POINT IT THAT WAY!
KA-BOOOOM

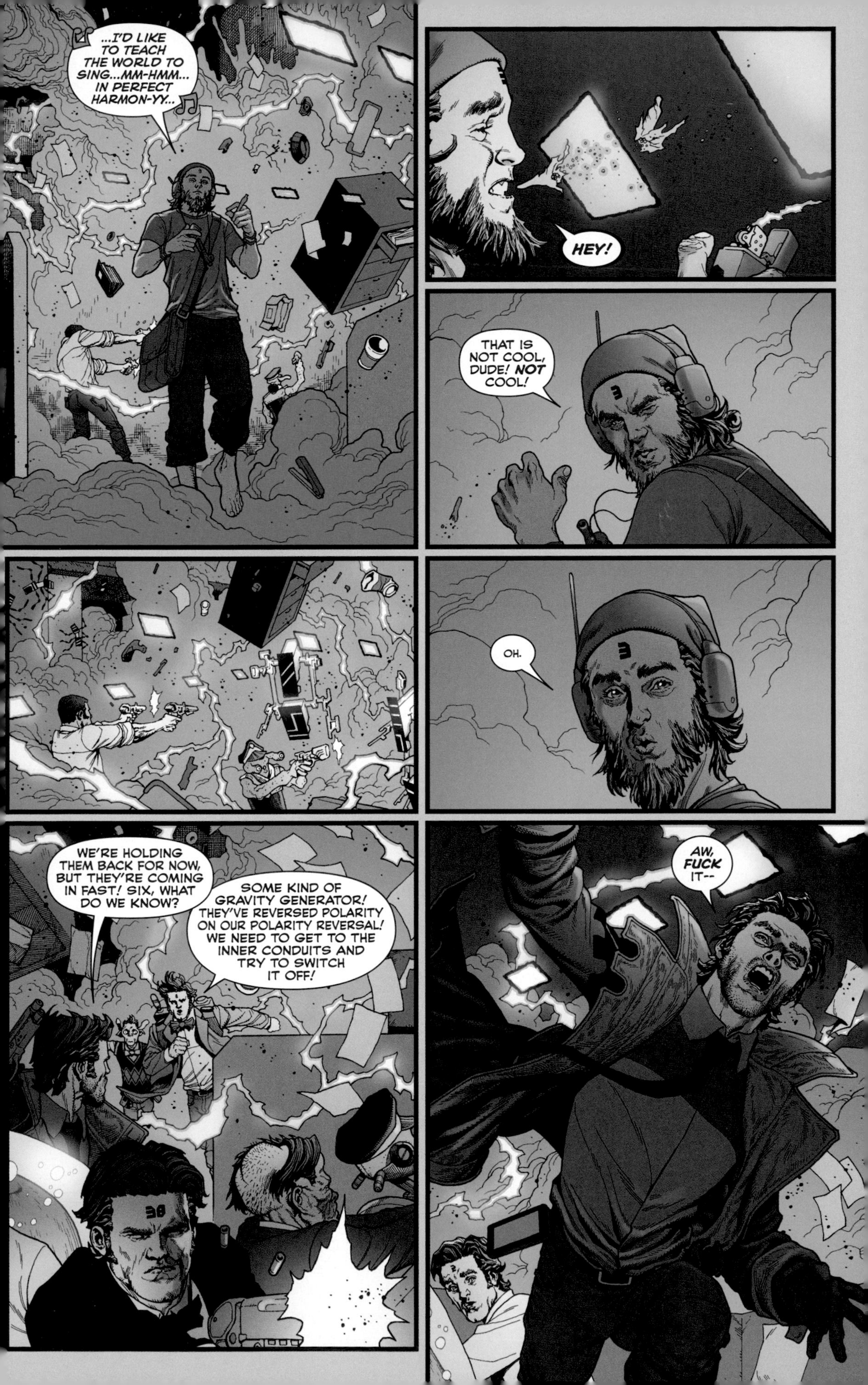

...I'D LIKE TO TEACH THE WORLD TO SING...MM-HMM... IN PERFECT HARMON-YY...
HEY!
THAT IS NOT COOL, DUDE! NOT COOL!
OH.
WE'RE HOLDING THEM BACK FOR NOW, BUT THEY'RE COMING IN FAST! SIX, WHAT DO WE KNOW?
SOME KIND OF GRAVITY GENERATOR! THEY'VE REVERSED POLARITY ON OUR POLARITY REVERSAL! WE NEED TO GET TO THE INNER CONDUITS AND TRY TO SWITCH IT OFF!
AW, FUCK IT--

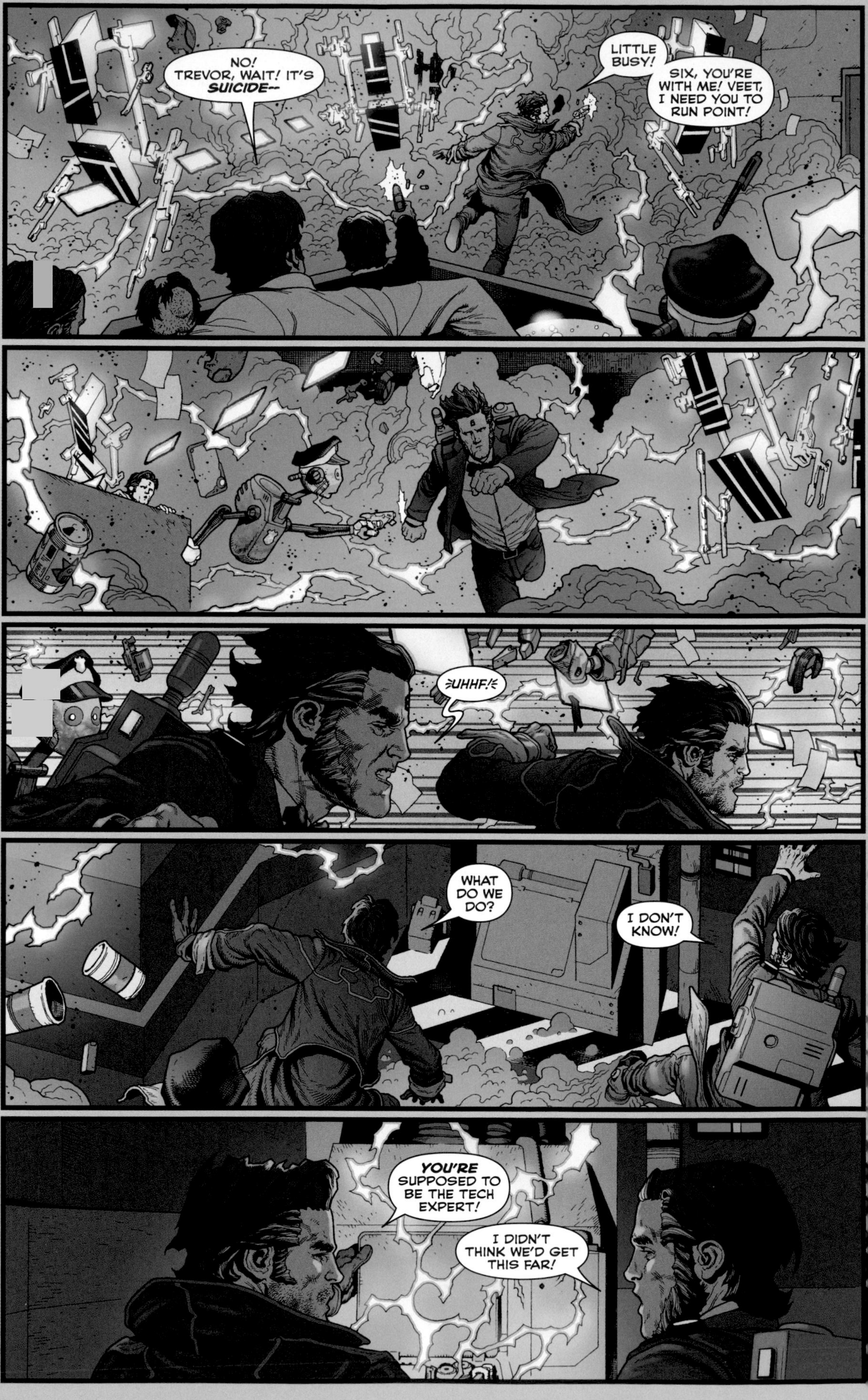
NO! TREVOR, WAIT! IT'S SUICIDE--
LITTLE BUSY!
SIX, YOU'RE WITH ME! VEET, I NEED YOU TO RUN POINT!
UHHF!
WHAT DO WE DO?
I DON'T KNOW!
YOU'RE SUPPOSED TO BE THE TECH EXPERT!
I DIDN'T THINK WE'D GET THIS FAR!

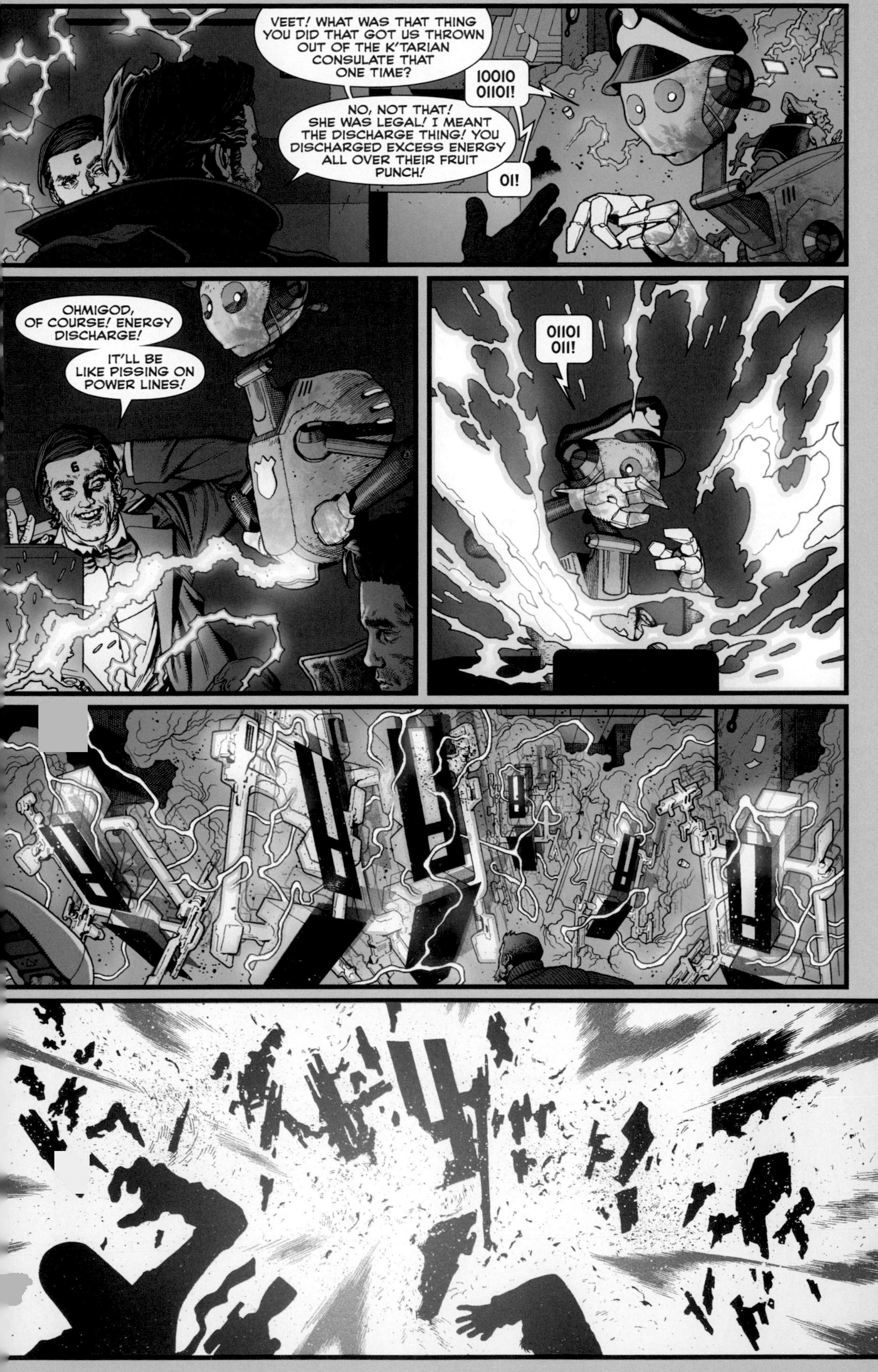
VEET! WHAT WAS THAT THING YOU DID THAT GOT US THROWN OUT OF THE K'TARIAN CONSULATE THAT ONE TIME?
10010 01101!
NO, NOT THAT! SHE WAS LEGAL! I MEANT THE DISCHARGE THING! YOU DISCHARGED EXCESS ENERGY ALL OVER THEIR FRUIT PUNCH!
01!
OHMIGOD, OF COURSE! ENERGY DISCHARGE!
IT'LL BE LIKE PISSING ON POWER LINES!
01101 011!

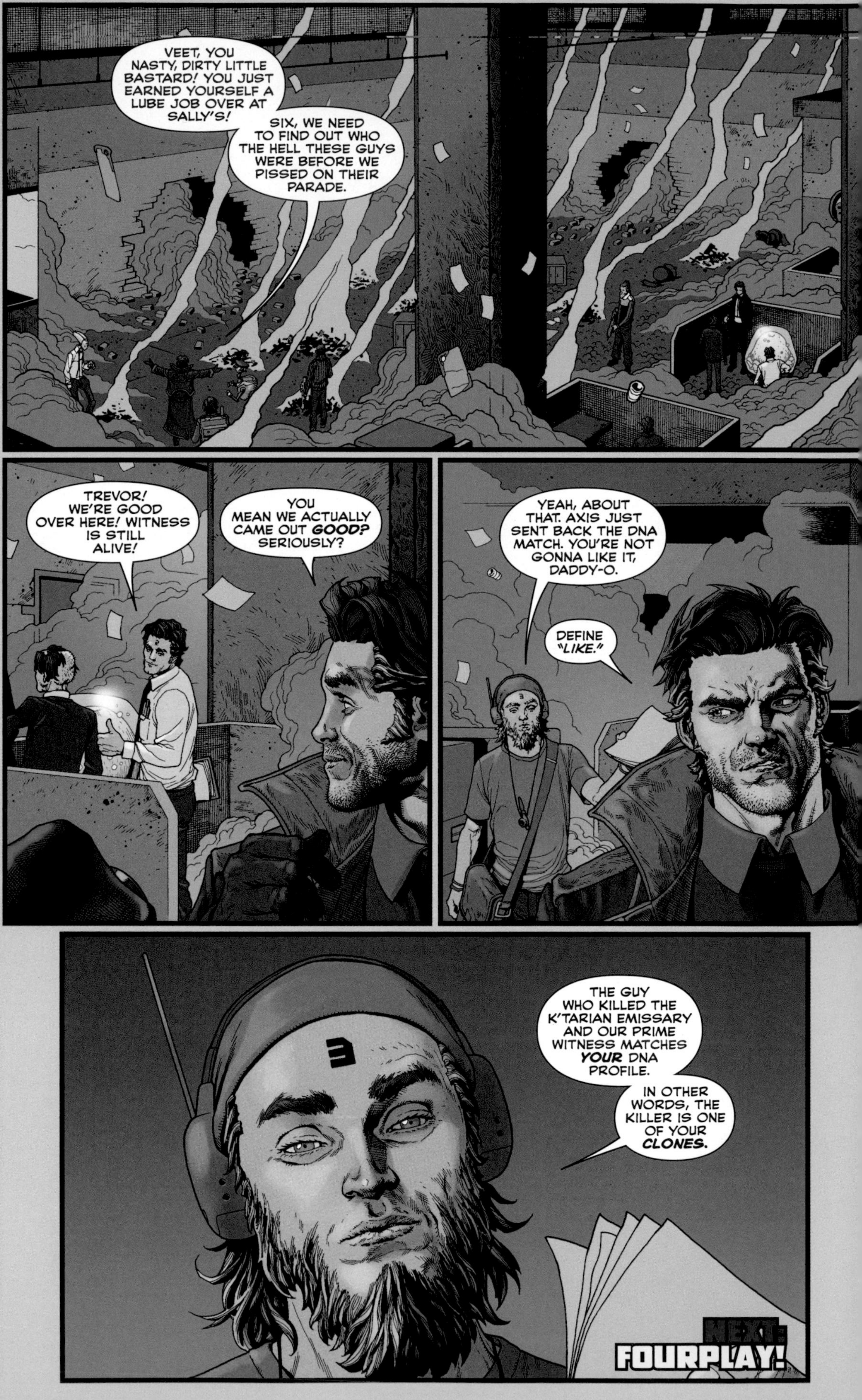
VEET, YOU NASTY, DIRTY LITTLE BASTARD! YOU JUST EARNED YOURSELF A LUBE JOB OVER AT SALLY'S!
SIX, WE NEED TO FIND OUT WHO THE HELL THESE GUYS WERE BEFORE WE PISSED ON THEIR PARADE.
TREVOR! WE'RE GOOD OVER HERE! WITNESS IS STILL ALIVE!
YOU MEAN WE ACTUALLY CAME OUT GOOD? SERIOUSLY?
YEAH, ABOUT THAT. AXIS JUST SENT BACK THE DNA MATCH. YOU'RE NOT GONNA LIKE IT, DADDY-O.
DEFINE "LIKE."
THE GUY WHO KILLED THE K'TARIAN EMISSARY AND OUR PRIME WITNESS MATCHES YOUR DNA PROFILE.
IN OTHER WORDS, THE KILLER IS ONE OF YOUR CLONES.
NEXT: FOURPLAY!

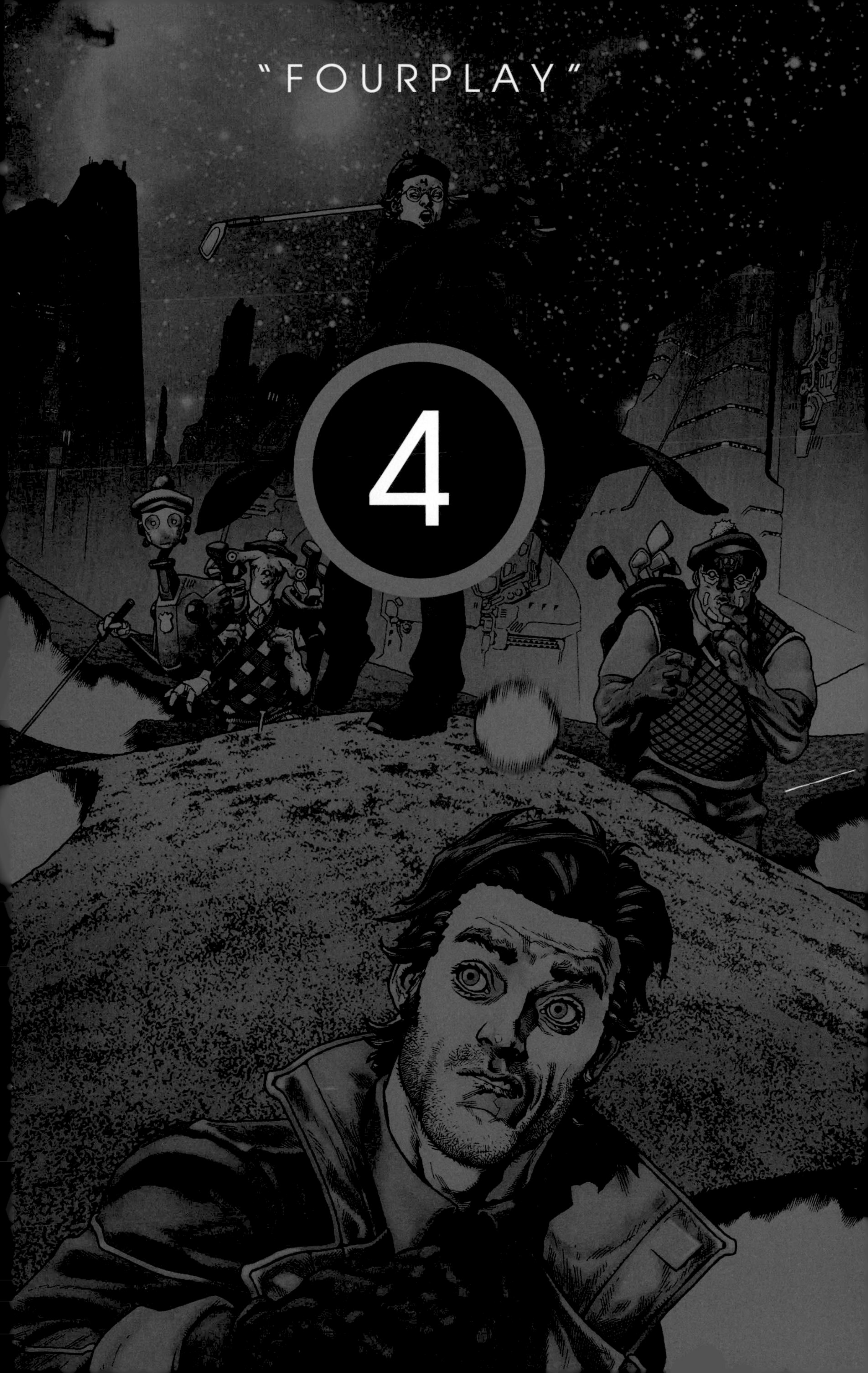
"FOURPLAY"
4

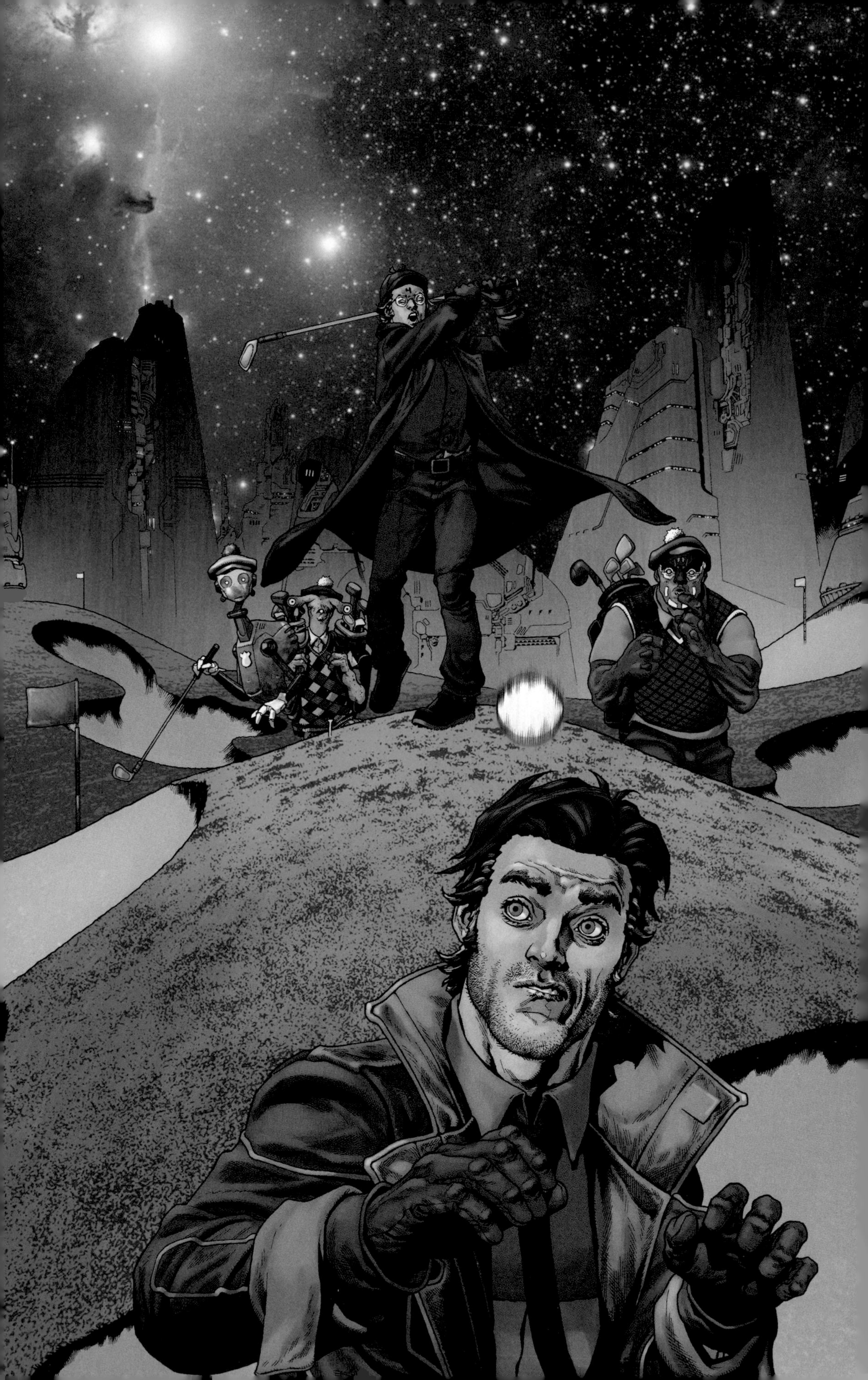

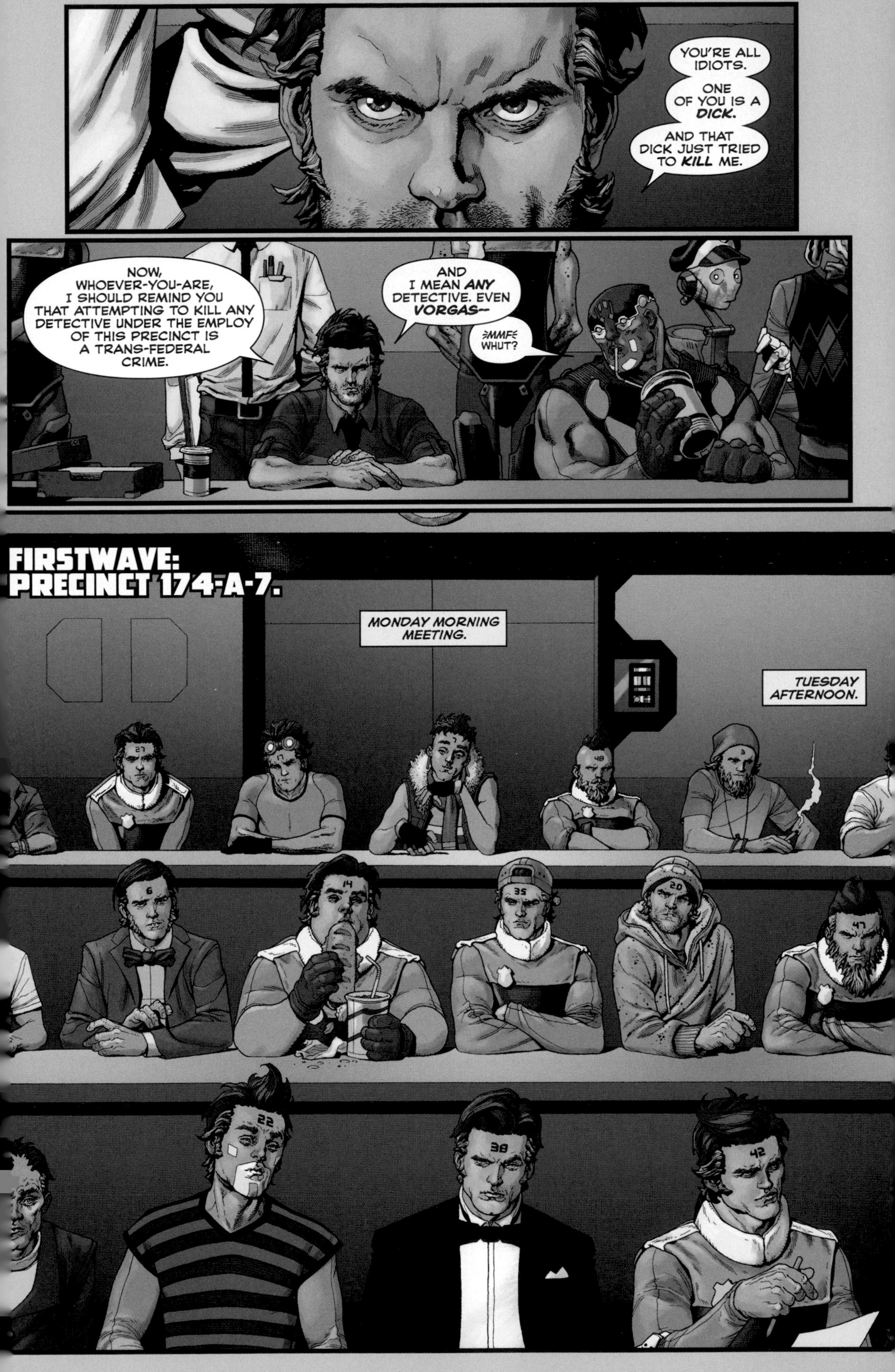
YOU'RE ALL IDIOTS.
ONE OF YOU IS A DICK.
AND THAT DICK JUST TRIED TO KILL ME.
NOW, WHOEVER-YOU-ARE, I SHOULD REMIND YOU THAT ATTEMPTING TO KILL ANY DETECTIVE UNDER THE EMPLOY OF THIS PRECINCT IS A TRANS-FEDERAL CRIME.
AND I MEAN ANY DETECTIVE. EVEN VORGAS--
MMF WHUT?
FIRSTWAVE: PRECINCT 174-A-7.
MONDAY MORNING MEETING.
TUESDAY AFTERNOON.

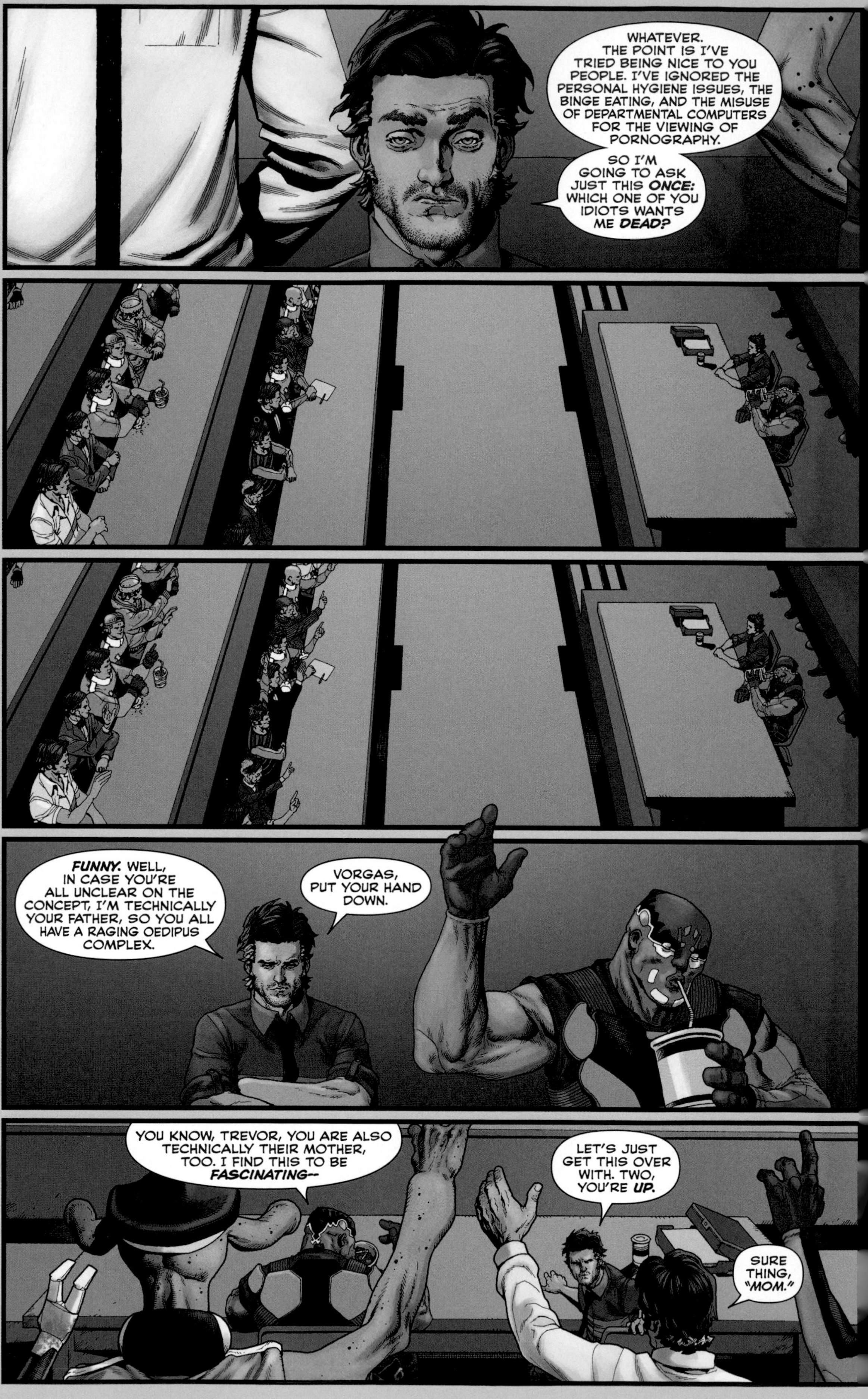
WHATEVER. THE POINT IS I'VE TRIED BEING NICE TO YOU PEOPLE. I'VE IGNORED THE PERSONAL HYGIENE ISSUES, THE BINGE EATING, AND THE MISUSE OF DEPARTMENTAL COMPUTERS FOR THE VIEWING OF PORNOGRAPHY.
SO I'M GOING TO ASK JUST THIS ONCE: WHICH ONE OF YOU IDIOTS WANTS ME DEAD?
FUNNY. WELL, IN CASE YOU'RE ALL UNCLEAR ON THE CONCEPT, I'M TECHNICALLY YOUR FATHER, SO YOU ALL HAVE A RAGING OEDIPUS COMPLEX.
VORGAS, PUT YOUR HAND DOWN.
YOU KNOW, TREVOR, YOU ARE ALSO TECHNICALLY THEIR MOTHER, TOO. I FIND THIS TO BE FASCINATING--
LET'S JUST GET THIS OVER WITH. TWO, YOU'RE UP.
SURE THING, "MOM."

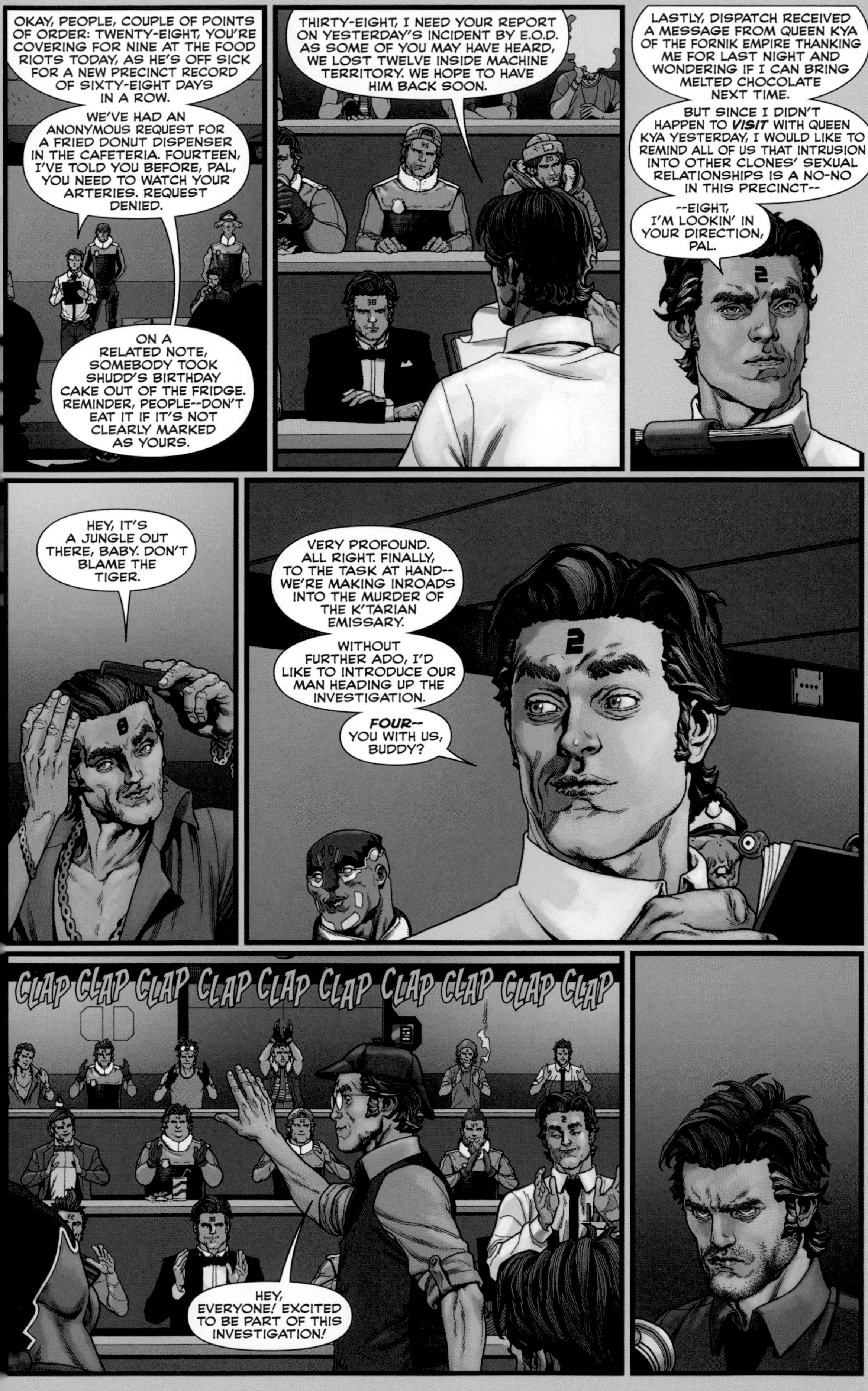

OKAY, PEOPLE, COUPLE OF POINTS OF ORDER: TWENTY-EIGHT, YOU'RE COVERING FOR NINE AT THE FOOD RIOTS TODAY, AS HE'S OFF SICK FOR A NEW PRECINCT RECORD OF SIXTY-EIGHT DAYS IN A ROW.
WE'VE HAD AN ANONYMOUS REQUEST FOR A FRIED DONUT DISPENSER IN THE CAFETERIA. FOURTEEN, I'VE TOLD YOU BEFORE, PAL, YOU NEED TO WATCH YOUR ARTERIES. REQUEST DENIED.
ON A RELATED NOTE, SOMEBODY TOOK SHUDD'S BIRTHDAY CAKE OUT OF THE FRIDGE. REMINDER, PEOPLE--DON'T EAT IT IF IT'S NOT CLEARLY MARKED AS YOURS.
THIRTY-EIGHT, I NEED YOUR REPORT ON YESTERDAY'S INCIDENT BY E.O.D. AS SOME OF YOU MAY HAVE HEARD, WE LOST TWELVE INSIDE MACHINE TERRITORY. WE HOPE TO HAVE HIM BACK SOON.
LASTLY, DISPATCH RECEIVED A MESSAGE FROM QUEEN KYA OF THE FORNIK EMPIRE THANKING ME FOR LAST NIGHT AND WONDERING IF I CAN BRING MELTED CHOCOLATE NEXT TIME.
BUT SINCE I DIDN'T HAPPEN TO *VISIT* WITH QUEEN KYA YESTERDAY, I WOULD LIKE TO REMIND ALL OF US THAT INTRUSION INTO OTHER CLONES' SEXUAL RELATIONSHIPS IS A NO-NO IN THIS PRECINCT--
--EIGHT, I'M LOOKIN' IN YOUR DIRECTION, PAL.
HEY, IT'S A JUNGLE OUT THERE, BABY. DON'T BLAME THE TIGER.
VERY PROFOUND. ALL RIGHT. FINALLY, TO THE TASK AT HAND--WE'RE MAKING INROADS INTO THE MURDER OF THE K'TARIAN EMISSARY.
WITHOUT FURTHER ADO, I'D LIKE TO INTRODUCE OUR MAN HEADING UP THE INVESTIGATION.
***FOUR--*** YOU WITH US, BUDDY?
CLAP CLAP CLAP CLAP CLAP CLAP CLAP CLAP CLAP CLAP
HEY, EVERYONE! EXCITED TO BE PART OF THIS INVESTIGATION!

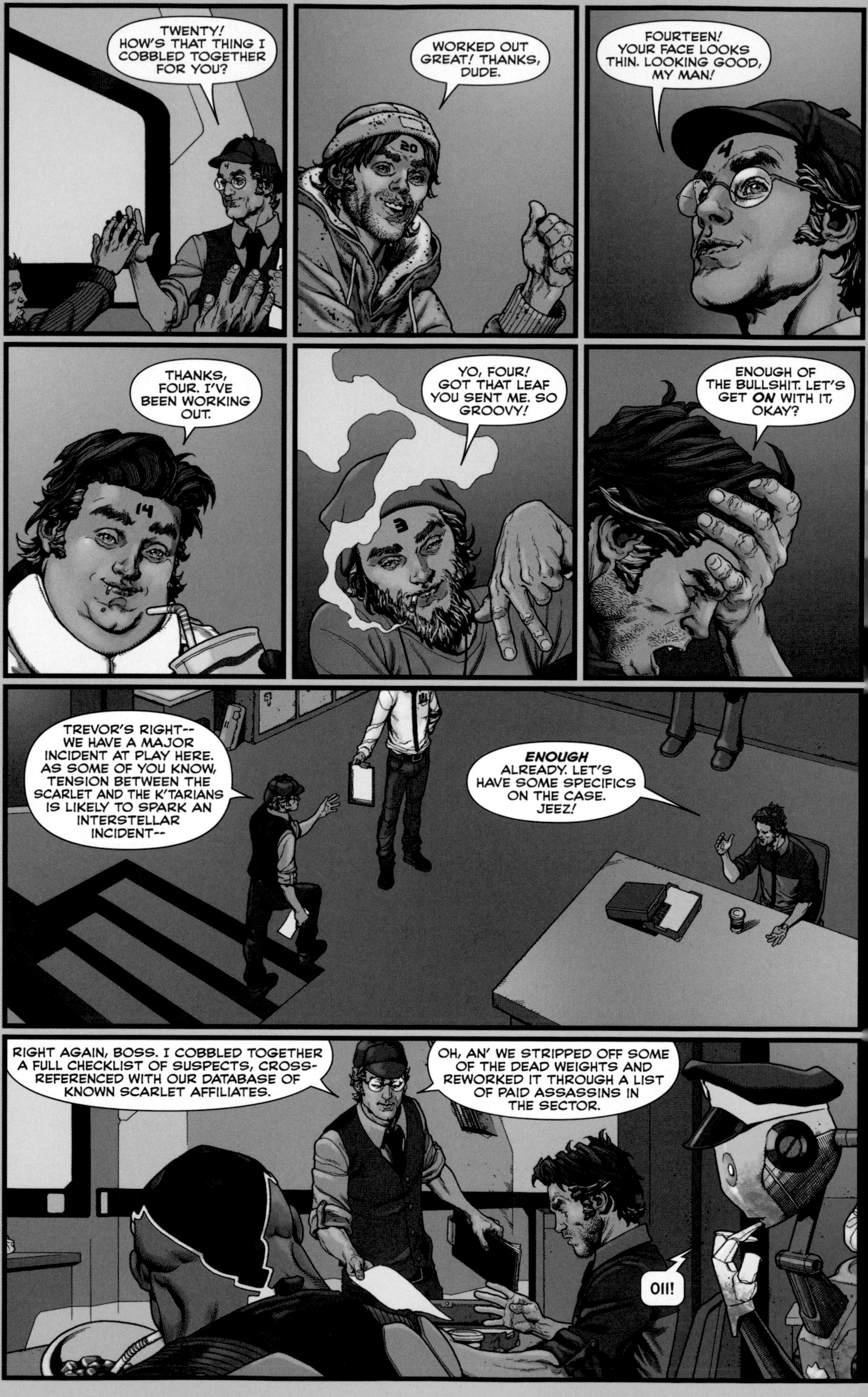
TWENTY! HOW'S THAT THING I COBBLED TOGETHER FOR YOU?
WORKED OUT GREAT! THANKS, DUDE.
FOURTEEN! YOUR FACE LOOKS THIN. LOOKING GOOD, MY MAN!
THANKS, FOUR. I'VE BEEN WORKING OUT.
YO, FOUR! GOT THAT LEAF YOU SENT ME. SO GROOVY!
ENOUGH OF THE BULLSHIT. LET'S GET ON WITH IT, OKAY?
TREVOR'S RIGHT-- WE HAVE A MAJOR INCIDENT AT PLAY HERE. AS SOME OF YOU KNOW, TENSION BETWEEN THE SCARLET AND THE K'TARIANS IS LIKELY TO SPARK AN INTERSTELLAR INCIDENT--
ENOUGH ALREADY. LET'S HAVE SOME SPECIFICS ON THE CASE. JEEZ!
RIGHT AGAIN, BOSS. I COBBLED TOGETHER A FULL CHECKLIST OF SUSPECTS, CROSS-REFERENCED WITH OUR DATABASE OF KNOWN SCARLET AFFILIATES.
OH, AN' WE STRIPPED OFF SOME OF THE DEAD WEIGHTS AND REWORKED IT THROUGH A LIST OF PAID ASSASSINS IN THE SECTOR.
OII!

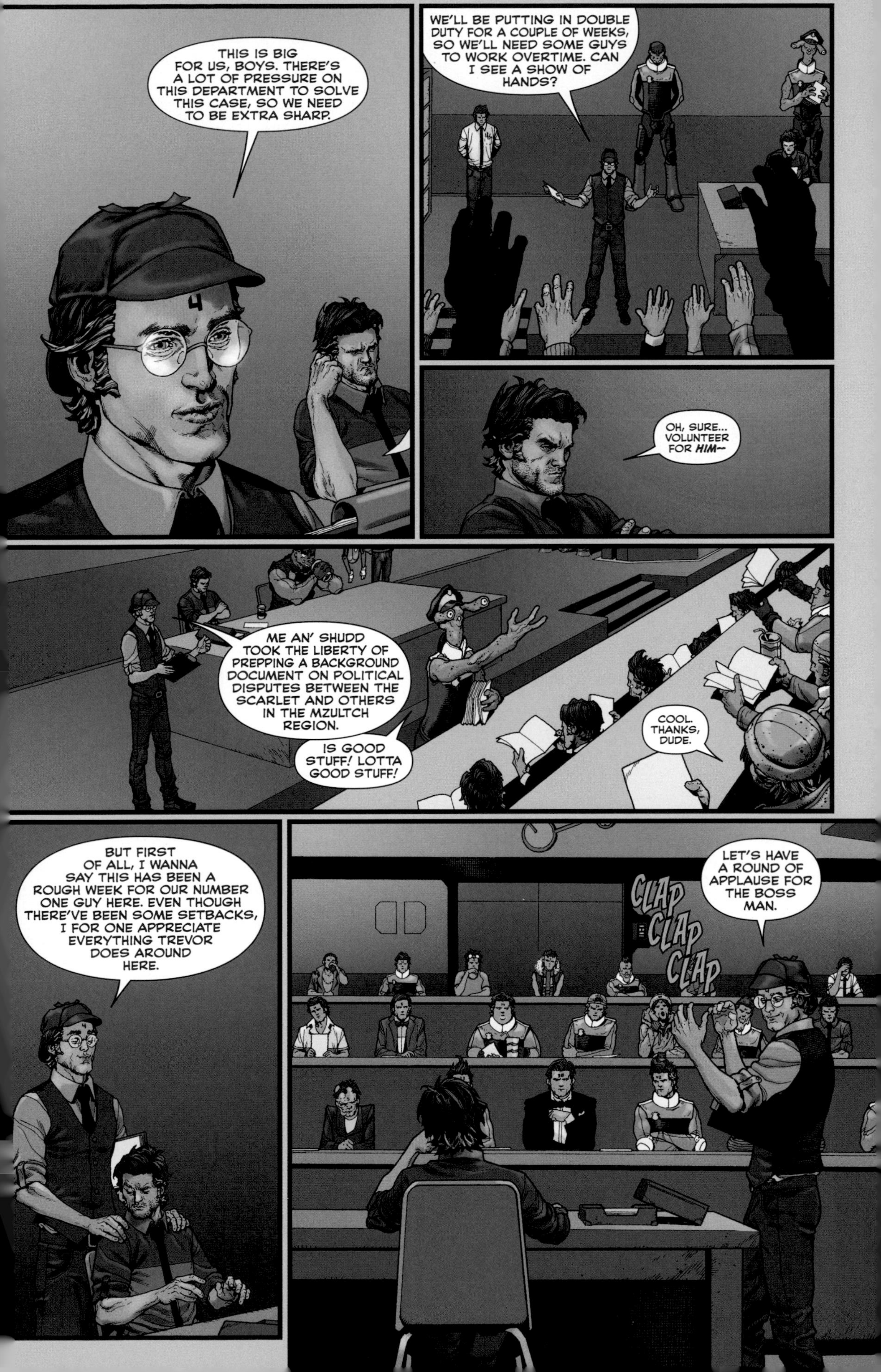

THIS IS BIG FOR US, BOYS. THERE'S A LOT OF PRESSURE ON THIS DEPARTMENT TO SOLVE THIS CASE, SO WE NEED TO BE EXTRA SHARP.
WE'LL BE PUTTING IN DOUBLE DUTY FOR A COUPLE OF WEEKS, SO WE'LL NEED SOME GUYS TO WORK OVERTIME. CAN I SEE A SHOW OF HANDS?
OH, SURE... VOLUNTEER FOR *HIM*--
ME AN' SHUDD TOOK THE LIBERTY OF PREPPING A BACKGROUND DOCUMENT ON POLITICAL DISPUTES BETWEEN THE SCARLET AND OTHERS IN THE MZULTCH REGION.
IS GOOD STUFF! LOTTA GOOD STUFF!
COOL. THANKS, DUDE.
BUT FIRST OF ALL, I WANNA SAY THIS HAS BEEN A ROUGH WEEK FOR OUR NUMBER ONE GUY HERE. EVEN THOUGH THERE'VE BEEN SOME SETBACKS, I FOR ONE APPRECIATE EVERYTHING TREVOR DOES AROUND HERE.
LET'S HAVE A ROUND OF APPLAUSE FOR THE BOSS MAN.
CLAP CLAP CLAP

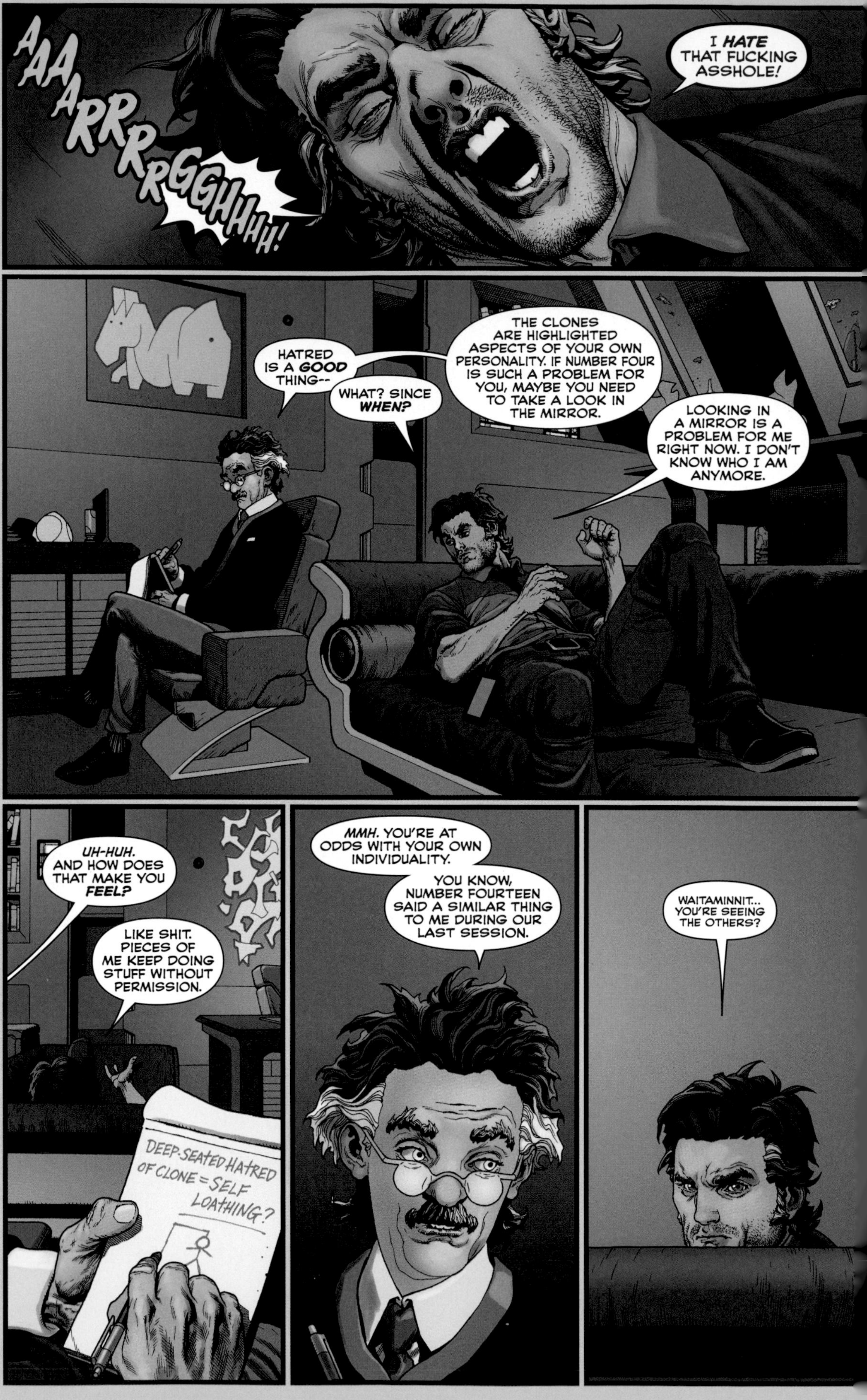

AAAARRRRGGHHHH!
I HATE THAT FUCKING ASSHOLE!
HATRED IS A GOOD THING--
WHAT? SINCE WHEN?
THE CLONES ARE HIGHLIGHTED ASPECTS OF YOUR OWN PERSONALITY. IF NUMBER FOUR IS SUCH A PROBLEM FOR YOU, MAYBE YOU NEED TO TAKE A LOOK IN THE MIRROR.
LOOKING IN A MIRROR IS A PROBLEM FOR ME RIGHT NOW. I DON'T KNOW WHO I AM ANYMORE.
UH-HUH. AND HOW DOES THAT MAKE YOU FEEL?
LIKE SHIT. PIECES OF ME KEEP DOING STUFF WITHOUT PERMISSION.
DEEP-SEATED HATRED OF CLONE = SELF LOATHING?
MMH. YOU'RE AT ODDS WITH YOUR OWN INDIVIDUALITY.
YOU KNOW, NUMBER FOURTEEN SAID A SIMILAR THING TO ME DURING OUR LAST SESSION.
WAITAMINNIT... YOU'RE SEEING THE OTHERS?

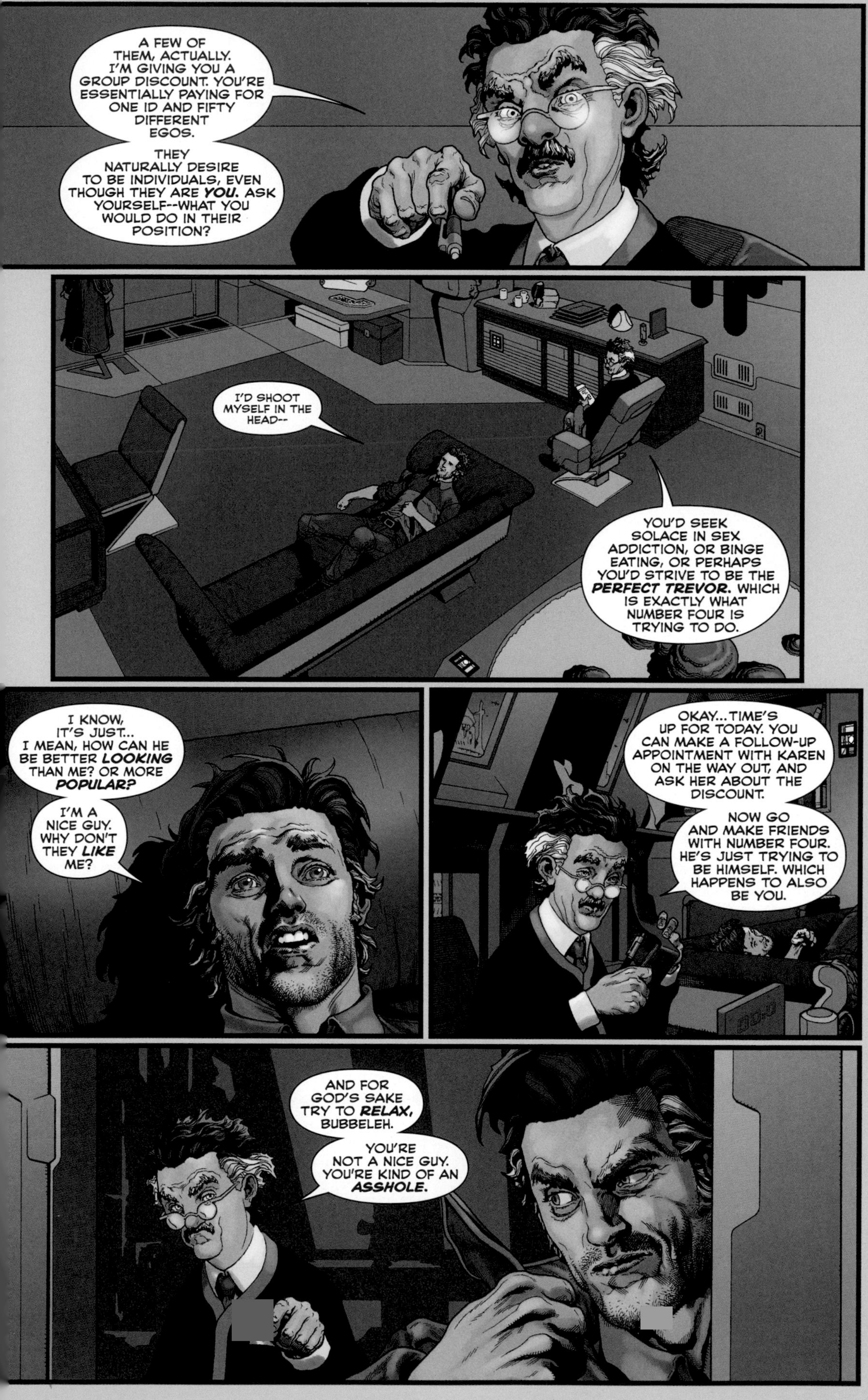
A FEW OF THEM, ACTUALLY. I'M GIVING YOU A GROUP DISCOUNT. YOU'RE ESSENTIALLY PAYING FOR ONE ID AND FIFTY DIFFERENT EGOS.
THEY NATURALLY DESIRE TO BE INDIVIDUALS, EVEN THOUGH THEY ARE ***YOU.*** ASK YOURSELF--WHAT YOU WOULD DO IN THEIR POSITION?
I'D SHOOT MYSELF IN THE HEAD--
YOU'D SEEK SOLACE IN SEX ADDICTION, OR BINGE EATING, OR PERHAPS YOU'D STRIVE TO BE THE ***PERFECT TREVOR.*** WHICH IS EXACTLY WHAT NUMBER FOUR IS TRYING TO DO.
I KNOW, IT'S JUST... I MEAN, HOW CAN HE BE BETTER ***LOOKING*** THAN ME? OR MORE ***POPULAR?***
I'M A NICE GUY. WHY DON'T THEY ***LIKE*** ME?
OKAY...TIME'S UP FOR TODAY. YOU CAN MAKE A FOLLOW-UP APPOINTMENT WITH KAREN ON THE WAY OUT, AND ASK HER ABOUT THE DISCOUNT.
NOW GO AND MAKE FRIENDS WITH NUMBER FOUR. HE'S JUST TRYING TO BE HIMSELF. WHICH HAPPENS TO ALSO BE YOU.
AND FOR GOD'S SAKE TRY TO ***RELAX,*** BUBBELEH.
YOU'RE NOT A NICE GUY. YOU'RE KIND OF AN ***ASSHOLE.***

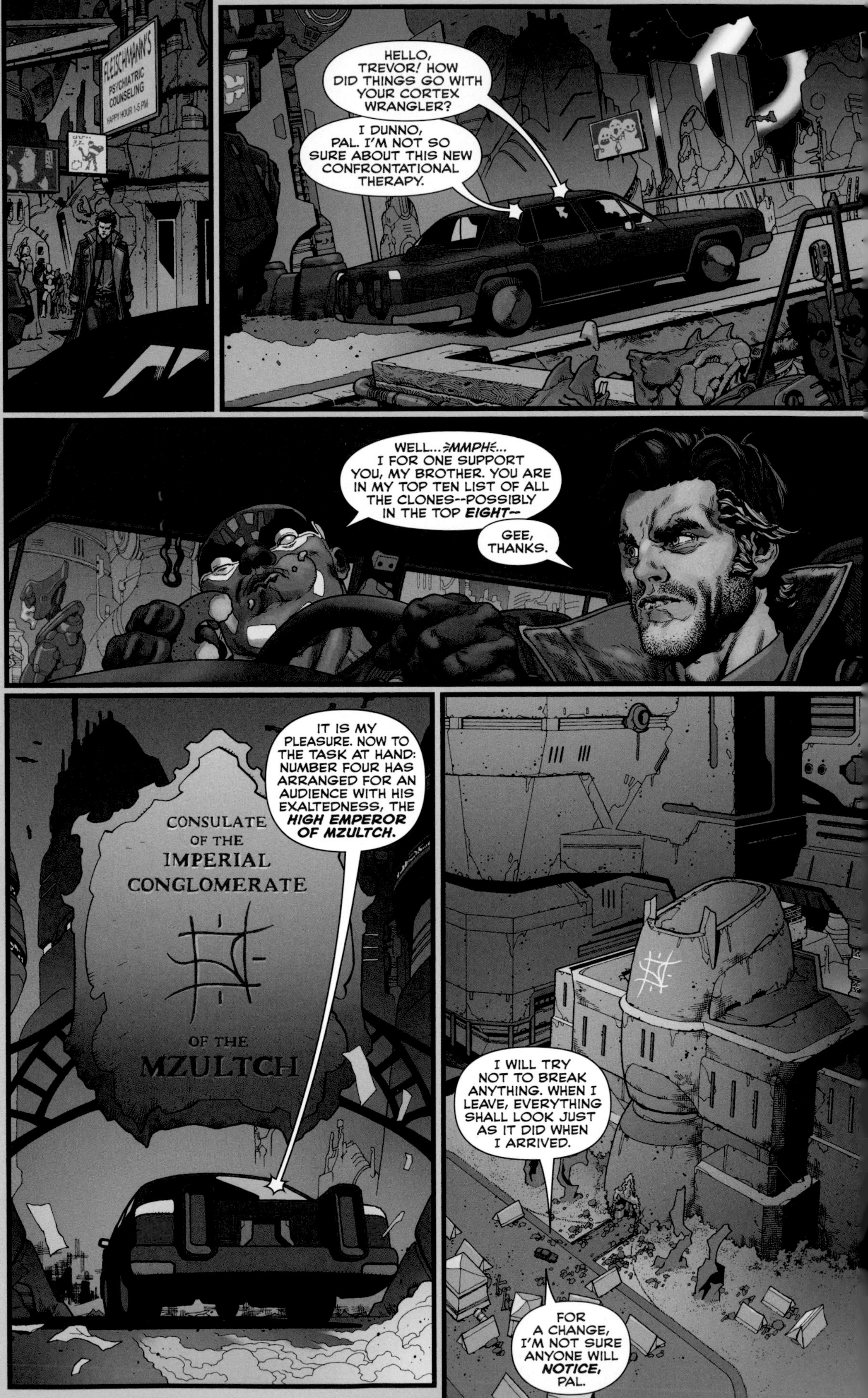
FLEISCHMANN'S
PSYCHIATRIC COUNSELING
HAPPY HOUR 1-5 PM
HELLO, TREVOR! HOW DID THINGS GO WITH YOUR CORTEX WRANGLER?
I DUNNO, PAL. I'M NOT SO SURE ABOUT THIS NEW CONFRONTATIONAL THERAPY.
WELL... MMPH... I FOR ONE SUPPORT YOU, MY BROTHER. YOU ARE IN MY TOP TEN LIST OF ALL THE CLONES--POSSIBLY IN THE TOP EIGHT--
GEE, THANKS.
CONSULATE OF THE IMPERIAL CONGLOMERATE
OF THE MZULTCH
IT IS MY PLEASURE. NOW TO THE TASK AT HAND: NUMBER FOUR HAS ARRANGED FOR AN AUDIENCE WITH HIS EXALTEDNESS, THE HIGH EMPEROR OF MZULTCH.
I WILL TRY NOT TO BREAK ANYTHING. WHEN I LEAVE, EVERYTHING SHALL LOOK JUST AS IT DID WHEN I ARRIVED.
FOR A CHANGE, I'M NOT SURE ANYONE WILL NOTICE, PAL.

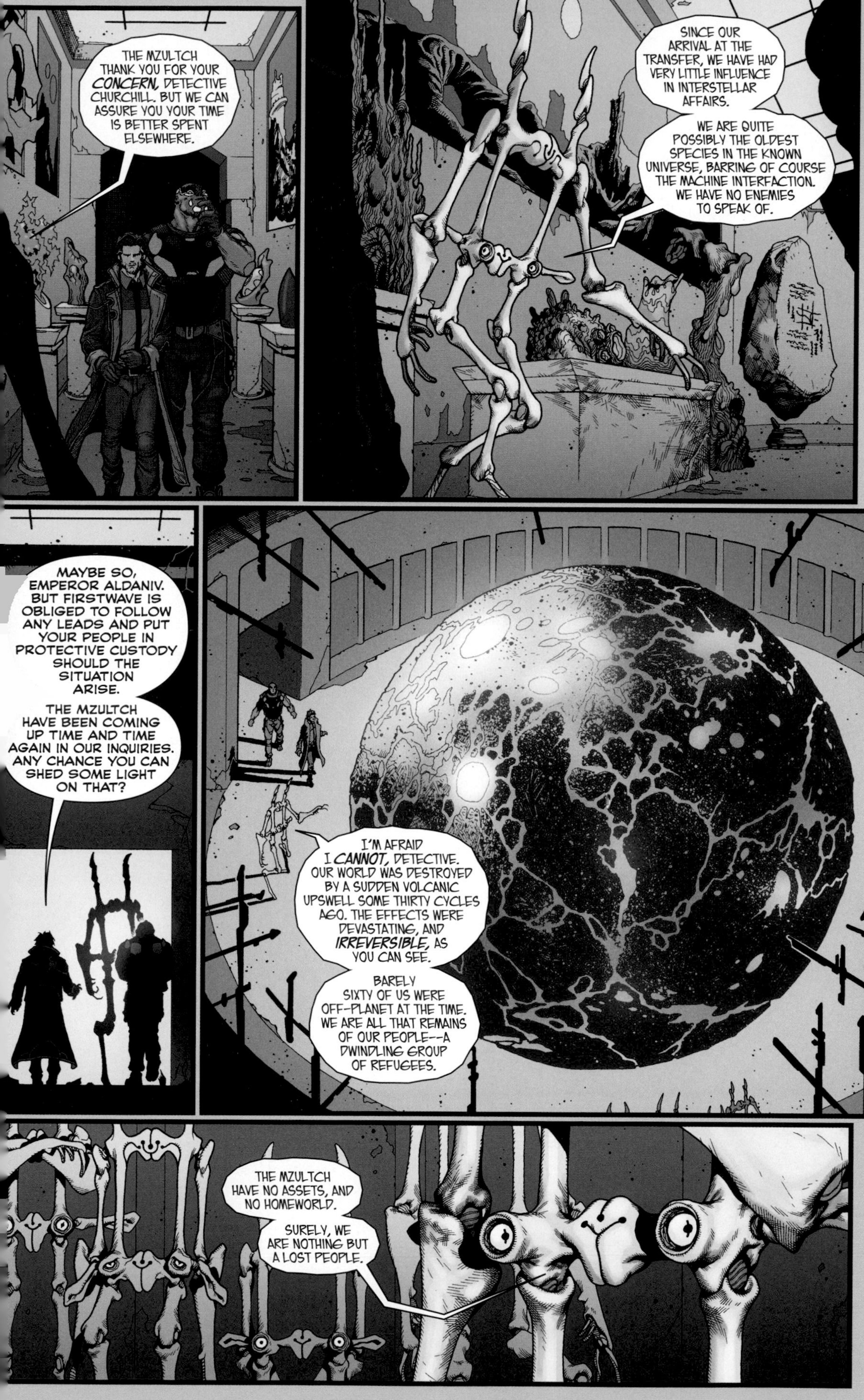
THE MZULTCH THANK YOU FOR YOUR CONCERN, DETECTIVE CHURCHILL. BUT WE CAN ASSURE YOU YOUR TIME IS BETTER SPENT ELSEWHERE.
SINCE OUR ARRIVAL AT THE TRANSFER, WE HAVE HAD VERY LITTLE INFLUENCE IN INTERSTELLAR AFFAIRS.
WE ARE QUITE POSSIBLY THE OLDEST SPECIES IN THE KNOWN UNIVERSE, BARRING OF COURSE THE MACHINE INTERFACTION. WE HAVE NO ENEMIES TO SPEAK OF.
MAYBE SO, EMPEROR ALDANIV. BUT FIRSTWAVE IS OBLIGED TO FOLLOW ANY LEADS AND PUT YOUR PEOPLE IN PROTECTIVE CUSTODY SHOULD THE SITUATION ARISE.
THE MZULTCH HAVE BEEN COMING UP TIME AND TIME AGAIN IN OUR INQUIRIES. ANY CHANCE YOU CAN SHED SOME LIGHT ON THAT?
I'M AFRAID I CANNOT, DETECTIVE. OUR WORLD WAS DESTROYED BY A SUDDEN VOLCANIC UPSWELL SOME THIRTY CYCLES AGO. THE EFFECTS WERE DEVASTATING, AND IRREVERSIBLE, AS YOU CAN SEE.
BARELY SIXTY OF US WERE OFF-PLANET AT THE TIME. WE ARE ALL THAT REMAINS OF OUR PEOPLE--A DWINDLING GROUP OF REFUGEES.
THE MZULTCH HAVE NO ASSETS, AND NO HOMEWORLD.
SURELY, WE ARE NOTHING BUT A LOST PEOPLE.

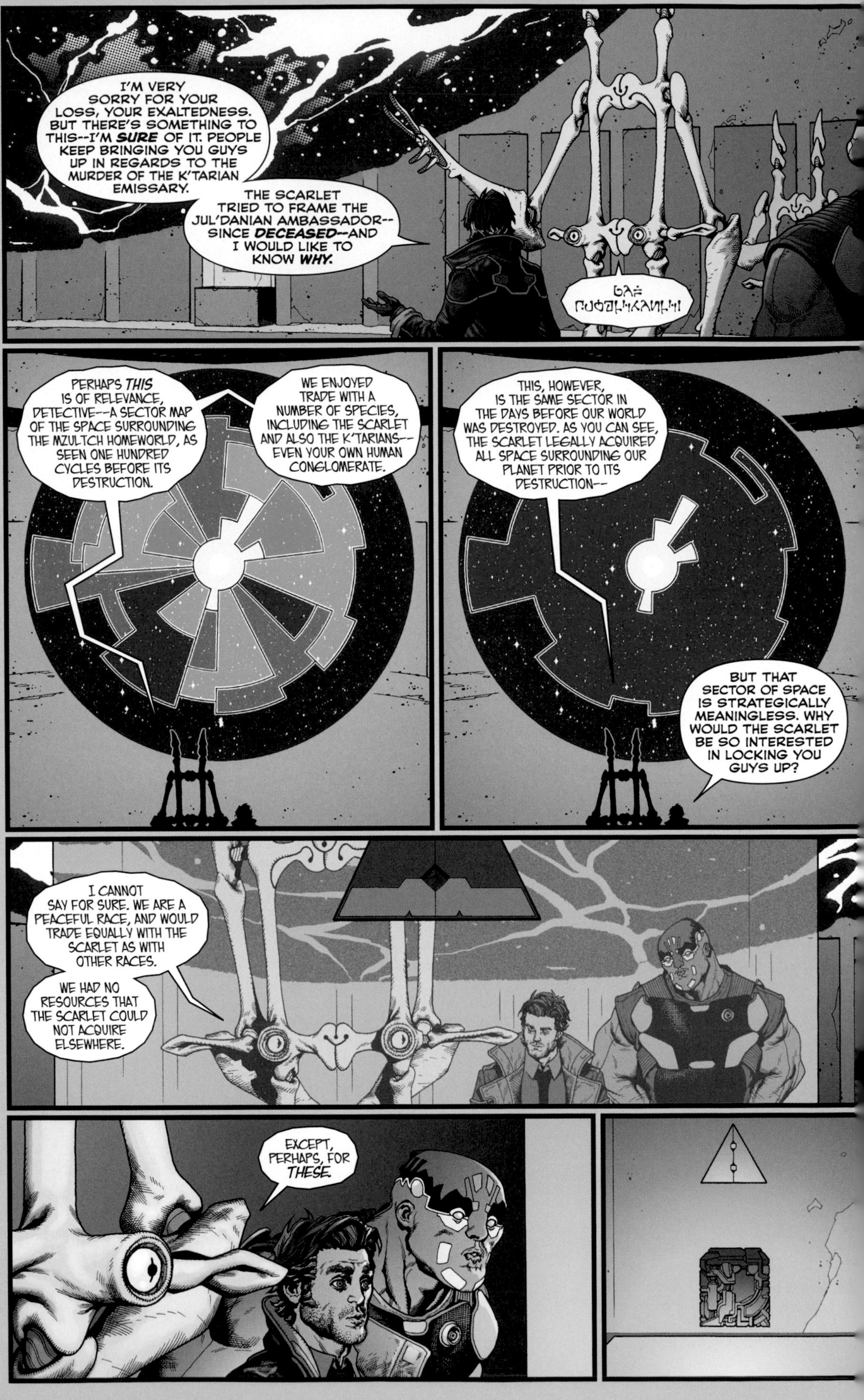
I'M VERY SORRY FOR YOUR LOSS, YOUR EXALTEDNESS. BUT THERE'S SOMETHING TO THIS--I'M SURE OF IT. PEOPLE KEEP BRINGING YOU GUYS UP IN REGARDS TO THE MURDER OF THE K'TARIAN EMISSARY.
THE SCARLET TRIED TO FRAME THE JUL'DANIAN AMBASSADOR--SINCE DECEASED--AND I WOULD LIKE TO KNOW WHY.
PERHAPS THIS IS OF RELEVANCE, DETECTIVE--A SECTOR MAP OF THE SPACE SURROUNDING THE MZULTCH HOMEWORLD, AS SEEN ONE HUNDRED CYCLES BEFORE ITS DESTRUCTION.
WE ENJOYED TRADE WITH A NUMBER OF SPECIES, INCLUDING THE SCARLET AND ALSO THE K'TARIANS--EVEN YOUR OWN HUMAN CONGLOMERATE.
THIS, HOWEVER, IS THE SAME SECTOR IN THE DAYS BEFORE OUR WORLD WAS DESTROYED. AS YOU CAN SEE, THE SCARLET LEGALLY ACQUIRED ALL SPACE SURROUNDING OUR PLANET PRIOR TO ITS DESTRUCTION--
BUT THAT SECTOR OF SPACE IS STRATEGICALLY MEANINGLESS. WHY WOULD THE SCARLET BE SO INTERESTED IN LOCKING YOU GUYS UP?
I CANNOT SAY FOR SURE. WE ARE A PEACEFUL RACE, AND WOULD TRADE EQUALLY WITH THE SCARLET AS WITH OTHER RACES.
WE HAD NO RESOURCES THAT THE SCARLET COULD NOT ACQUIRE ELSEWHERE.
EXCEPT, PERHAPS, FOR THESE.

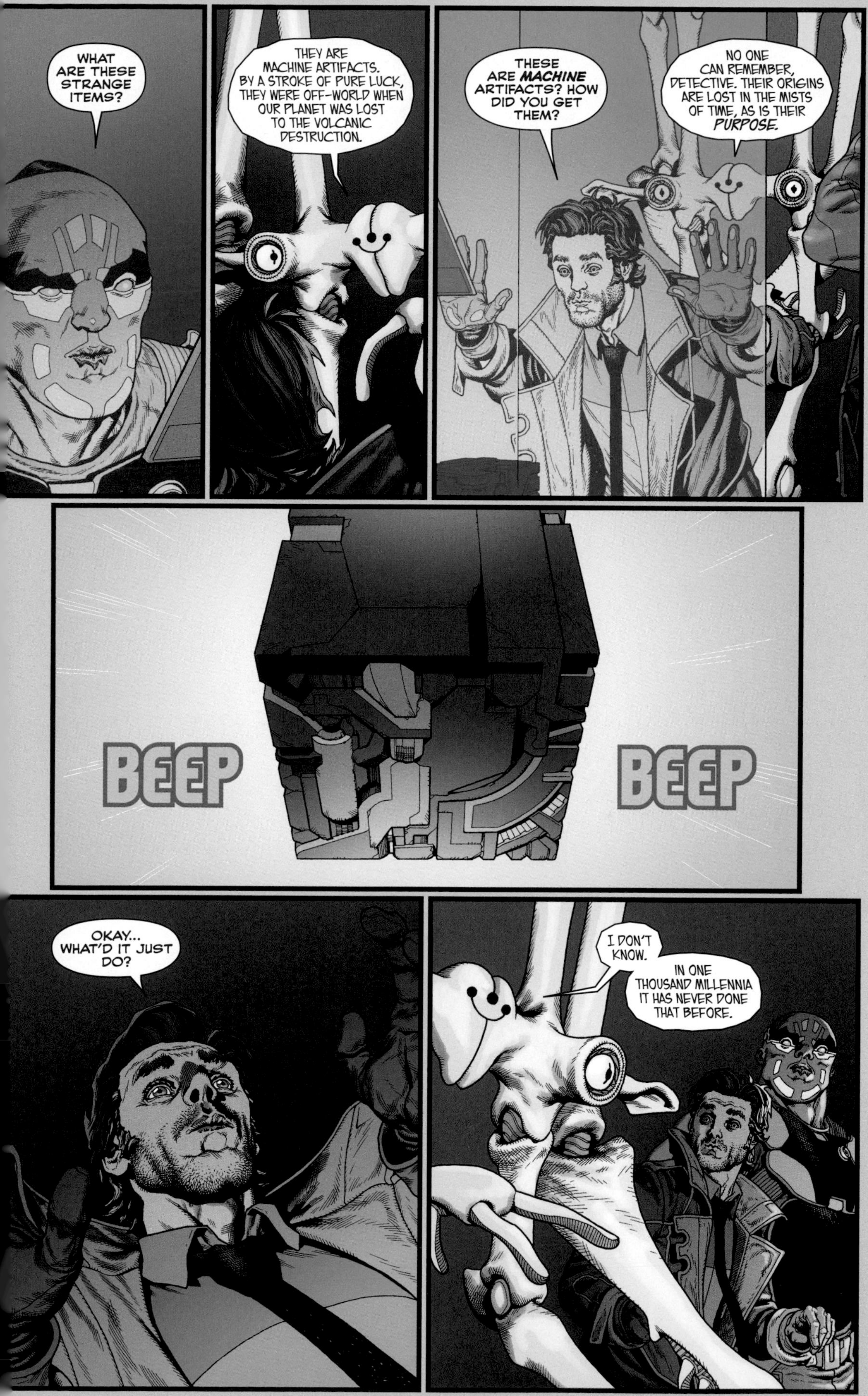
WHAT ARE THESE STRANGE ITEMS?
THEY ARE MACHINE ARTIFACTS. BY A STROKE OF PURE LUCK, THEY WERE OFF-WORLD WHEN OUR PLANET WAS LOST TO THE VOLCANIC DESTRUCTION.
THESE ARE *MACHINE* ARTIFACTS? HOW DID YOU GET THEM?
NO ONE CAN REMEMBER, DETECTIVE. THEIR ORIGINS ARE LOST IN THE MISTS OF TIME, AS IS THEIR *PURPOSE.*
BEEP
BEEP
OKAY... WHAT'D IT JUST DO?
I DON'T KNOW.
IN ONE THOUSAND MILLENNIA IT HAS NEVER DONE THAT BEFORE.

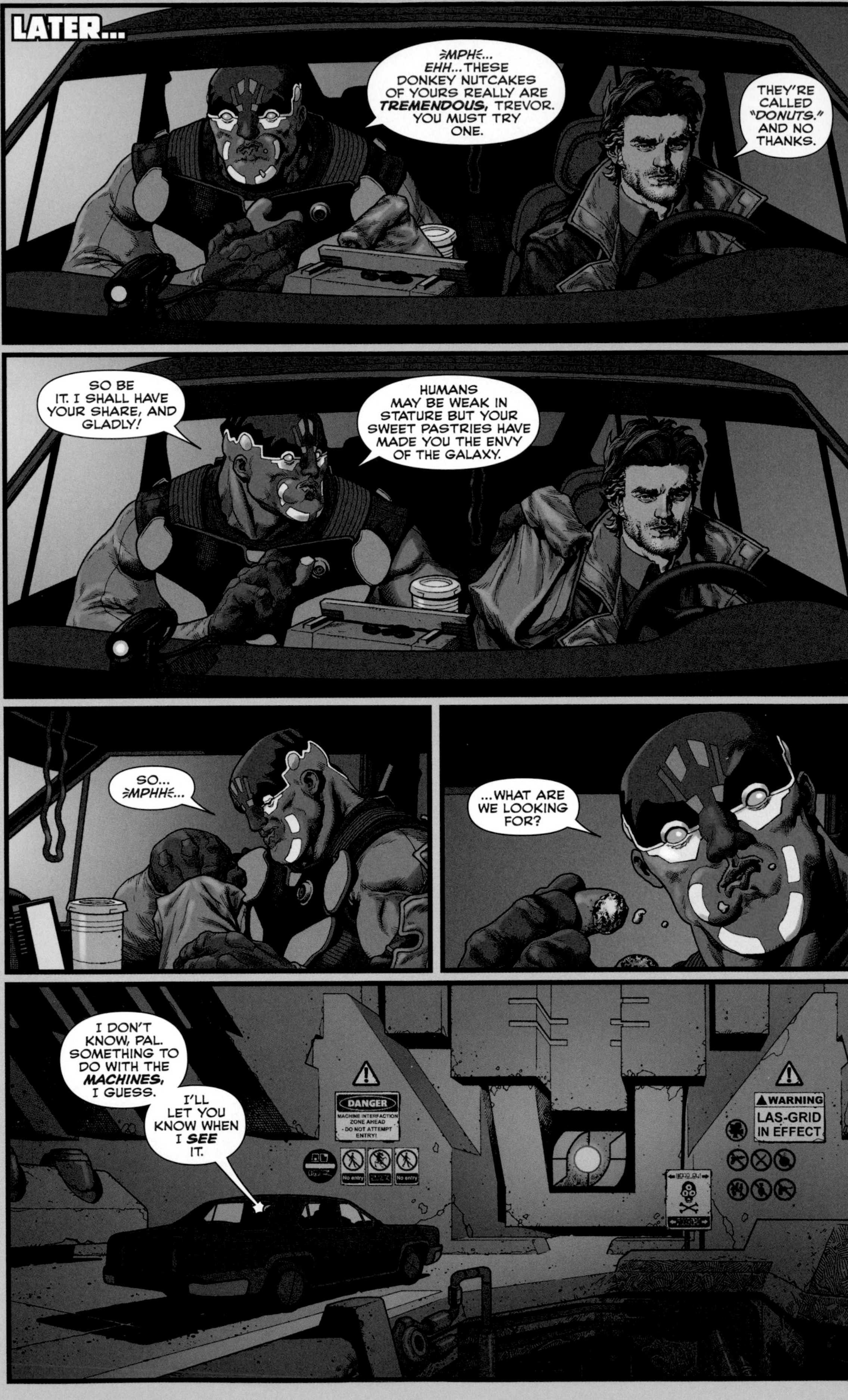
LATER...
≥MPH≤... EHH... THESE DONKEY NUTCAKES OF YOURS REALLY ARE TREMENDOUS, TREVOR. YOU MUST TRY ONE.
THEY'RE CALLED "DONUTS." AND NO THANKS.
SO BE IT. I SHALL HAVE YOUR SHARE, AND GLADLY!
HUMANS MAY BE WEAK IN STATURE BUT YOUR SWEET PASTRIES HAVE MADE YOU THE ENVY OF THE GALAXY.
SO... ≥MPHH≤...
...WHAT ARE WE LOOKING FOR?
I DON'T KNOW, PAL. SOMETHING TO DO WITH THE MACHINES, I GUESS.
I'LL LET YOU KNOW WHEN I SEE IT.
DANGER
MACHINE INTERFACTION ZONE AHEAD - DO NOT ATTEMPT ENTRY!
No entry
No entry
WARNING
LAS-GRID IN EFFECT

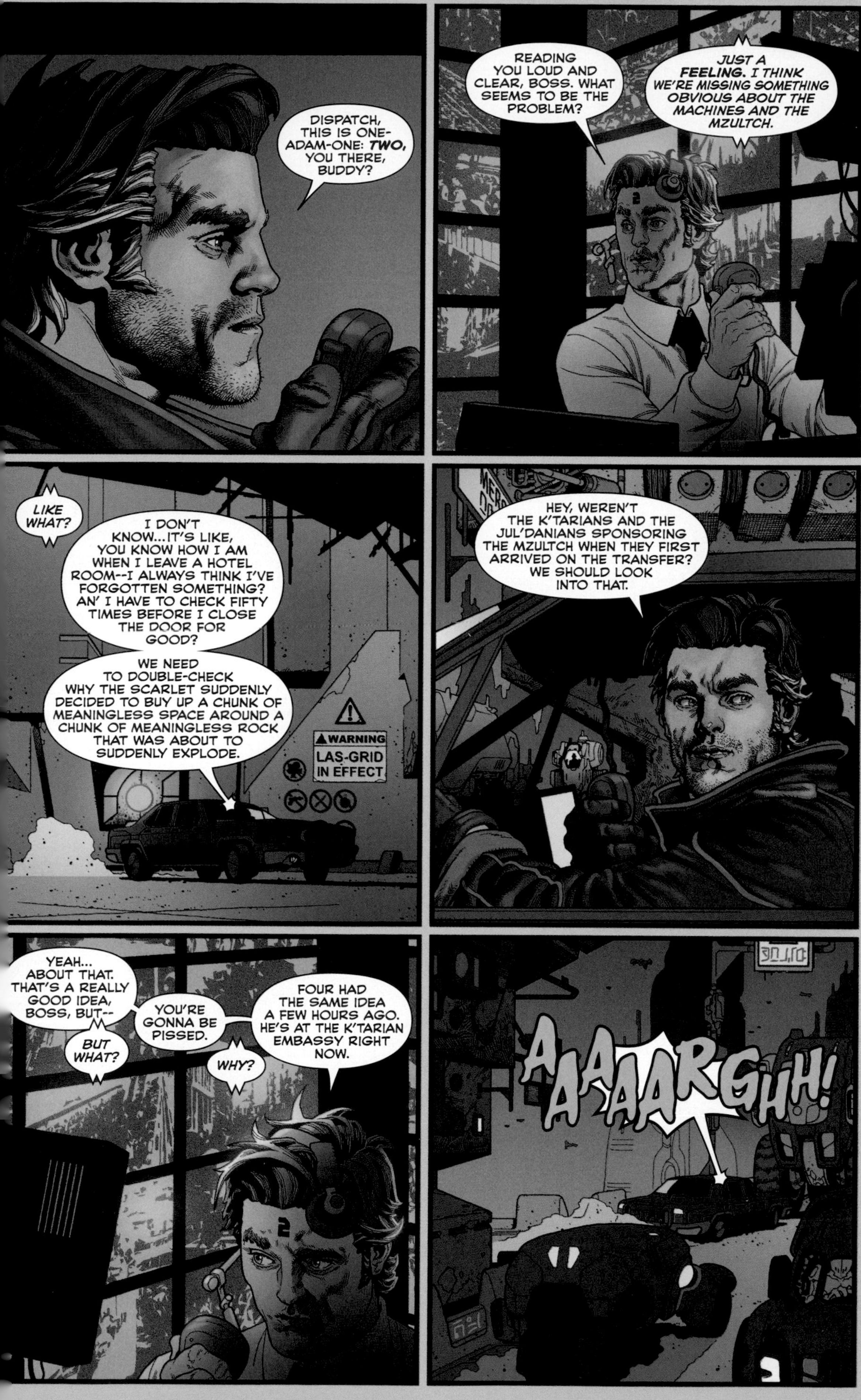
DISPATCH, THIS IS ONE-ADAM-ONE: *TWO,* YOU THERE, BUDDY?
READING YOU LOUD AND CLEAR, BOSS. WHAT SEEMS TO BE THE PROBLEM?
*JUST A **FEELING.** I THINK WE'RE MISSING SOMETHING OBVIOUS ABOUT THE MACHINES AND THE MZULTCH.*
*LIKE WHAT?*
I DON'T KNOW...IT'S LIKE, YOU KNOW HOW I AM WHEN I LEAVE A HOTEL ROOM--I ALWAYS THINK I'VE FORGOTTEN SOMETHING? AN' I HAVE TO CHECK FIFTY TIMES BEFORE I CLOSE THE DOOR FOR GOOD?
WE NEED TO DOUBLE-CHECK WHY THE SCARLET SUDDENLY DECIDED TO BUY UP A CHUNK OF MEANINGLESS SPACE AROUND A CHUNK OF MEANINGLESS ROCK THAT WAS ABOUT TO SUDDENLY EXPLODE.
WARNING
LAS-GRID IN EFFECT
HEY, WEREN'T THE K'TARIANS AND THE JUL'DANIANS SPONSORING THE MZULTCH WHEN THEY FIRST ARRIVED ON THE TRANSFER? WE SHOULD LOOK INTO THAT.
YEAH... ABOUT THAT. THAT'S A REALLY GOOD IDEA, BOSS, BUT--
*BUT WHAT?*
YOU'RE GONNA BE PISSED.
*WHY?*
FOUR HAD THE SAME IDEA A FEW HOURS AGO. HE'S AT THE K'TARIAN EMBASSY RIGHT NOW.
AAAAARGHH!

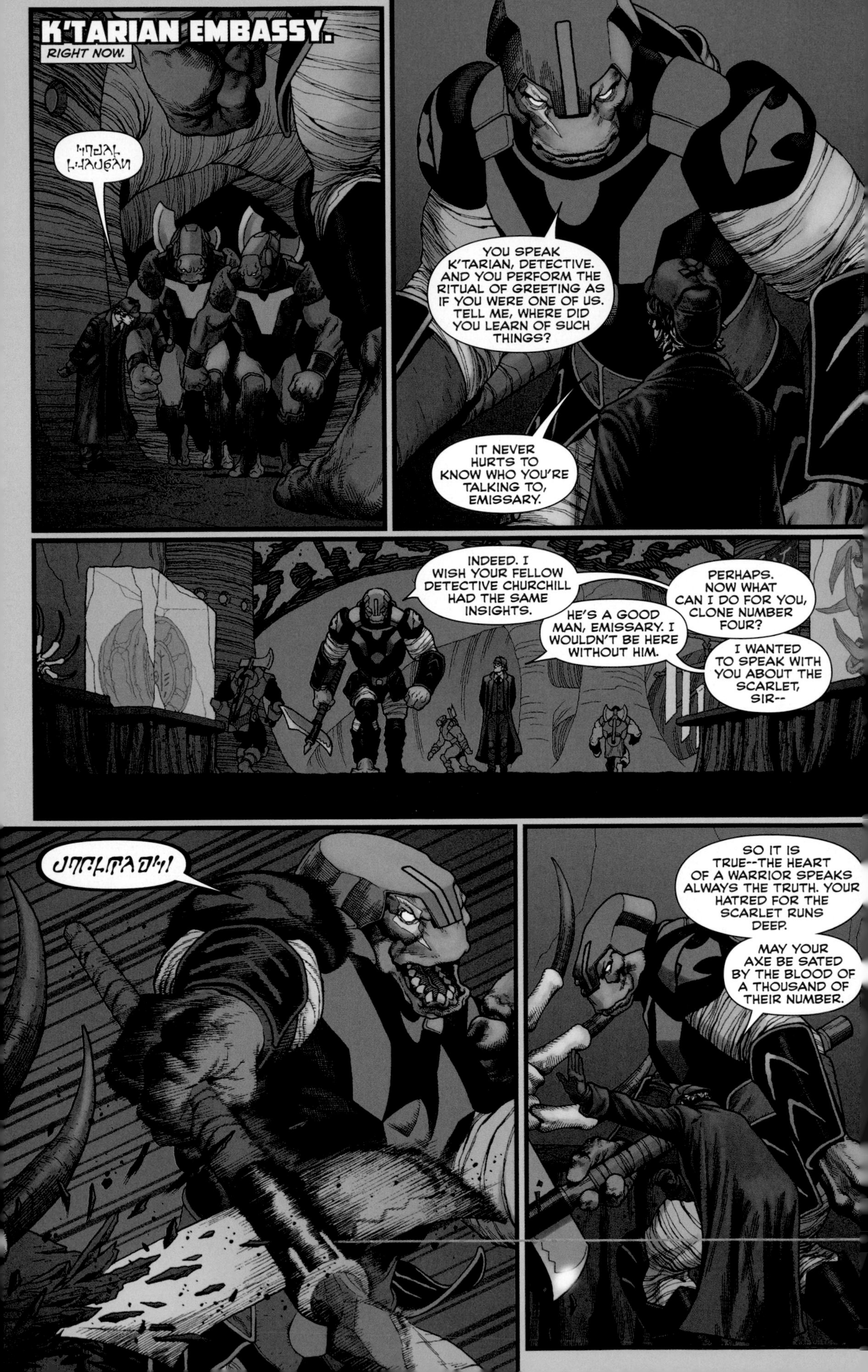
K'TARIAN EMBASSY.
RIGHT NOW.
YOU SPEAK K'TARIAN, DETECTIVE. AND YOU PERFORM THE RITUAL OF GREETING AS IF YOU WERE ONE OF US. TELL ME, WHERE DID YOU LEARN OF SUCH THINGS?
IT NEVER HURTS TO KNOW WHO YOU'RE TALKING TO, EMISSARY.
INDEED. I WISH YOUR FELLOW DETECTIVE CHURCHILL HAD THE SAME INSIGHTS.
HE'S A GOOD MAN, EMISSARY. I WOULDN'T BE HERE WITHOUT HIM.
PERHAPS. NOW WHAT CAN I DO FOR YOU, CLONE NUMBER FOUR?
I WANTED TO SPEAK WITH YOU ABOUT THE SCARLET, SIR--
SO IT IS TRUE--THE HEART OF A WARRIOR SPEAKS ALWAYS THE TRUTH. YOUR HATRED FOR THE SCARLET RUNS DEEP.
MAY YOUR AXE BE SATED BY THE BLOOD OF A THOUSAND OF THEIR NUMBER.

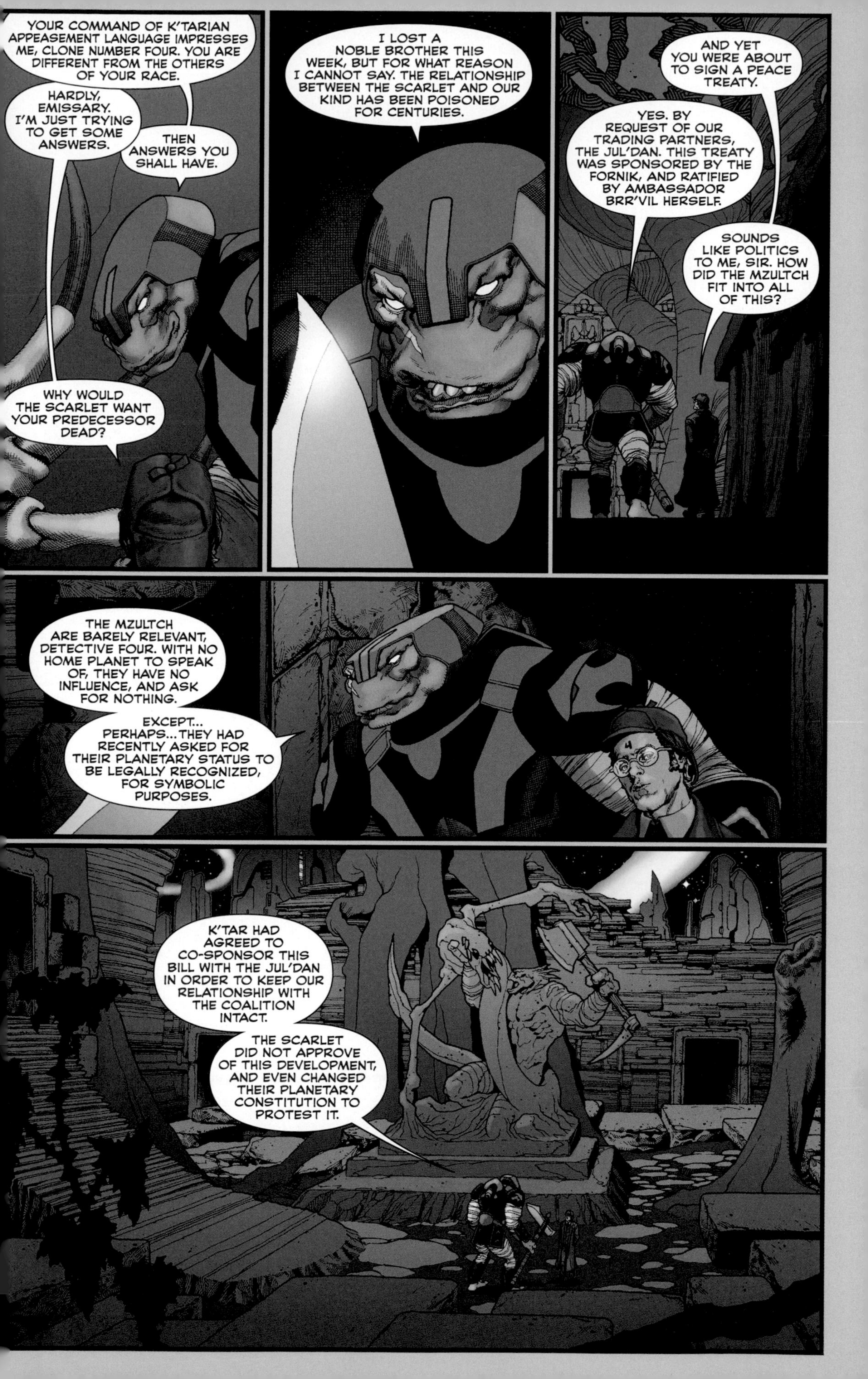
YOUR COMMAND OF K'TARIAN APPEASEMENT LANGUAGE IMPRESSES ME, CLONE NUMBER FOUR. YOU ARE DIFFERENT FROM THE OTHERS OF YOUR RACE.
HARDLY, EMISSARY. I'M JUST TRYING TO GET SOME ANSWERS.
THEN ANSWERS YOU SHALL HAVE.
WHY WOULD THE SCARLET WANT YOUR PREDECESSOR DEAD?
I LOST A NOBLE BROTHER THIS WEEK, BUT FOR WHAT REASON I CANNOT SAY. THE RELATIONSHIP BETWEEN THE SCARLET AND OUR KIND HAS BEEN POISONED FOR CENTURIES.
AND YET YOU WERE ABOUT TO SIGN A PEACE TREATY.
YES. BY REQUEST OF OUR TRADING PARTNERS, THE JUL'DAN. THIS TREATY WAS SPONSORED BY THE FORNIK, AND RATIFIED BY AMBASSADOR BRR'VIL HERSELF.
SOUNDS LIKE POLITICS TO ME, SIR. HOW DID THE MZULTCH FIT INTO ALL OF THIS?
THE MZULTCH ARE BARELY RELEVANT, DETECTIVE FOUR. WITH NO HOME PLANET TO SPEAK OF, THEY HAVE NO INFLUENCE, AND ASK FOR NOTHING.
EXCEPT... PERHAPS... THEY HAD RECENTLY ASKED FOR THEIR PLANETARY STATUS TO BE LEGALLY RECOGNIZED, FOR SYMBOLIC PURPOSES.
K'TAR HAD AGREED TO CO-SPONSOR THIS BILL WITH THE JUL'DAN IN ORDER TO KEEP OUR RELATIONSHIP WITH THE COALITION INTACT.
THE SCARLET DID NOT APPROVE OF THIS DEVELOPMENT, AND EVEN CHANGED THEIR PLANETARY CONSTITUTION TO PROTEST IT.

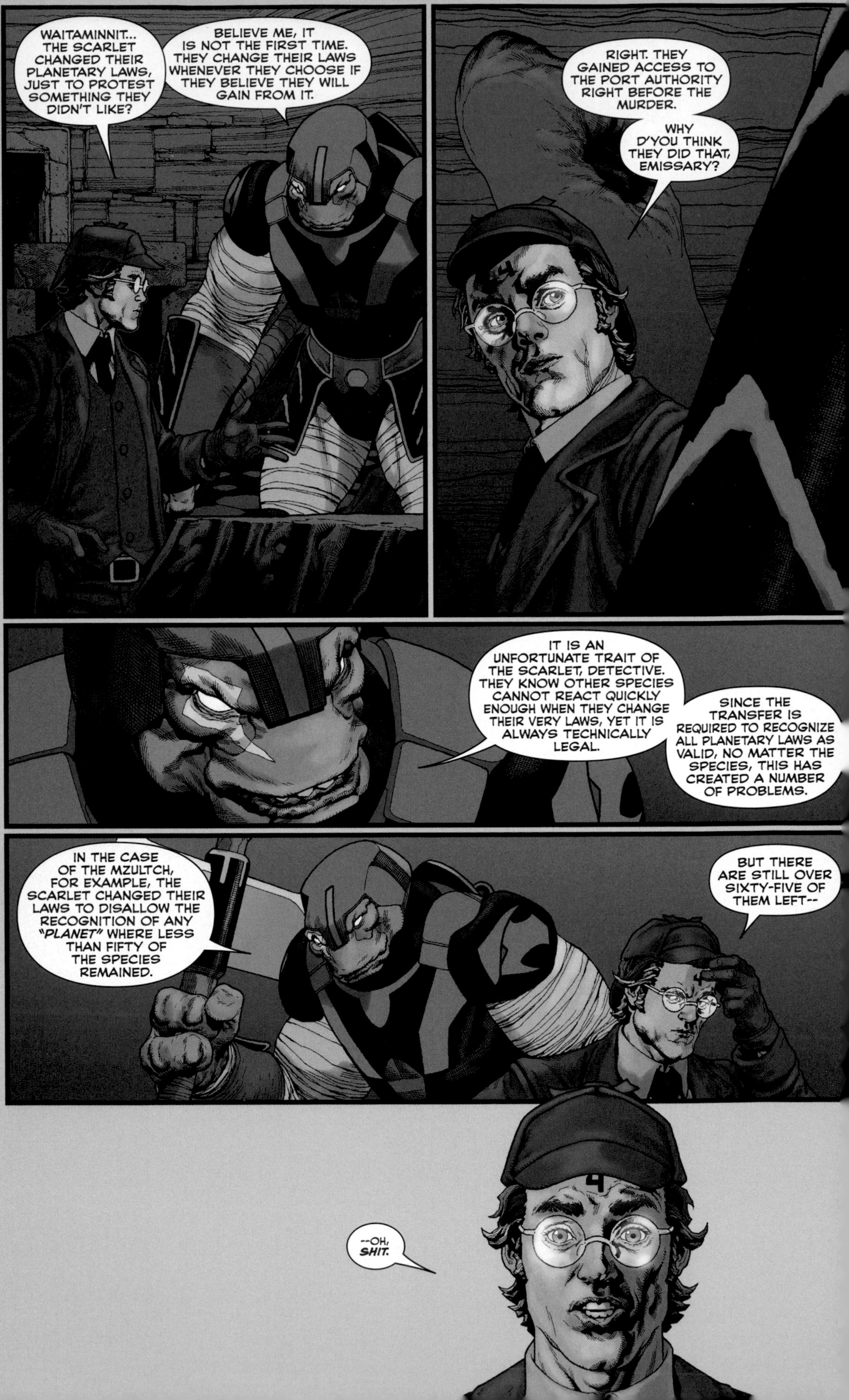

WAITAMINNIT... THE SCARLET CHANGED THEIR PLANETARY LAWS, JUST TO PROTEST SOMETHING THEY DIDN'T LIKE?
BELIEVE ME, IT IS NOT THE FIRST TIME. THEY CHANGE THEIR LAWS WHENEVER THEY CHOOSE IF THEY BELIEVE THEY WILL GAIN FROM IT.
RIGHT. THEY GAINED ACCESS TO THE PORT AUTHORITY RIGHT BEFORE THE MURDER.
WHY D'YOU THINK THEY DID THAT, EMISSARY?
IT IS AN UNFORTUNATE TRAIT OF THE SCARLET, DETECTIVE. THEY KNOW OTHER SPECIES CANNOT REACT QUICKLY ENOUGH WHEN THEY CHANGE THEIR VERY LAWS, YET IT IS ALWAYS TECHNICALLY LEGAL.
SINCE THE TRANSFER IS REQUIRED TO RECOGNIZE ALL PLANETARY LAWS AS VALID, NO MATTER THE SPECIES, THIS HAS CREATED A NUMBER OF PROBLEMS.
IN THE CASE OF THE MZULTCH, FOR EXAMPLE, THE SCARLET CHANGED THEIR LAWS TO DISALLOW THE RECOGNITION OF ANY *"PLANET"* WHERE LESS THAN FIFTY OF THE SPECIES REMAINED.
BUT THERE ARE STILL OVER SIXTY-FIVE OF THEM LEFT--
--OH, ***SHIT.***

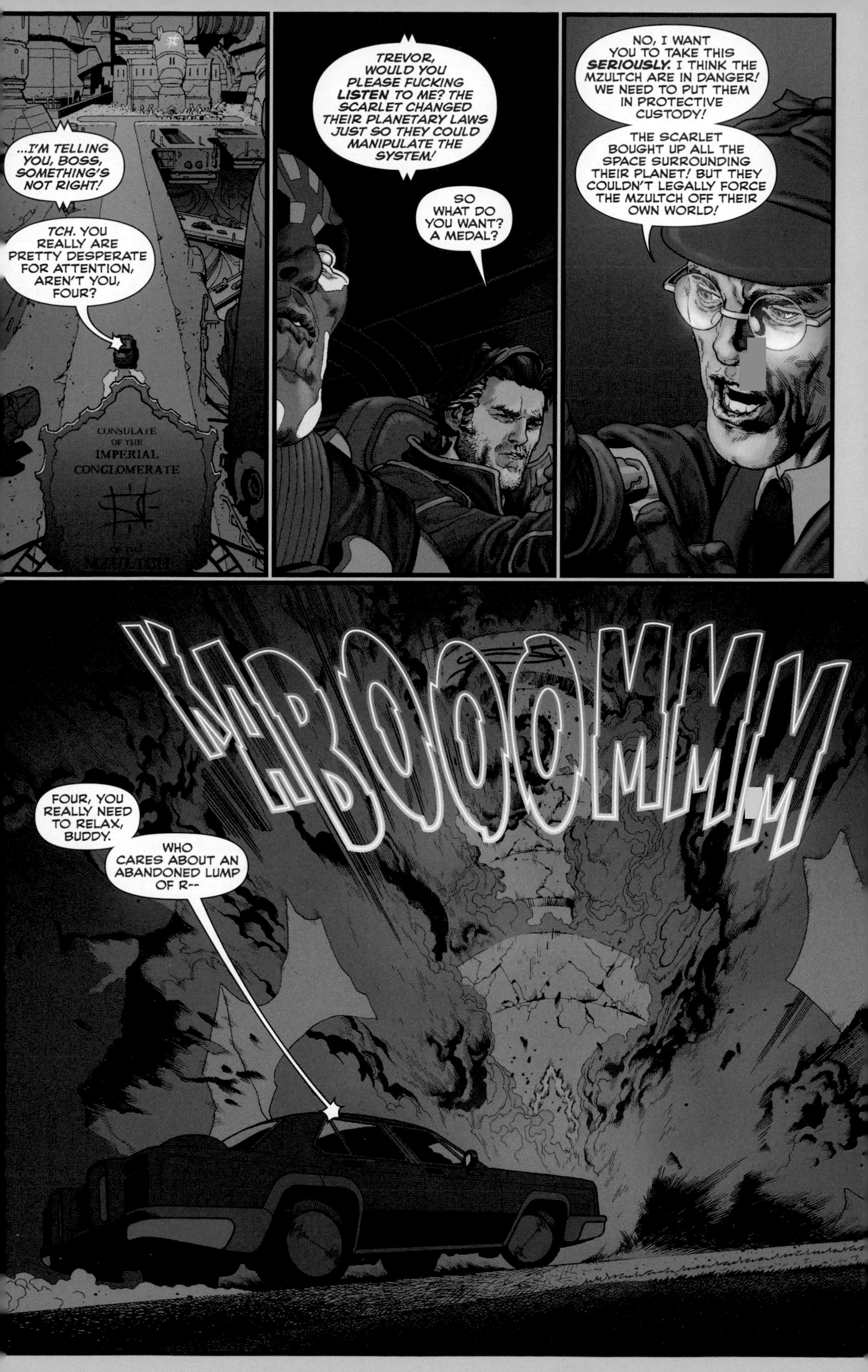

...I'M TELLING YOU, BOSS, SOMETHING'S NOT RIGHT!
TCH. YOU REALLY ARE PRETTY DESPERATE FOR ATTENTION, AREN'T YOU, FOUR?
CONSULATE OF THE IMPERIAL CONGLOMERATE
TREVOR, WOULD YOU PLEASE FUCKING LISTEN TO ME? THE SCARLET CHANGED THEIR PLANETARY LAWS JUST SO THEY COULD MANIPULATE THE SYSTEM!
SO WHAT DO YOU WANT? A MEDAL?
NO, I WANT YOU TO TAKE THIS SERIOUSLY. I THINK THE MZULTCH ARE IN DANGER! WE NEED TO PUT THEM IN PROTECTIVE CUSTODY!
THE SCARLET BOUGHT UP ALL THE SPACE SURROUNDING THEIR PLANET! BUT THEY COULDN'T LEGALLY FORCE THE MZULTCH OFF THEIR OWN WORLD!
'VRBOOOMMM
FOUR, YOU REALLY NEED TO RELAX, BUDDY.
WHO CARES ABOUT AN ABANDONED LUMP OF R--

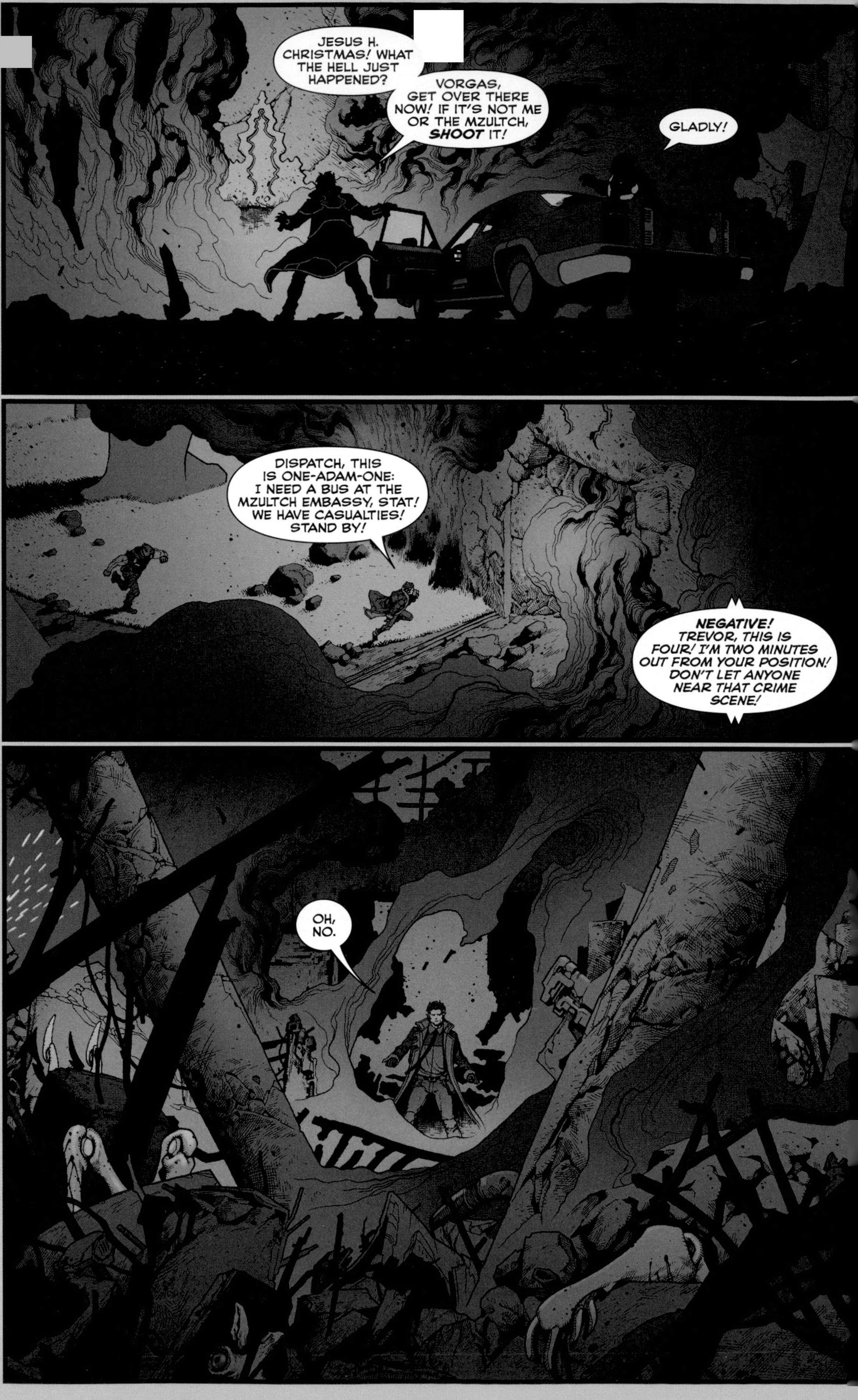
JESUS H. CHRISTMAS! WHAT THE HELL JUST HAPPENED?
VORGAS, GET OVER THERE NOW! IF IT'S NOT ME OR THE MZULTCH, SHOOT IT!
GLADLY!
DISPATCH, THIS IS ONE-ADAM-ONE: I NEED A BUS AT THE MZULTCH EMBASSY, STAT! WE HAVE CASUALTIES! STAND BY!
NEGATIVE! TREVOR, THIS IS FOUR! I'M TWO MINUTES OUT FROM YOUR POSITION! DON'T LET ANYONE NEAR THAT CRIME SCENE!
OH, NO.

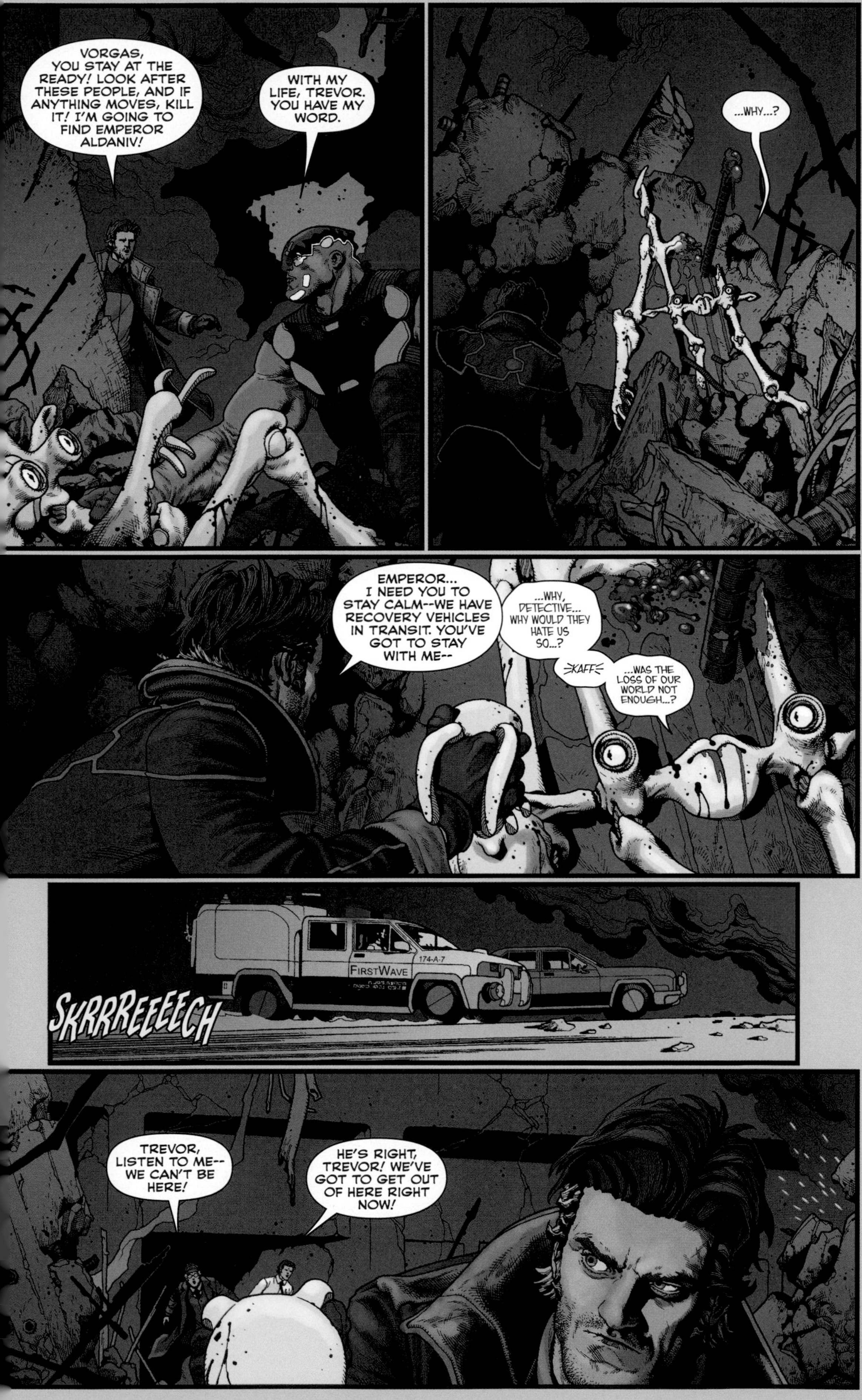
VORGAS, YOU STAY AT THE READY! LOOK AFTER THESE PEOPLE, AND IF ANYTHING MOVES, KILL IT! I'M GOING TO FIND EMPEROR ALDANIV!
WITH MY LIFE, TREVOR. YOU HAVE MY WORD.
...WHY...?
EMPEROR... I NEED YOU TO STAY CALM--WE HAVE RECOVERY VEHICLES IN TRANSIT. YOU'VE GOT TO STAY WITH ME--
...WHY, DETECTIVE... WHY WOULD THEY HATE US SO...?
KAFF
...WAS THE LOSS OF OUR WORLD NOT ENOUGH...?
174-A-7
FIRSTWAVE
SKRRREEEECH
TREVOR, LISTEN TO ME-- WE CAN'T BE HERE!
HE'S RIGHT, TREVOR! WE'VE GOT TO GET OUT OF HERE RIGHT NOW!

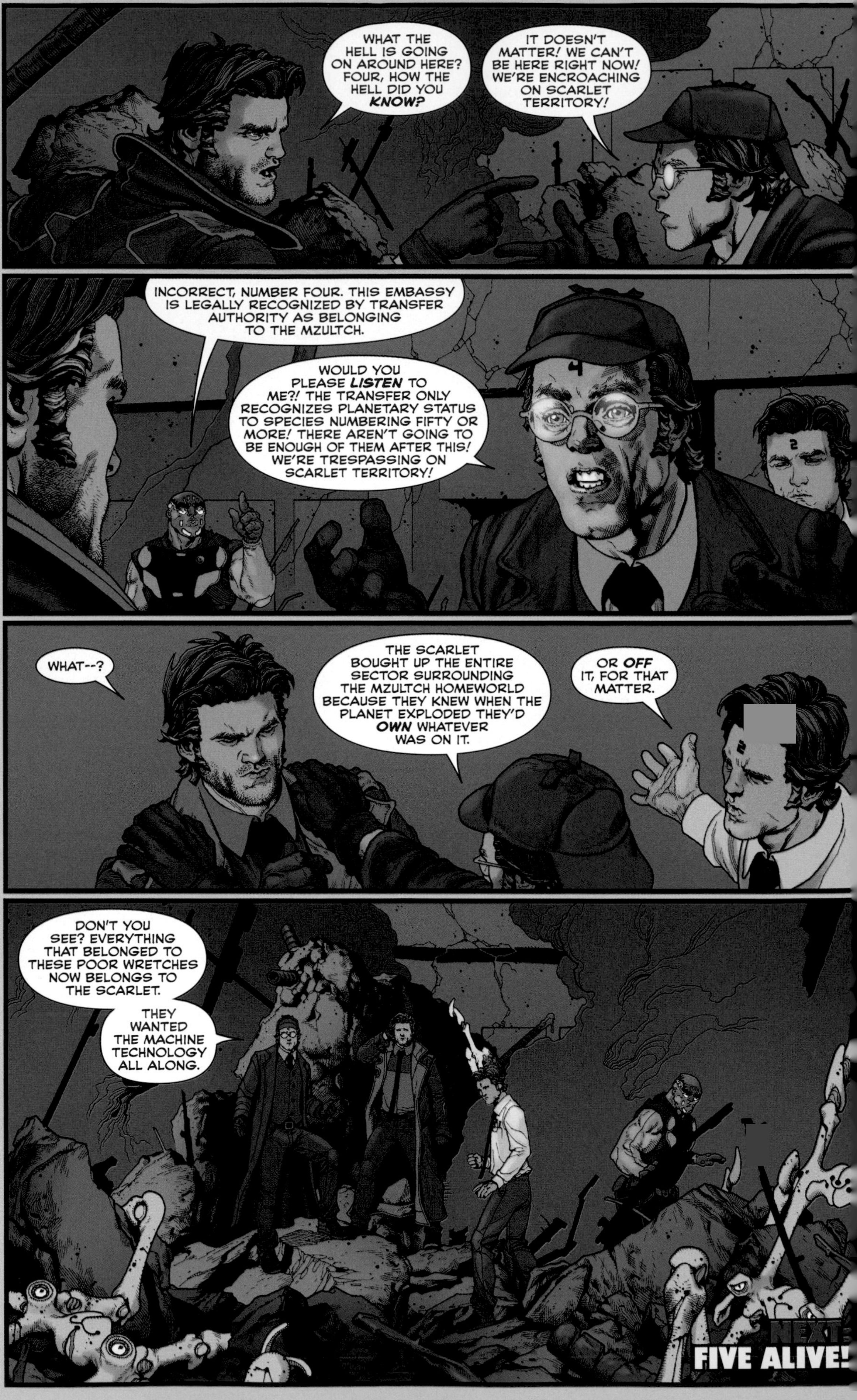
WHAT THE HELL IS GOING ON AROUND HERE? FOUR, HOW THE HELL DID YOU KNOW?
IT DOESN'T MATTER! WE CAN'T BE HERE RIGHT NOW! WE'RE ENCROACHING ON SCARLET TERRITORY!
INCORRECT, NUMBER FOUR. THIS EMBASSY IS LEGALLY RECOGNIZED BY TRANSFER AUTHORITY AS BELONGING TO THE MZULTCH.
WOULD YOU PLEASE LISTEN TO ME?! THE TRANSFER ONLY RECOGNIZES PLANETARY STATUS TO SPECIES NUMBERING FIFTY OR MORE! THERE AREN'T GOING TO BE ENOUGH OF THEM AFTER THIS! WE'RE TRESPASSING ON SCARLET TERRITORY!
WHAT--?
THE SCARLET BOUGHT UP THE ENTIRE SECTOR SURROUNDING THE MZULTCH HOMEWORLD BECAUSE THEY KNEW WHEN THE PLANET EXPLODED THEY'D OWN WHATEVER WAS ON IT.
OR OFF IT, FOR THAT MATTER.
DON'T YOU SEE? EVERYTHING THAT BELONGED TO THESE POOR WRETCHES NOW BELONGS TO THE SCARLET.
THEY WANTED THE MACHINE TECHNOLOGY ALL ALONG.
NEXT: FIVE ALIVE!

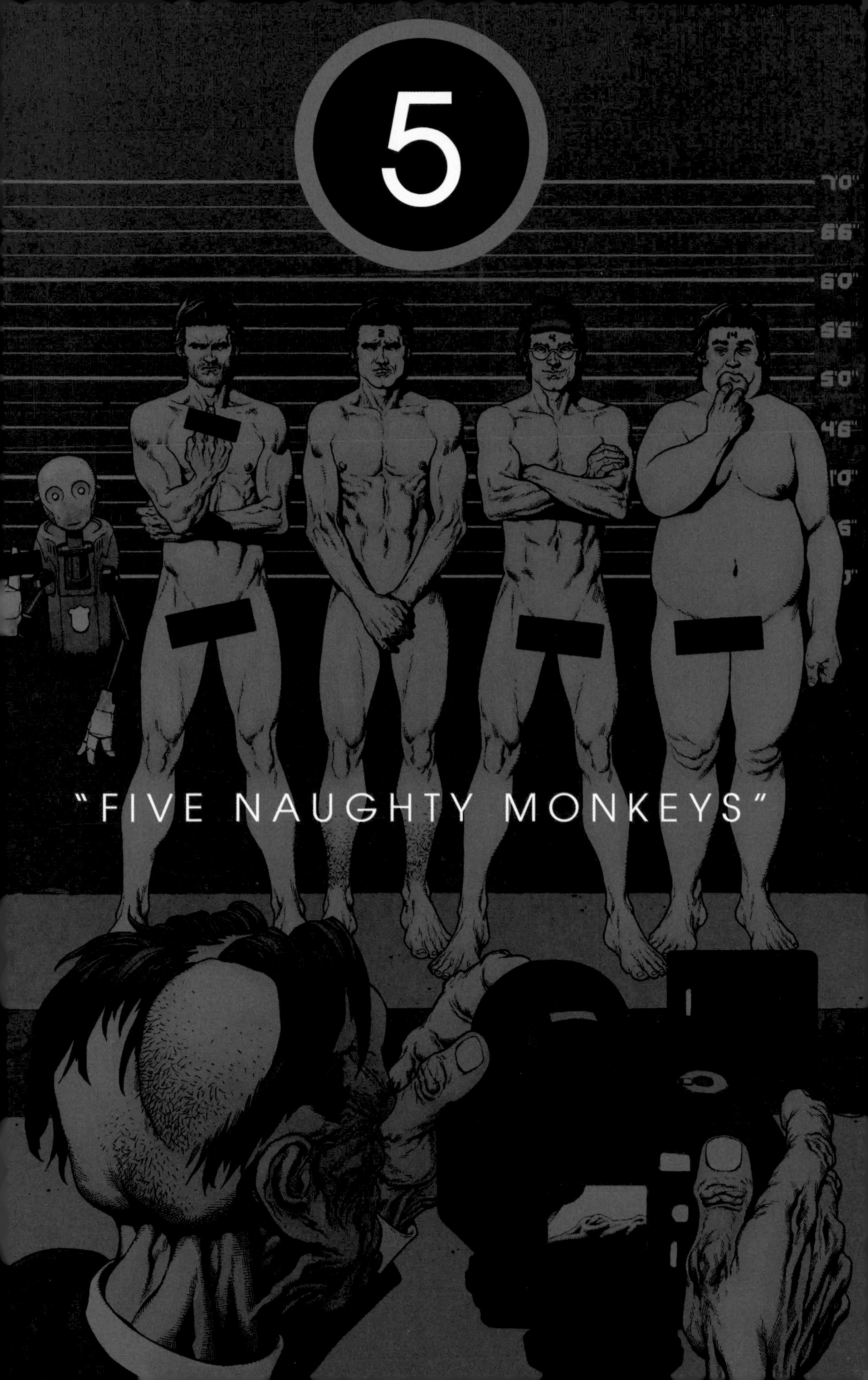
5
"FIVE NAUGHTY MONKEYS"

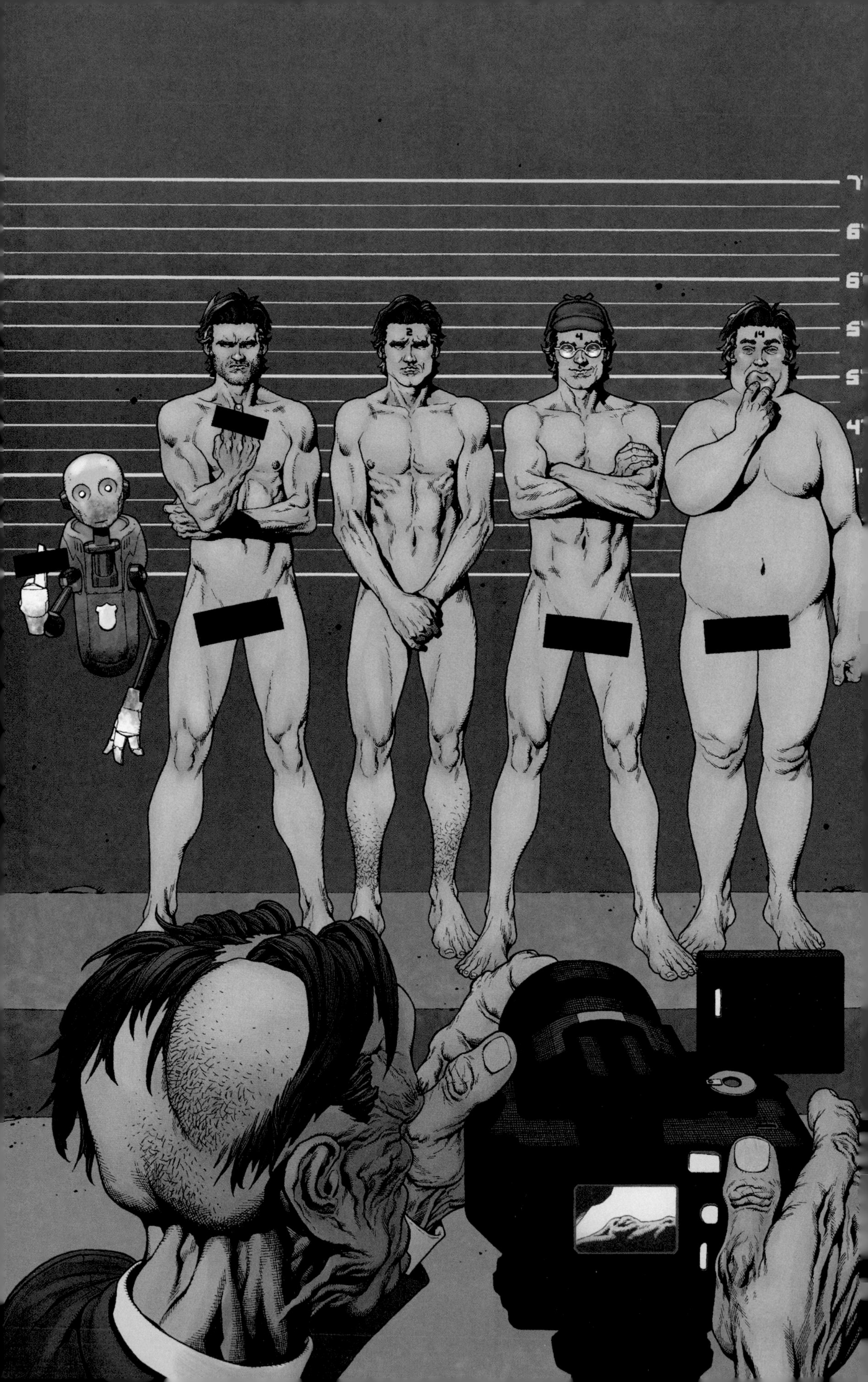
2
4
14

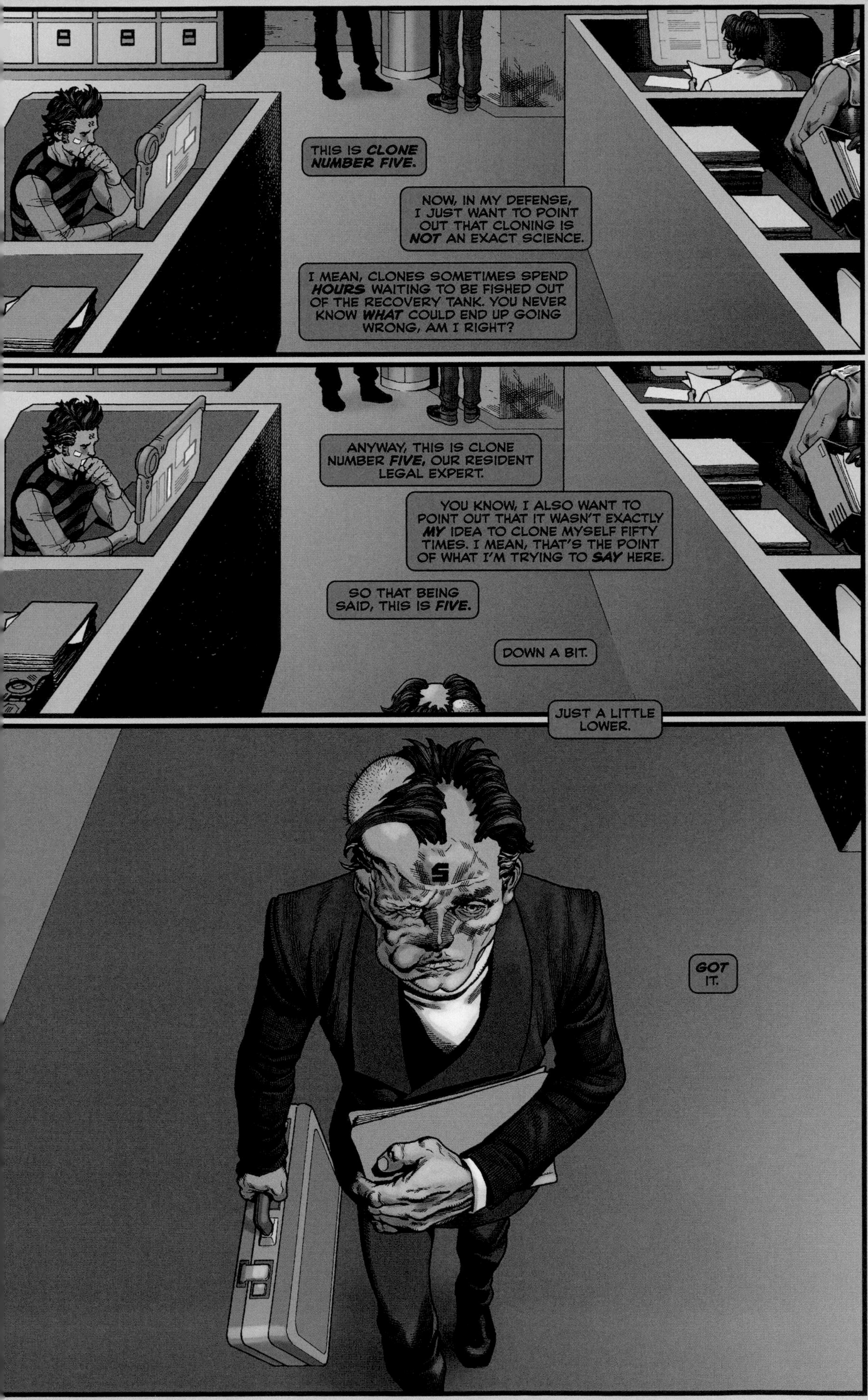
THIS IS CLONE NUMBER FIVE.
NOW, IN MY DEFENSE, I JUST WANT TO POINT OUT THAT CLONING IS NOT AN EXACT SCIENCE.
I MEAN, CLONES SOMETIMES SPEND HOURS WAITING TO BE FISHED OUT OF THE RECOVERY TANK. YOU NEVER KNOW WHAT COULD END UP GOING WRONG, AM I RIGHT?
ANYWAY, THIS IS CLONE NUMBER FIVE, OUR RESIDENT LEGAL EXPERT.
YOU KNOW, I ALSO WANT TO POINT OUT THAT IT WASN'T EXACTLY MY IDEA TO CLONE MYSELF FIFTY TIMES. I MEAN, THAT'S THE POINT OF WHAT I'M TRYING TO SAY HERE.
SO THAT BEING SAID, THIS IS FIVE.
DOWN A BIT.
JUST A LITTLE LOWER.
GOT IT.

YO, *QUASI!* THANKS FOR GETTING BACK TO ME ON THAT CASE FILE. YOU REALLY SAVED MY ASS WITH STOLTEH.

HEY, QUASI. LEGAL QUESTION-- IF YOU BURN SOMETHING REMOTELY AND YOU AREN'T AROUND TO *SEE* IT, ARE YOU LEGALLY RESPONSIBLE?

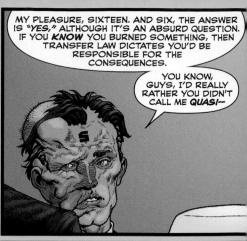

MY PLEASURE, SIXTEEN. AND SIX, THE ANSWER IS "YES," ALTHOUGH IT'S AN ABSURD QUESTION. IF YOU *KNOW* YOU BURNED SOMETHING, THEN TRANSFER LAW DICTATES YOU'D BE RESPONSIBLE FOR THE CONSEQUENCES.

YOU KNOW, GUYS, I'D REALLY RATHER YOU DIDN'T CALL ME *QUASI*--

*HUH.* GOOD TO KNOW.

THANKS, QUASI! YOU'RE A LEGAL GENIUS, MY MAN!

...SO I SAY, *"HE'S A FREAK AN' HIS HEAD LOOKS LIKE A PAIR OF GONADS."* AND THAT FRUIT LOOP SEVEN'S ALL, LIKE, *"LIVE AND LET LIVE, MAN"*--

*IXNAY! IXNAY!*

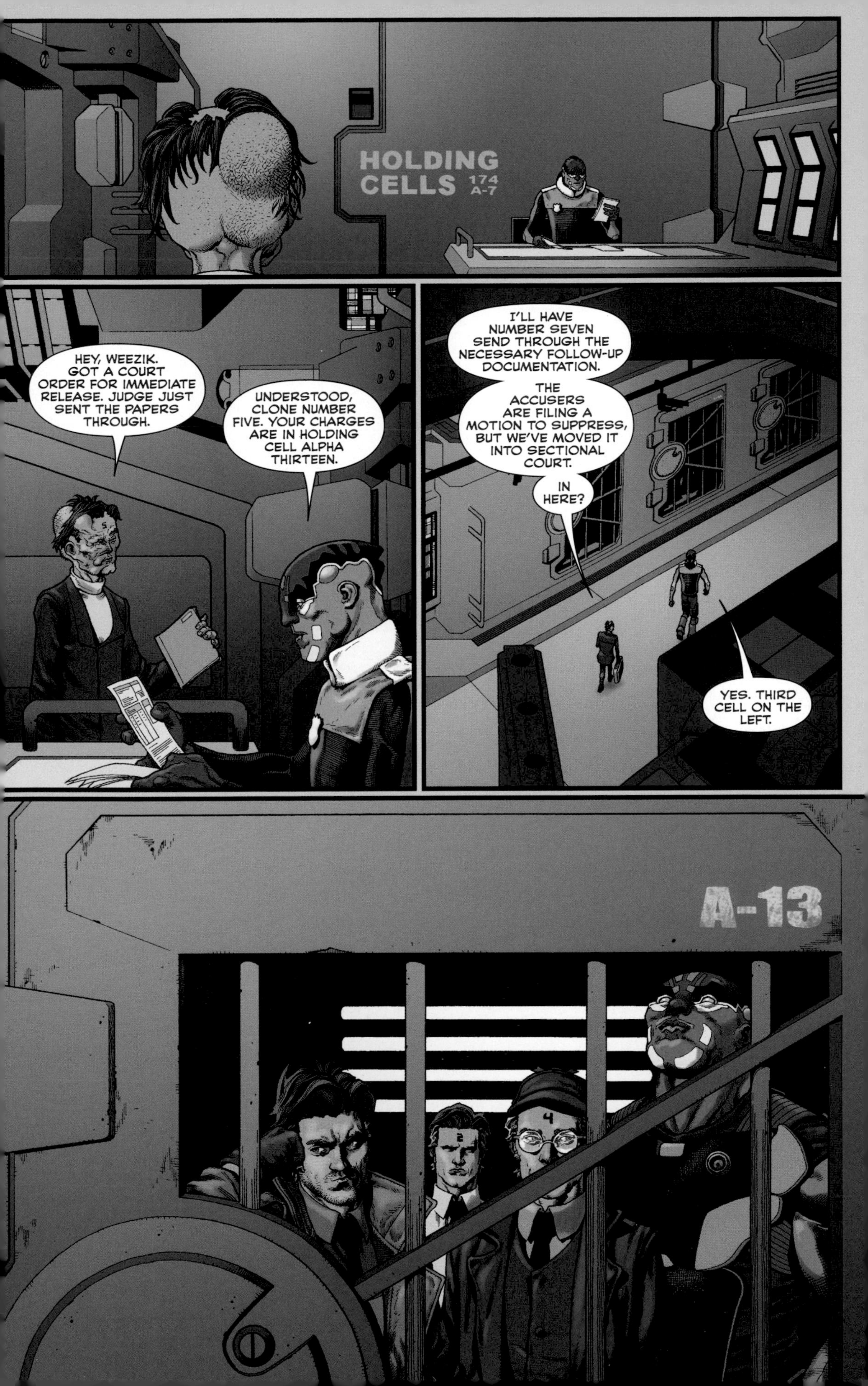
HOLDING CELLS 174 A-7
HEY, WEEZIK. GOT A COURT ORDER FOR IMMEDIATE RELEASE. JUDGE JUST SENT THE PAPERS THROUGH.
UNDERSTOOD, CLONE NUMBER FIVE. YOUR CHARGES ARE IN HOLDING CELL ALPHA THIRTEEN.
I'LL HAVE NUMBER SEVEN SEND THROUGH THE NECESSARY FOLLOW-UP DOCUMENTATION.
THE ACCUSERS ARE FILING A MOTION TO SUPPRESS, BUT WE'VE MOVED IT INTO SECTIONAL COURT.
IN HERE?
YES. THIRD CELL ON THE LEFT.
A-13

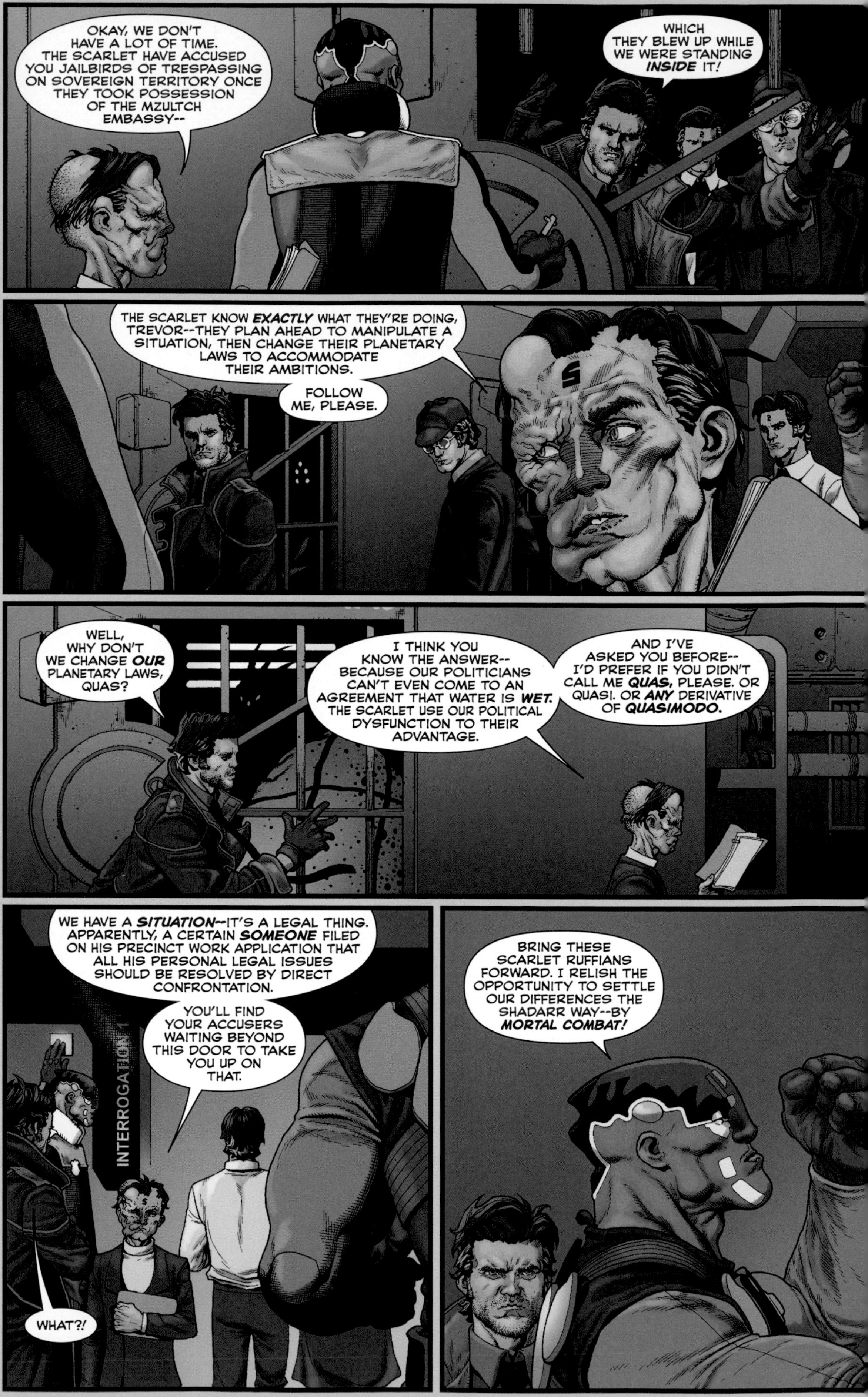
OKAY, WE DON'T HAVE A LOT OF TIME. THE SCARLET HAVE ACCUSED YOU JAILBIRDS OF TRESPASSING ON SOVEREIGN TERRITORY ONCE THEY TOOK POSSESSION OF THE MZULTCH EMBASSY--
WHICH THEY BLEW UP WHILE WE WERE STANDING *INSIDE* IT!
THE SCARLET KNOW *EXACTLY* WHAT THEY'RE DOING, TREVOR--THEY PLAN AHEAD TO MANIPULATE A SITUATION, THEN CHANGE THEIR PLANETARY LAWS TO ACCOMMODATE THEIR AMBITIONS.
FOLLOW ME, PLEASE.
WELL, WHY DON'T WE CHANGE *OUR* PLANETARY LAWS, QUAS?
I THINK YOU KNOW THE ANSWER-- BECAUSE OUR POLITICIANS CAN'T EVEN COME TO AN AGREEMENT THAT WATER IS *WET*. THE SCARLET USE OUR POLITICAL DYSFUNCTION TO THEIR ADVANTAGE.
AND I'VE ASKED YOU BEFORE-- I'D PREFER IF YOU DIDN'T CALL ME *QUAS*, PLEASE. OR QUASI. OR *ANY* DERIVATIVE OF *QUASIMODO*.
WE HAVE A *SITUATION*--IT'S A LEGAL THING. APPARENTLY, A CERTAIN *SOMEONE* FILED ON HIS PRECINCT WORK APPLICATION THAT ALL HIS PERSONAL LEGAL ISSUES SHOULD BE RESOLVED BY DIRECT CONFRONTATION.
YOU'LL FIND YOUR ACCUSERS WAITING BEYOND THIS DOOR TO TAKE YOU UP ON THAT.
INTERROGATION
WHAT?!
BRING THESE SCARLET RUFFIANS FORWARD. I RELISH THE OPPORTUNITY TO SETTLE OUR DIFFERENCES THE SHADARR WAY--BY *MORTAL COMBAT!*

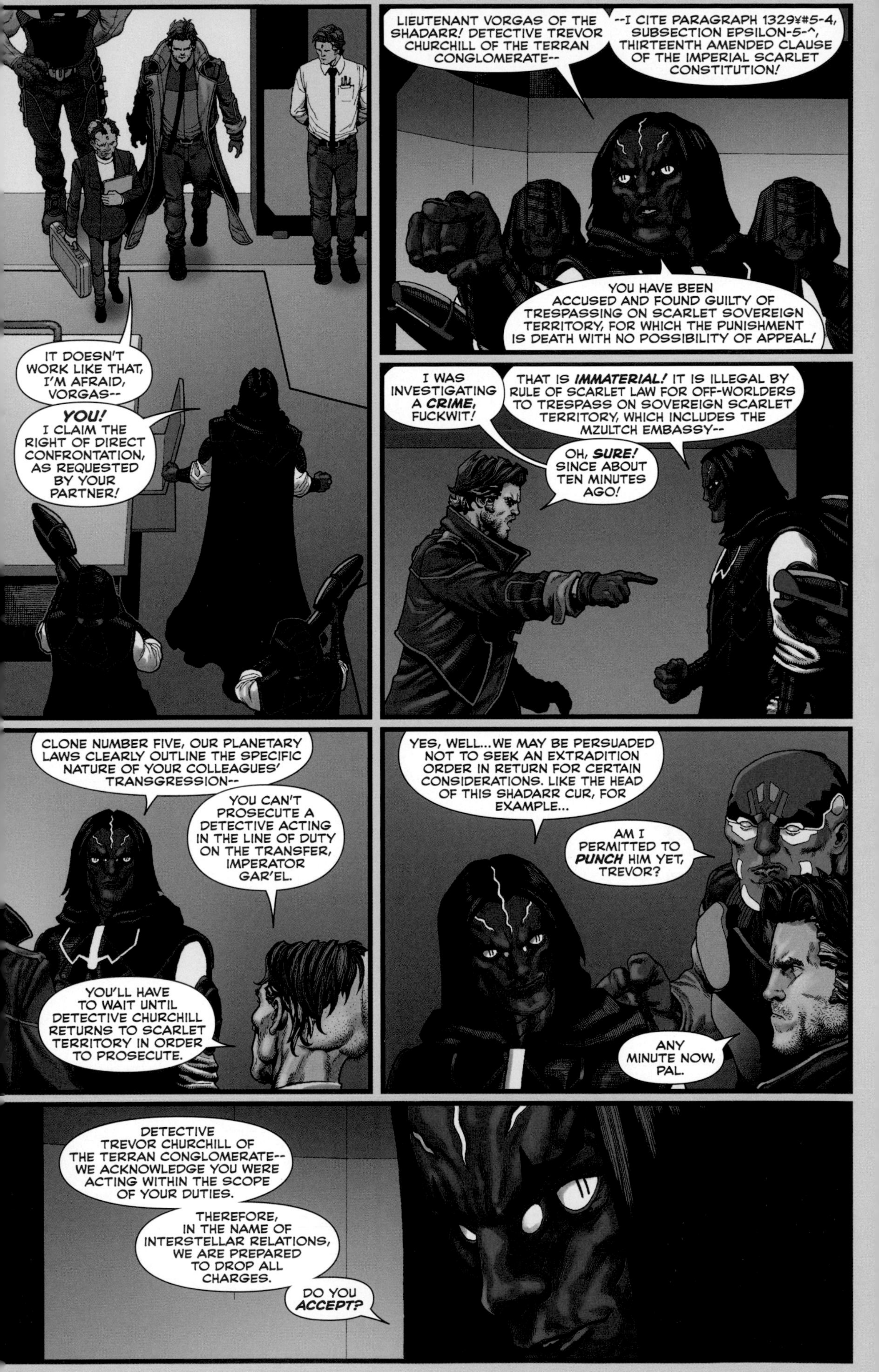

IT DOESN'T WORK LIKE THAT, I'M AFRAID, VORGAS--
YOU! I CLAIM THE RIGHT OF DIRECT CONFRONTATION, AS REQUESTED BY YOUR PARTNER!
LIEUTENANT VORGAS OF THE SHADARR! DETECTIVE TREVOR CHURCHILL OF THE TERRAN CONGLOMERATE--
--I CITE PARAGRAPH 1329¥#5-4, SUBSECTION EPSILON-5-^, THIRTEENTH AMENDED CLAUSE OF THE IMPERIAL SCARLET CONSTITUTION!
YOU HAVE BEEN ACCUSED AND FOUND GUILTY OF TRESPASSING ON SCARLET SOVEREIGN TERRITORY, FOR WHICH THE PUNISHMENT IS DEATH WITH NO POSSIBILITY OF APPEAL!
I WAS INVESTIGATING A CRIME, FUCKWIT!
THAT IS IMMATERIAL! IT IS ILLEGAL BY RULE OF SCARLET LAW FOR OFF-WORLDERS TO TRESPASS ON SOVEREIGN SCARLET TERRITORY, WHICH INCLUDES THE MZULTCH EMBASSY--
OH, SURE! SINCE ABOUT TEN MINUTES AGO!
CLONE NUMBER FIVE, OUR PLANETARY LAWS CLEARLY OUTLINE THE SPECIFIC NATURE OF YOUR COLLEAGUES' TRANSGRESSION--
YOU CAN'T PROSECUTE A DETECTIVE ACTING IN THE LINE OF DUTY ON THE TRANSFER, IMPERATOR GAR'EL.
YOU'LL HAVE TO WAIT UNTIL DETECTIVE CHURCHILL RETURNS TO SCARLET TERRITORY IN ORDER TO PROSECUTE.
YES, WELL...WE MAY BE PERSUADED NOT TO SEEK AN EXTRADITION ORDER IN RETURN FOR CERTAIN CONSIDERATIONS. LIKE THE HEAD OF THIS SHADARR CUR, FOR EXAMPLE...
AM I PERMITTED TO PUNCH HIM YET, TREVOR?
ANY MINUTE NOW, PAL.
DETECTIVE TREVOR CHURCHILL OF THE TERRAN CONGLOMERATE-- WE ACKNOWLEDGE YOU WERE ACTING WITHIN THE SCOPE OF YOUR DUTIES.
THEREFORE, IN THE NAME OF INTERSTELLAR RELATIONS, WE ARE PREPARED TO DROP ALL CHARGES.
DO YOU ACCEPT?

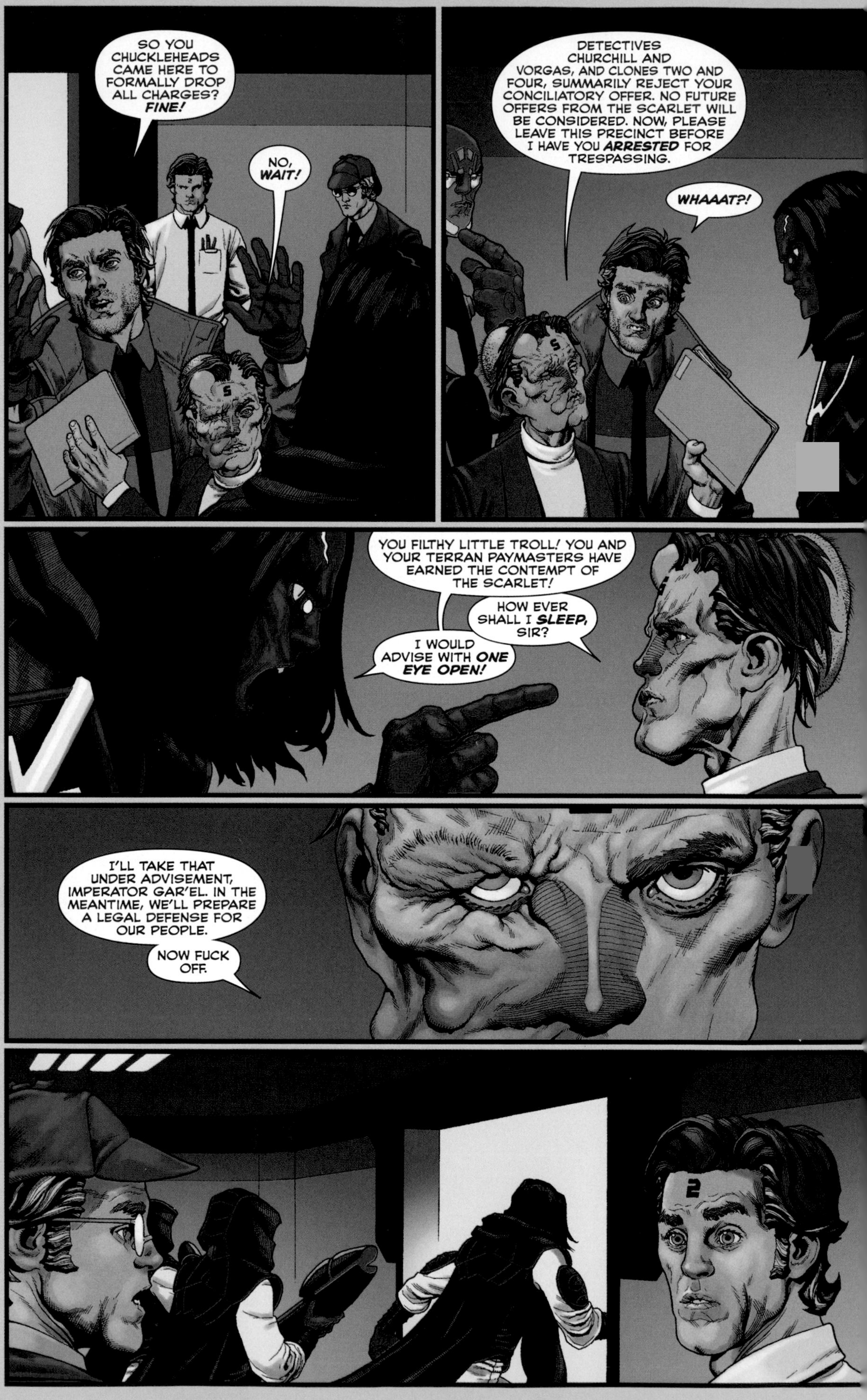
SO YOU CHUCKLEHEADS CAME HERE TO FORMALLY DROP ALL CHARGES? **FINE!**
NO, **WAIT!**
DETECTIVES CHURCHILL AND VORGAS, AND CLONES TWO AND FOUR, SUMMARILY REJECT YOUR CONCILIATORY OFFER. NO FUTURE OFFERS FROM THE SCARLET WILL BE CONSIDERED. NOW, PLEASE LEAVE THIS PRECINCT BEFORE I HAVE YOU **ARRESTED** FOR TRESPASSING.
**WHAAAT?!**
YOU FILTHY LITTLE TROLL! YOU AND YOUR TERRAN PAYMASTERS HAVE EARNED THE CONTEMPT OF THE SCARLET!
HOW EVER SHALL I **SLEEP,** SIR?
I WOULD ADVISE WITH **ONE EYE OPEN!**
I'LL TAKE THAT UNDER ADVISEMENT, IMPERATOR GAR'EL. IN THE MEANTIME, WE'LL PREPARE A LEGAL DEFENSE FOR OUR PEOPLE.
NOW FUCK OFF.

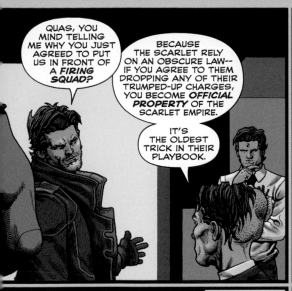

QUAS, YOU MIND TELLING ME WHY YOU JUST AGREED TO PUT US IN FRONT OF A *FIRING SQUAD?*

BECAUSE THE SCARLET RELY ON AN OBSCURE LAW-- IF YOU AGREE TO THEM DROPPING ANY OF THEIR TRUMPED-UP CHARGES, YOU BECOME *OFFICIAL PROPERTY* OF THE SCARLET EMPIRE.

IT'S THE OLDEST TRICK IN THEIR *PLAYBOOK.*

QUASI, YOU LITTLE BULLSHITTER. YOU MADE THEM THINK YOU WERE STUPID, AND THEN YOU GAVE THEM BOTH BARRELS.

I'D HUG YOU IF YOU DIDN'T HAVE SUCH A REVOLTING SKIN CONDITION, YOU NASTY LITTLE GOBLIN.

I *ALSO* MADE THEM THINK I WAS STUPID.

YEAH. YOU DID GREAT, PAL.

I'VE BOUGHT US SOME TIME, BUT THE SCARLET ARE RELENTLESS--THEY'LL BE BACK ONCE THEY WORK OUT WHAT LAWS THEY NEED TO CHANGE IN THEIR FAVOR.

THIS IS GOING TO BE A LEGAL NIGHTMARE, AND THEY'LL BE LOOKING FOR ANY OPPORTUNITY TO EXPLOIT IT WHILE YOU'RE ACTING IN THE LINE OF DUTY.

SO I'M BEGGING YOU-- ALL *FOUR* OF YOU-- TAKE THE DAY OFF. GO PLAY GOLF OR SOMETHING. ANYTHING. AS LONG AS YOU TAKE A BACK SEAT ON THIS AND LET ME WORK OUT WHAT TO DO.

GET IT? GOT IT? *GOOD.*

SO. *GOLF?*

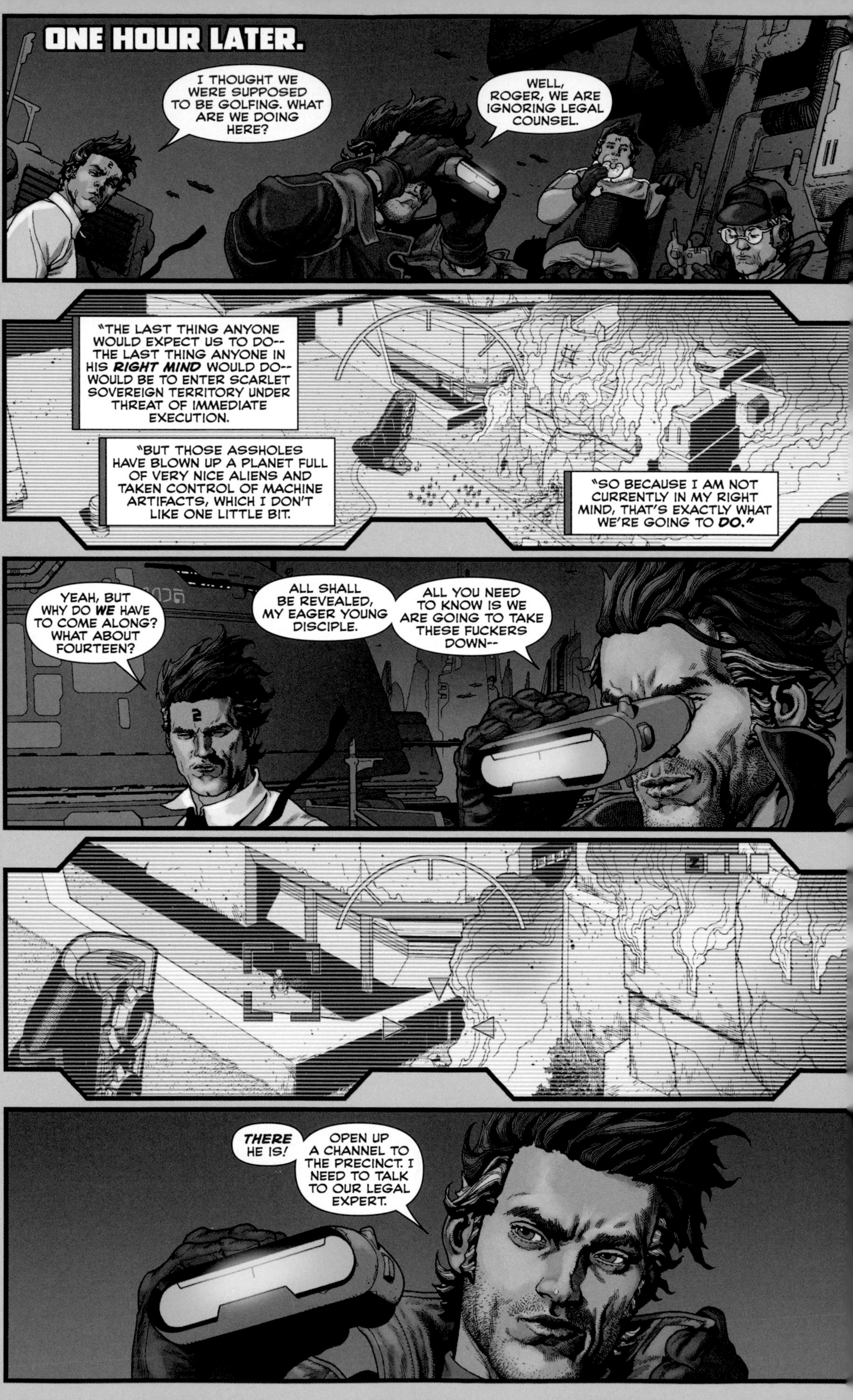
ONE HOUR LATER.
I THOUGHT WE WERE SUPPOSED TO BE GOLFING. WHAT ARE WE DOING HERE?
WELL, ROGER, WE ARE IGNORING LEGAL COUNSEL.
"THE LAST THING ANYONE WOULD EXPECT US TO DO-- THE LAST THING ANYONE IN HIS *RIGHT MIND* WOULD DO-- WOULD BE TO ENTER SCARLET SOVEREIGN TERRITORY UNDER THREAT OF IMMEDIATE EXECUTION.
"BUT THOSE ASSHOLES HAVE BLOWN UP A PLANET FULL OF VERY NICE ALIENS AND TAKEN CONTROL OF MACHINE ARTIFACTS, WHICH I DON'T LIKE ONE LITTLE BIT.
"SO BECAUSE I AM NOT CURRENTLY IN MY RIGHT MIND, THAT'S EXACTLY WHAT WE'RE GOING TO *DO.*"
YEAH, BUT WHY DO *WE* HAVE TO COME ALONG? WHAT ABOUT FOURTEEN?
ALL SHALL BE REVEALED, MY EAGER YOUNG DISCIPLE.
ALL YOU NEED TO KNOW IS WE ARE GOING TO TAKE THESE FUCKERS DOWN--
*THERE* HE IS!
OPEN UP A CHANNEL TO THE PRECINCT. I NEED TO TALK TO OUR LEGAL EXPERT.

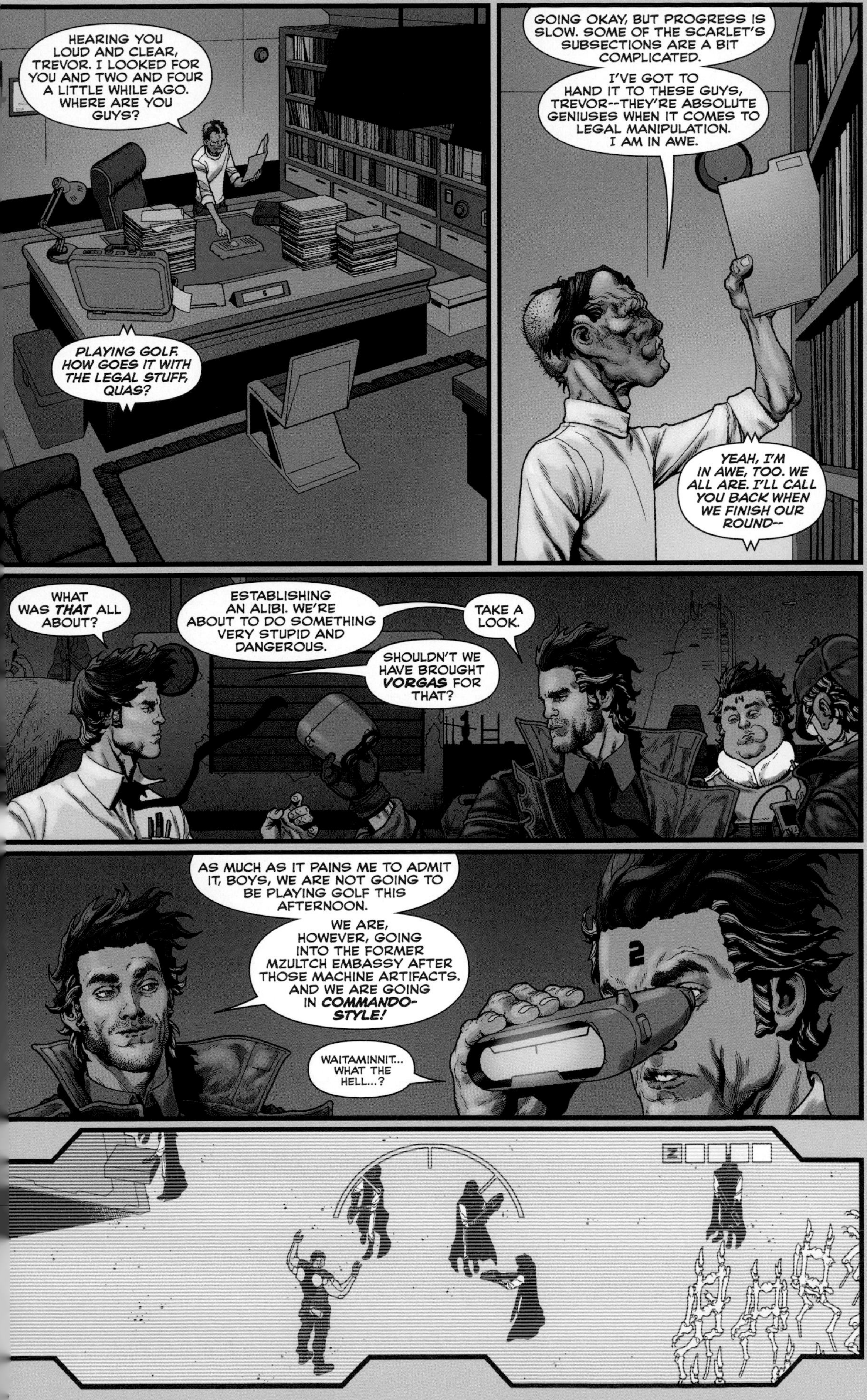
HEARING YOU LOUD AND CLEAR, TREVOR. I LOOKED FOR YOU AND TWO AND FOUR A LITTLE WHILE AGO. WHERE ARE YOU GUYS?
PLAYING GOLF. HOW GOES IT WITH THE LEGAL STUFF, QUAS?
GOING OKAY, BUT PROGRESS IS SLOW. SOME OF THE SCARLET'S SUBSECTIONS ARE A BIT COMPLICATED.
I'VE GOT TO HAND IT TO THESE GUYS, TREVOR--THEY'RE ABSOLUTE GENIUSES WHEN IT COMES TO LEGAL MANIPULATION. I AM IN AWE.
YEAH, I'M IN AWE, TOO. WE ALL ARE. I'LL CALL YOU BACK WHEN WE FINISH OUR ROUND--
WHAT WAS THAT ALL ABOUT?
ESTABLISHING AN ALIBI. WE'RE ABOUT TO DO SOMETHING VERY STUPID AND DANGEROUS.
SHOULDN'T WE HAVE BROUGHT VORGAS FOR THAT?
TAKE A LOOK.
AS MUCH AS IT PAINS ME TO ADMIT IT, BOYS, WE ARE NOT GOING TO BE PLAYING GOLF THIS AFTERNOON.
WE ARE, HOWEVER, GOING INTO THE FORMER MZULTCH EMBASSY AFTER THOSE MACHINE ARTIFACTS. AND WE ARE GOING IN COMMANDO-STYLE!
WAITAMINNIT... WHAT THE HELL...?

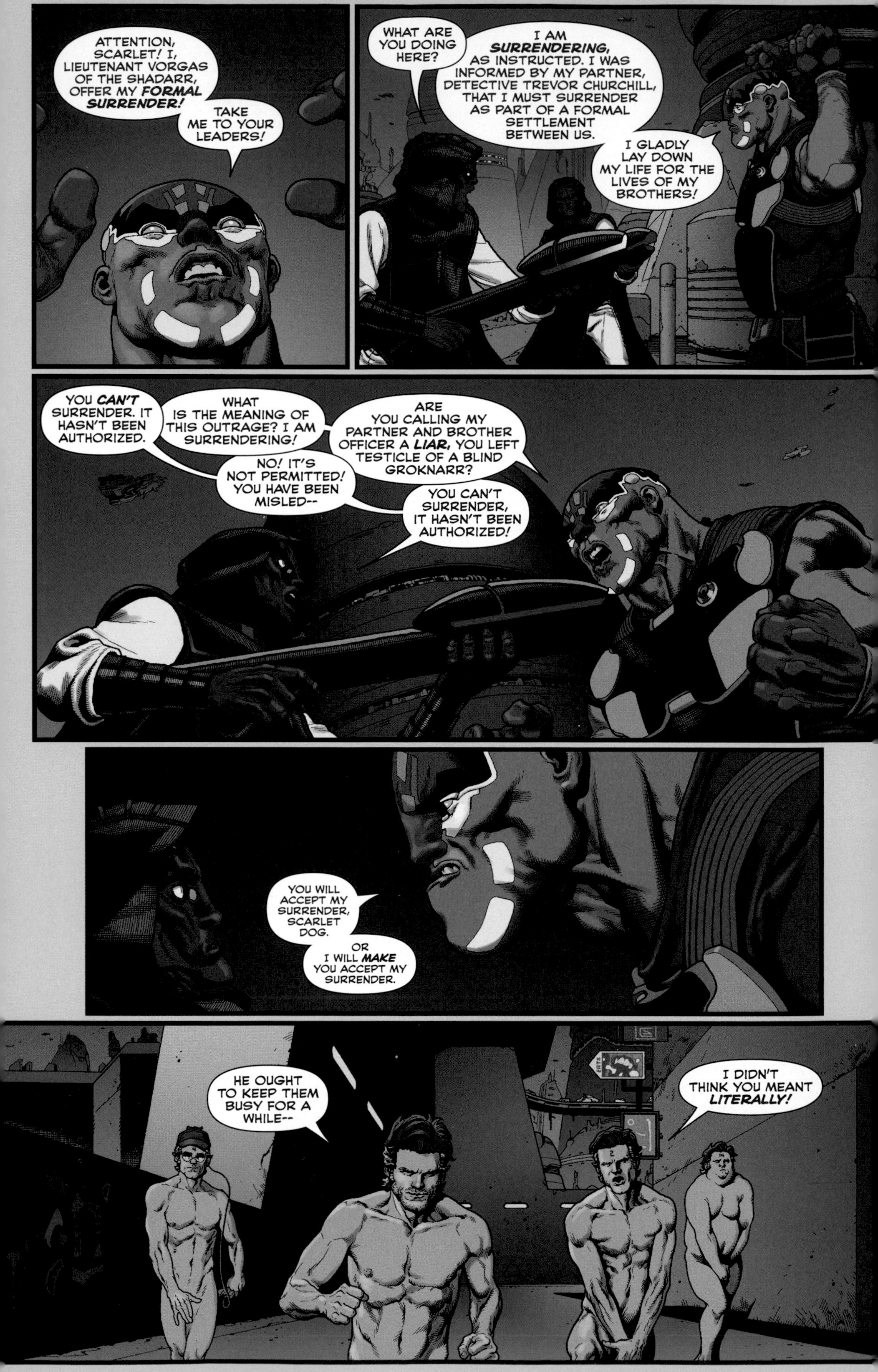
ATTENTION, SCARLET! I, LIEUTENANT VORGAS OF THE SHADARR, OFFER MY ***FORMAL SURRENDER!***
TAKE ME TO YOUR LEADERS!
WHAT ARE YOU DOING HERE?
I AM ***SURRENDERING,*** AS INSTRUCTED. I WAS INFORMED BY MY PARTNER, DETECTIVE TREVOR CHURCHILL, THAT I MUST SURRENDER AS PART OF A FORMAL SETTLEMENT BETWEEN US.
I GLADLY LAY DOWN MY LIFE FOR THE LIVES OF MY BROTHERS!
YOU ***CAN'T*** SURRENDER. IT HASN'T BEEN AUTHORIZED.
WHAT IS THE MEANING OF THIS OUTRAGE? I AM SURRENDERING!
NO! IT'S NOT PERMITTED! YOU HAVE BEEN MISLED--
ARE YOU CALLING MY PARTNER AND BROTHER OFFICER A ***LIAR,*** YOU LEFT TESTICLE OF A BLIND GROKNARR?
YOU CAN'T SURRENDER, IT HASN'T BEEN AUTHORIZED!
YOU WILL ACCEPT MY SURRENDER, SCARLET DOG.
OR I WILL ***MAKE*** YOU ACCEPT MY SURRENDER.
HE OUGHT TO KEEP THEM BUSY FOR A WHILE--
I DIDN'T THINK YOU MEANT ***LITERALLY!***

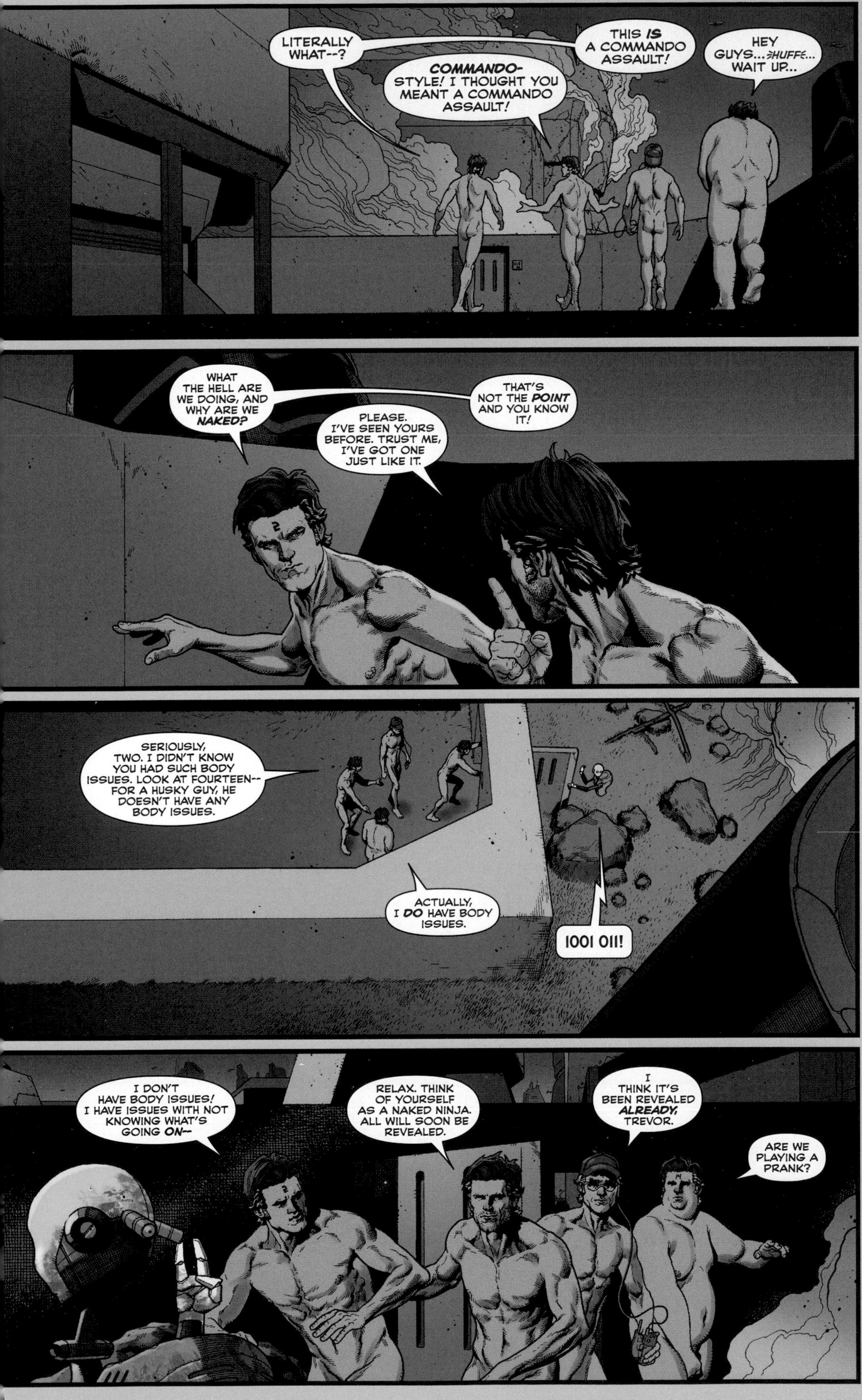

LITERALLY WHAT--?
THIS **IS** A COMMANDO ASSAULT!
**COMMANDO-**STYLE! I THOUGHT YOU MEANT A COMMANDO ASSAULT!
HEY GUYS... *HUFF*... WAIT UP...
WHAT THE HELL ARE WE DOING, AND WHY ARE WE **NAKED?**
THAT'S NOT THE **POINT** AND YOU KNOW IT!
PLEASE. I'VE SEEN YOURS BEFORE. TRUST ME, I'VE GOT ONE JUST LIKE IT.
SERIOUSLY, TWO. I DIDN'T KNOW YOU HAD SUCH BODY ISSUES. LOOK AT FOURTEEN-- FOR A HUSKY GUY, HE DOESN'T HAVE ANY BODY ISSUES.
ACTUALLY, I **DO** HAVE BODY ISSUES.
1001 011!
I DON'T HAVE BODY ISSUES! I HAVE ISSUES WITH NOT KNOWING WHAT'S GOING **ON--**
RELAX. THINK OF YOURSELF AS A NAKED NINJA. ALL WILL SOON BE REVEALED.
I THINK IT'S BEEN REVEALED **ALREADY,** TREVOR.
ARE WE PLAYING A PRANK?

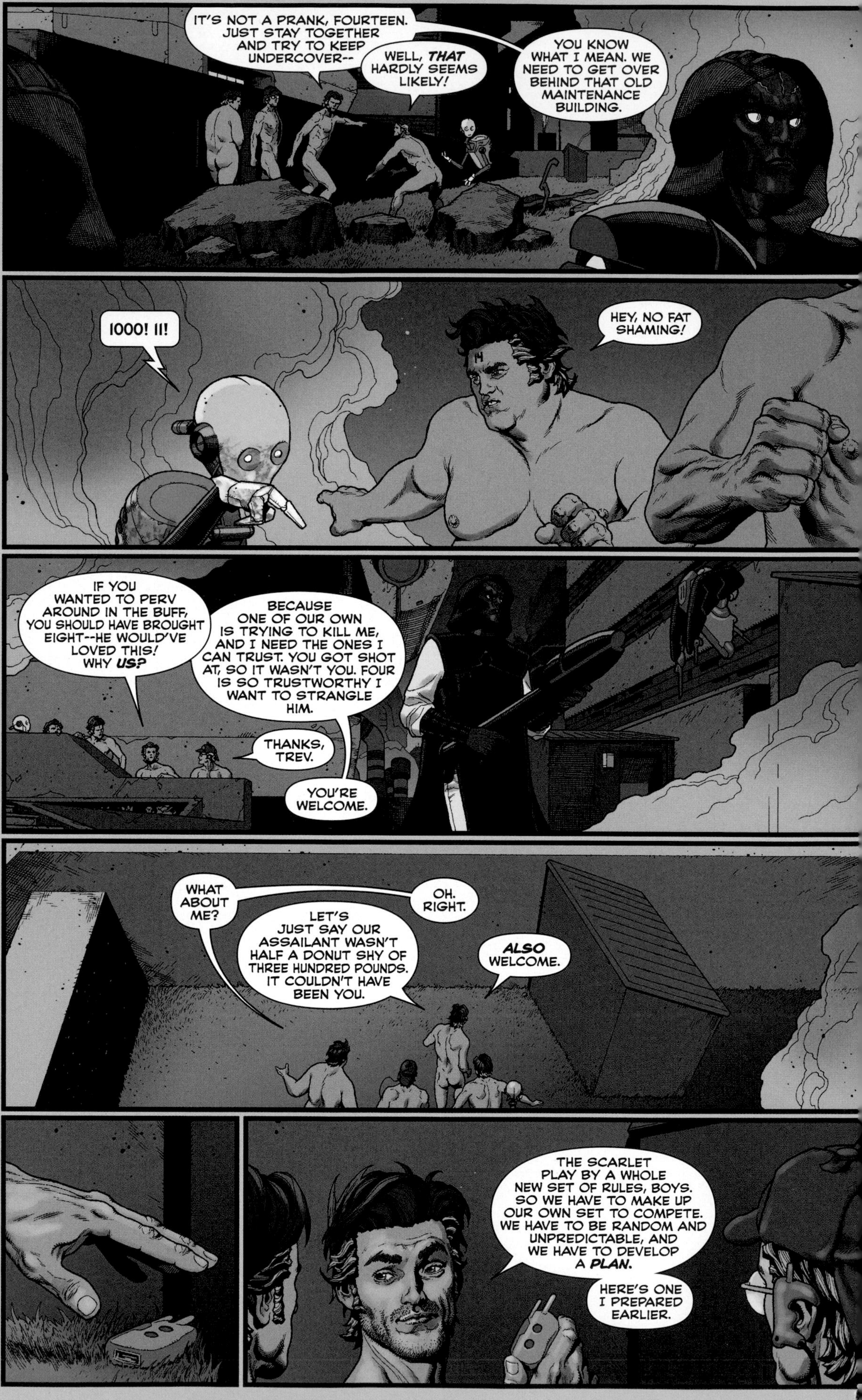
IT'S NOT A PRANK, FOURTEEN. JUST STAY TOGETHER AND TRY TO KEEP UNDERCOVER--
WELL, THAT HARDLY SEEMS LIKELY!
YOU KNOW WHAT I MEAN. WE NEED TO GET OVER BEHIND THAT OLD MAINTENANCE BUILDING.
IOOO! II!
HEY, NO FAT SHAMING!
IF YOU WANTED TO PERV AROUND IN THE BUFF, YOU SHOULD HAVE BROUGHT EIGHT--HE WOULD'VE LOVED THIS! WHY US?
BECAUSE ONE OF OUR OWN IS TRYING TO KILL ME, AND I NEED THE ONES I CAN TRUST. YOU GOT SHOT AT, SO IT WASN'T YOU. FOUR IS SO TRUSTWORTHY I WANT TO STRANGLE HIM.
THANKS, TREV.
YOU'RE WELCOME.
WHAT ABOUT ME?
OH. RIGHT.
LET'S JUST SAY OUR ASSAILANT WASN'T HALF A DONUT SHY OF THREE HUNDRED POUNDS. IT COULDN'T HAVE BEEN YOU.
ALSO WELCOME.
THE SCARLET PLAY BY A WHOLE NEW SET OF RULES, BOYS. SO WE HAVE TO MAKE UP OUR OWN SET TO COMPETE. WE HAVE TO BE RANDOM AND UNPREDICTABLE, AND WE HAVE TO DEVELOP A PLAN.
HERE'S ONE I PREPARED EARLIER.

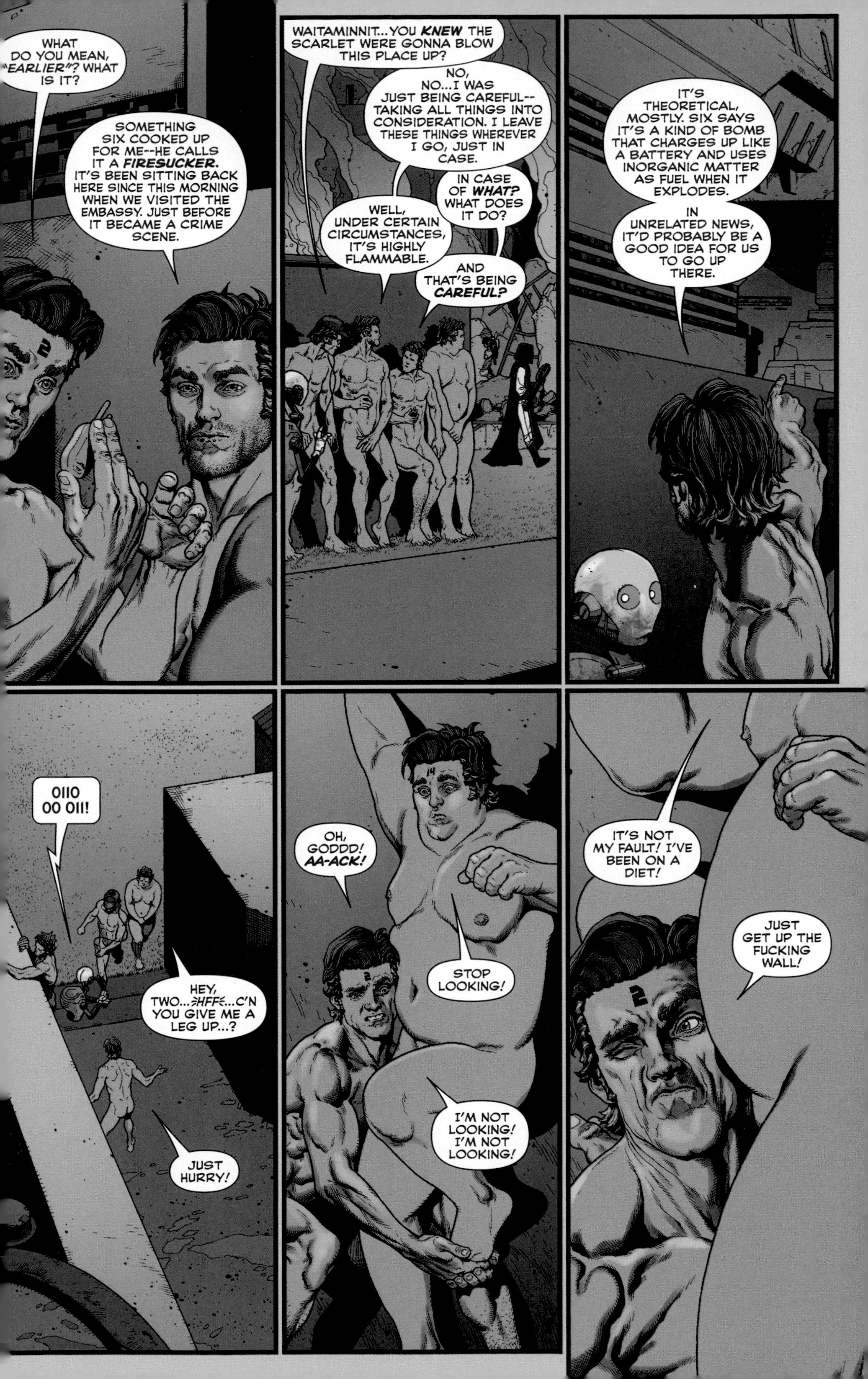
WHAT DO YOU MEAN, "EARLIER"? WHAT IS IT?
SOMETHING SIX COOKED UP FOR ME--HE CALLS IT A FIRESUCKER. IT'S BEEN SITTING BACK HERE SINCE THIS MORNING WHEN WE VISITED THE EMBASSY. JUST BEFORE IT BECAME A CRIME SCENE.
WAITAMINNIT...YOU KNEW THE SCARLET WERE GONNA BLOW THIS PLACE UP?
NO, NO...I WAS JUST BEING CAREFUL-- TAKING ALL THINGS INTO CONSIDERATION. I LEAVE THESE THINGS WHEREVER I GO, JUST IN CASE.
IN CASE OF WHAT? WHAT DOES IT DO?
WELL, UNDER CERTAIN CIRCUMSTANCES, IT'S HIGHLY FLAMMABLE.
AND THAT'S BEING CAREFUL?
IT'S THEORETICAL, MOSTLY. SIX SAYS IT'S A KIND OF BOMB THAT CHARGES UP LIKE A BATTERY AND USES INORGANIC MATTER AS FUEL WHEN IT EXPLODES.
IN UNRELATED NEWS, IT'D PROBABLY BE A GOOD IDEA FOR US TO GO UP THERE.
0110 00 011!
HEY, TWO...HFF...C'N YOU GIVE ME A LEG UP...?
JUST HURRY!
OH, GODDD! AA-ACK!
STOP LOOKING!
I'M NOT LOOKING! I'M NOT LOOKING!
IT'S NOT MY FAULT! I'VE BEEN ON A DIET!
JUST GET UP THE FUCKING WALL!

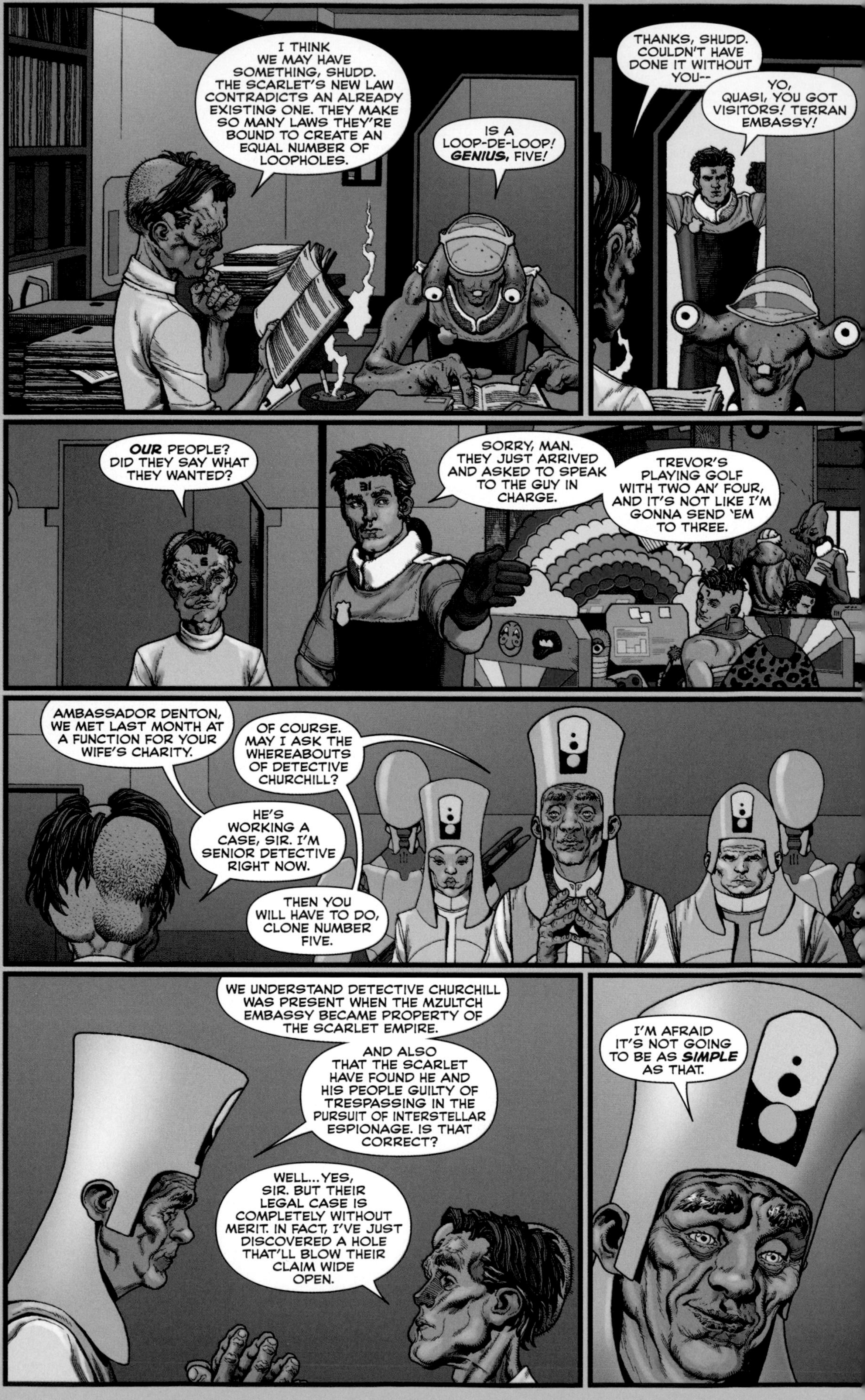
I THINK WE MAY HAVE SOMETHING, SHUDD. THE SCARLET'S NEW LAW CONTRADICTS AN ALREADY EXISTING ONE. THEY MAKE SO MANY LAWS THEY'RE BOUND TO CREATE AN EQUAL NUMBER OF LOOPHOLES.
IS A LOOP-DE-LOOP! GENIUS, FIVE!
THANKS, SHUDD. COULDN'T HAVE DONE IT WITHOUT YOU--
YO, QUASI, YOU GOT VISITORS! TERRAN EMBASSY!
OUR PEOPLE? DID THEY SAY WHAT THEY WANTED?
SORRY, MAN. THEY JUST ARRIVED AND ASKED TO SPEAK TO THE GUY IN CHARGE.
TREVOR'S PLAYING GOLF WITH TWO AN' FOUR, AND IT'S NOT LIKE I'M GONNA SEND 'EM TO THREE.
AMBASSADOR DENTON, WE MET LAST MONTH AT A FUNCTION FOR YOUR WIFE'S CHARITY.
OF COURSE. MAY I ASK THE WHEREABOUTS OF DETECTIVE CHURCHILL?
HE'S WORKING A CASE, SIR. I'M SENIOR DETECTIVE RIGHT NOW.
THEN YOU WILL HAVE TO DO, CLONE NUMBER FIVE.
WE UNDERSTAND DETECTIVE CHURCHILL WAS PRESENT WHEN THE MZULTCH EMBASSY BECAME PROPERTY OF THE SCARLET EMPIRE.
AND ALSO THAT THE SCARLET HAVE FOUND HE AND HIS PEOPLE GUILTY OF TRESPASSING IN THE PURSUIT OF INTERSTELLAR ESPIONAGE. IS THAT CORRECT?
WELL...YES, SIR. BUT THEIR LEGAL CASE IS COMPLETELY WITHOUT MERIT. IN FACT, I'VE JUST DISCOVERED A HOLE THAT'LL BLOW THEIR CLAIM WIDE OPEN.
I'M AFRAID IT'S NOT GOING TO BE AS SIMPLE AS THAT.

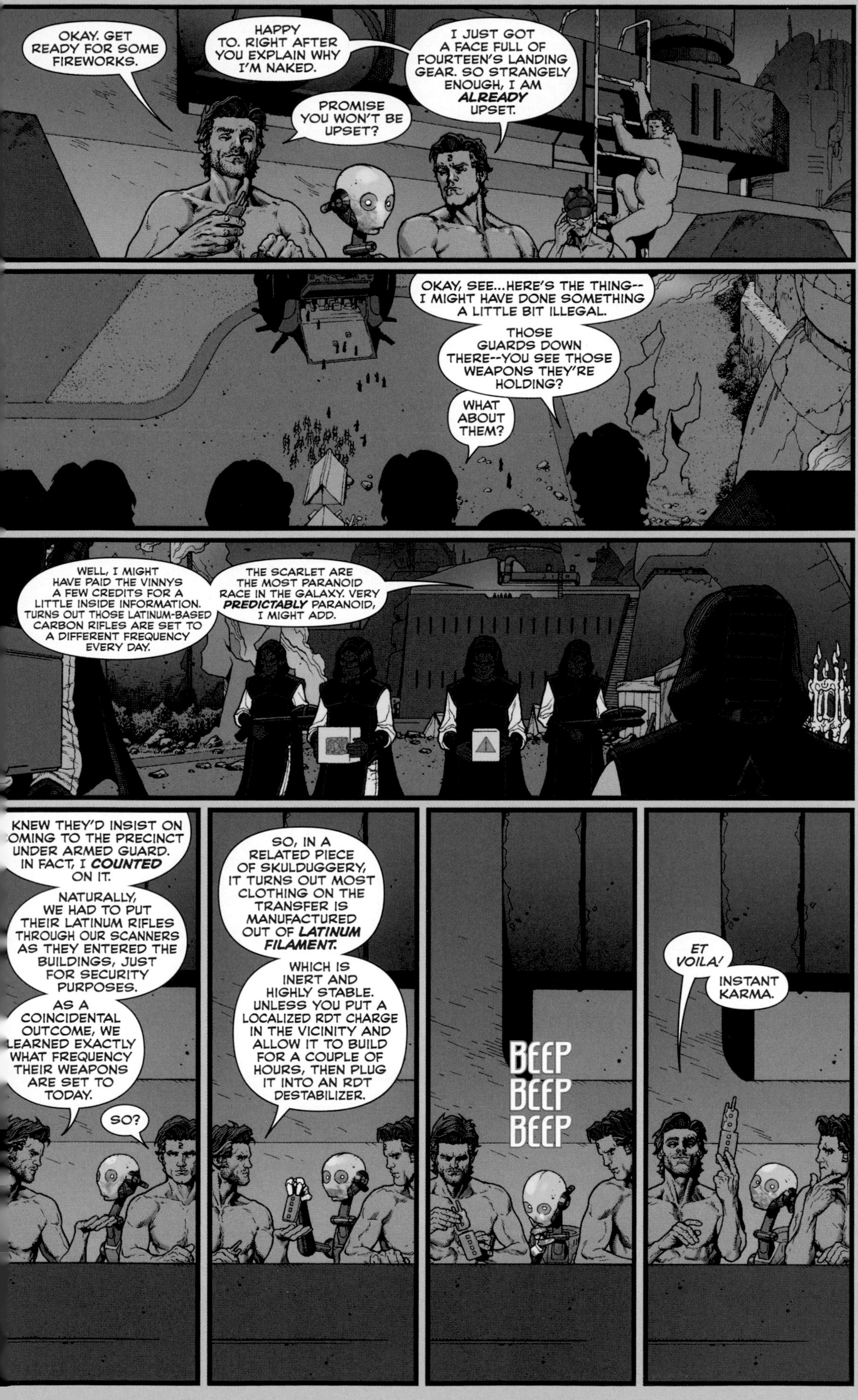
OKAY. GET READY FOR SOME FIREWORKS.
HAPPY TO. RIGHT AFTER YOU EXPLAIN WHY I'M NAKED.
PROMISE YOU WON'T BE UPSET?
I JUST GOT A FACE FULL OF FOURTEEN'S LANDING GEAR. SO STRANGELY ENOUGH, I AM ALREADY UPSET.
OKAY, SEE...HERE'S THE THING-- I MIGHT HAVE DONE SOMETHING A LITTLE BIT ILLEGAL.
THOSE GUARDS DOWN THERE--YOU SEE THOSE WEAPONS THEY'RE HOLDING?
WHAT ABOUT THEM?
WELL, I MIGHT HAVE PAID THE VINNYS A FEW CREDITS FOR A LITTLE INSIDE INFORMATION. TURNS OUT THOSE LATINUM-BASED CARBON RIFLES ARE SET TO A DIFFERENT FREQUENCY EVERY DAY.
THE SCARLET ARE THE MOST PARANOID RACE IN THE GALAXY. VERY PREDICTABLY PARANOID, I MIGHT ADD.
KNEW THEY'D INSIST ON OMING TO THE PRECINCT UNDER ARMED GUARD. IN FACT, I COUNTED ON IT.
NATURALLY, WE HAD TO PUT THEIR LATINUM RIFLES THROUGH OUR SCANNERS AS THEY ENTERED THE BUILDINGS, JUST FOR SECURITY PURPOSES.
AS A COINCIDENTAL OUTCOME, WE LEARNED EXACTLY WHAT FREQUENCY THEIR WEAPONS ARE SET TO TODAY.
SO?
SO, IN A RELATED PIECE OF SKULDUGGERY, IT TURNS OUT MOST CLOTHING ON THE TRANSFER IS MANUFACTURED OUT OF LATINUM FILAMENT.
WHICH IS INERT AND HIGHLY STABLE. UNLESS YOU PUT A LOCALIZED RDT CHARGE IN THE VICINITY AND ALLOW IT TO BUILD FOR A COUPLE OF HOURS, THEN PLUG IT INTO AN RDT DESTABILIZER.
BEEP BEEP BEEP
ET VOILA!
INSTANT KARMA.

NOW, YOU WILL ALSO NOTICE THAT THE MZULTCH-- WHILE VERY INTERESTING AND ALIEN-SHAPED-- ALSO HAPPEN TO BE TECHNICALLY *NAKED* ON ACCOUNT OF THE FACT THEY DON'T NEED CLOTHING.

SO THE REASON, ROGER, WHY YOU ARE CURRENTLY NAKED AS A JAYBIRD IS VERY SIMPLE-- I DID NOT WANT LITTLE ROGER TO EXPLODE WHEN I DID *THIS*.

OH.

BEEP

VEEPVEEPVEEPVEEPVEEP

NN-AAAH!

GYAAAAHHH

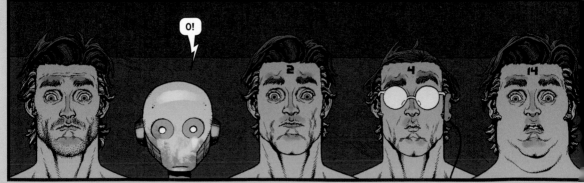

O!

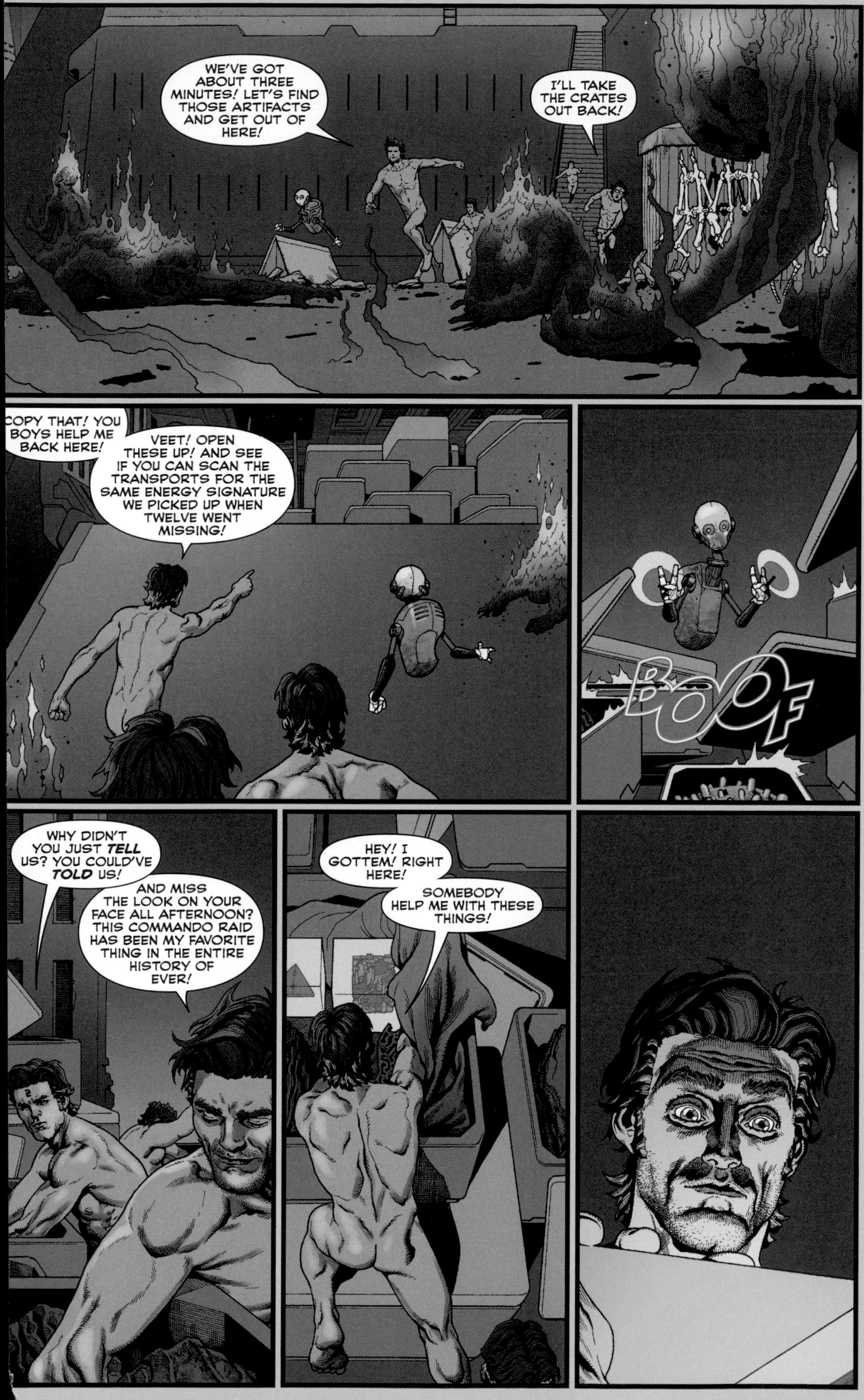
WE'VE GOT ABOUT THREE MINUTES! LET'S FIND THOSE ARTIFACTS AND GET OUT OF HERE!
I'LL TAKE THE CRATES OUT BACK!
COPY THAT! YOU BOYS HELP ME BACK HERE!
VEET! OPEN THESE UP! AND SEE IF YOU CAN SCAN THE TRANSPORTS FOR THE SAME ENERGY SIGNATURE WE PICKED UP WHEN TWELVE WENT MISSING!
BOOF
WHY DIDN'T YOU JUST TELL US? YOU COULD'VE TOLD US!
AND MISS THE LOOK ON YOUR FACE ALL AFTERNOON? THIS COMMANDO RAID HAS BEEN MY FAVORITE THING IN THE ENTIRE HISTORY OF EVER!
HEY! I GOTTEM! RIGHT HERE!
SOMEBODY HELP ME WITH THESE THINGS!

WE NEED TO GET THESE ARTIFACTS OUT THE FRONT GATE BEFORE THE SCARLET GET HERE!

THE FRONT GATE? WHY NOT OUT BACK?

JUST DO IT! *HURRY!*

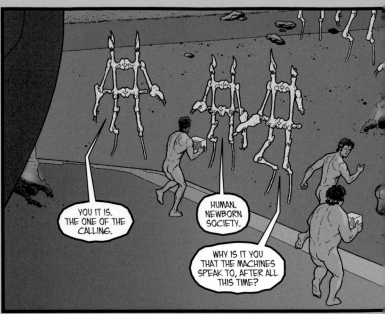

YOU IT IS. THE ONE OF THE CALLING.

HUMAN. NEWBORN SOCIETY.

WHY IS IT YOU THAT THE MACHINES SPEAK TO, AFTER ALL THIS TIME?

I WISH I HAD AN ANSWER. I JUST DON'T, I'M SORRY.

WE HAVE TO GO. BUT IF I HAVE IT IN MY POWER TO COME BACK FOR YOU PEOPLE, I PROMISE I *WILL.*

*HURRY!* WE'RE RUNNING OUT OF TIME!

I'M TRYING...

≳AH-HEHH≲...

...THIS THING IS *HEAVY!*

OUT THERE! *GO! GO!*

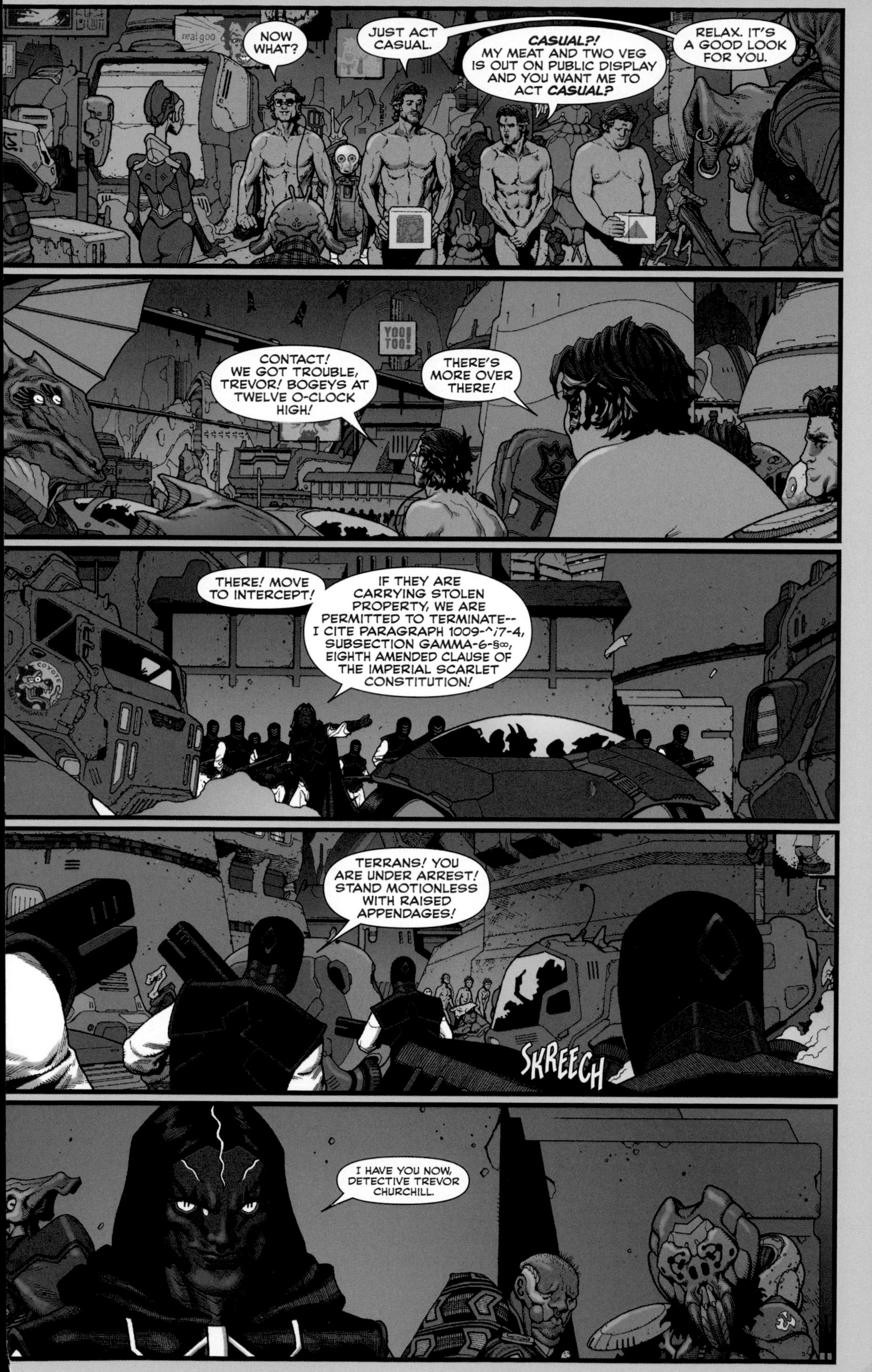
real goo
NOW WHAT?
JUST ACT CASUAL.
***CASUAL?!*** MY MEAT AND TWO VEG IS OUT ON PUBLIC DISPLAY AND YOU WANT ME TO ACT ***CASUAL?***
RELAX. IT'S A GOOD LOOK FOR YOU.
YOO TOO!
CONTACT! WE GOT TROUBLE, TREVOR! BOGEYS AT TWELVE O-CLOCK HIGH!
THERE'S MORE OVER THERE!
THERE! MOVE TO INTERCEPT!
IF THEY ARE CARRYING STOLEN PROPERTY, WE ARE PERMITTED TO TERMINATE-- I CITE PARAGRAPH 1009-^¡7-4, SUBSECTION GAMMA-6-§∞, EIGHTH AMENDED CLAUSE OF THE IMPERIAL SCARLET CONSTITUTION!
COYOTE
TERRANS! YOU ARE UNDER ARREST! STAND MOTIONLESS WITH RAISED APPENDAGES!
SKREECH
I HAVE YOU NOW, DETECTIVE TREVOR CHURCHILL.

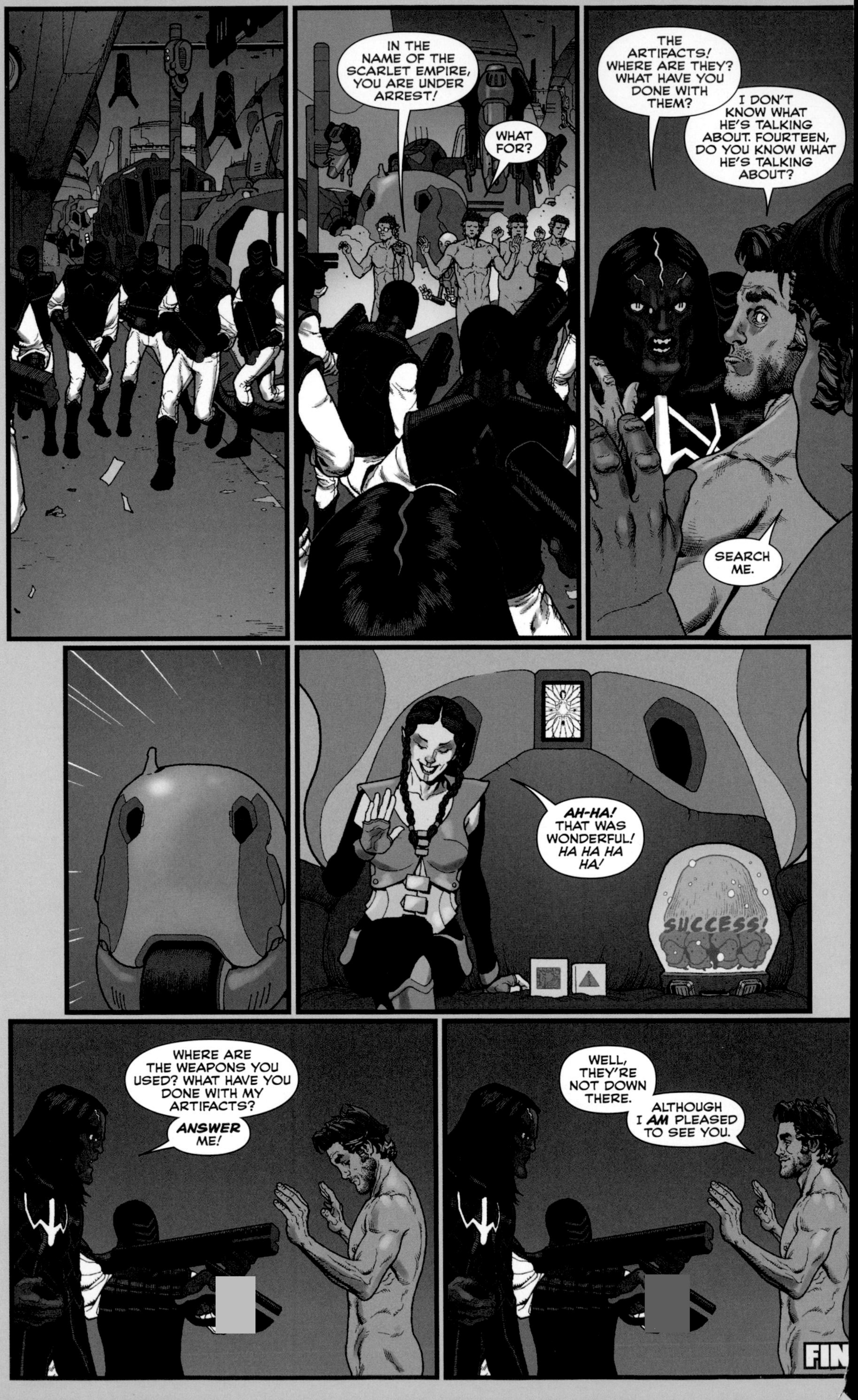
IN THE NAME OF THE SCARLET EMPIRE, YOU ARE UNDER ARREST!
WHAT FOR?
THE ARTIFACTS! WHERE ARE THEY? WHAT HAVE YOU DONE WITH THEM?
I DON'T KNOW WHAT HE'S TALKING ABOUT. FOURTEEN, DO YOU KNOW WHAT HE'S TALKING ABOUT?
SEARCH ME.
AH-HA! THAT WAS WONDERFUL! HA HA HA HA!
SUCCESS!
WHERE ARE THE WEAPONS YOU USED? WHAT HAVE YOU DONE WITH MY ARTIFACTS? ANSWER ME!
WELL, THEY'RE NOT DOWN THERE.
ALTHOUGH I AM PLEASED TO SEE YOU.
FIN

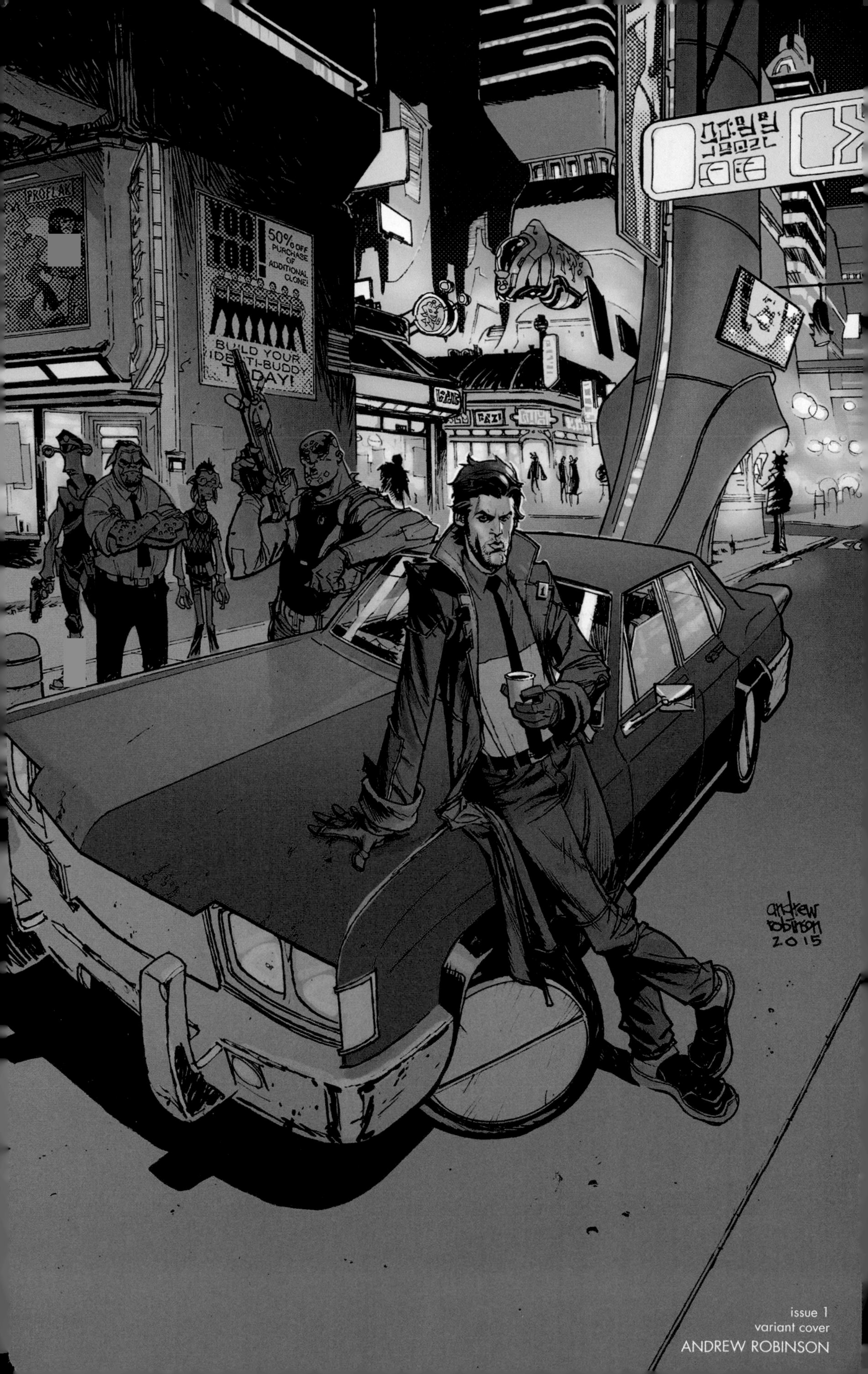
PROFLAK
YOO TOO!
50% OFF PURCHASE OF ADDITIONAL CLONE!
BUILD YOUR
andrew robinson 2015

issue 1
variant cover
ANDREW ROBINSON

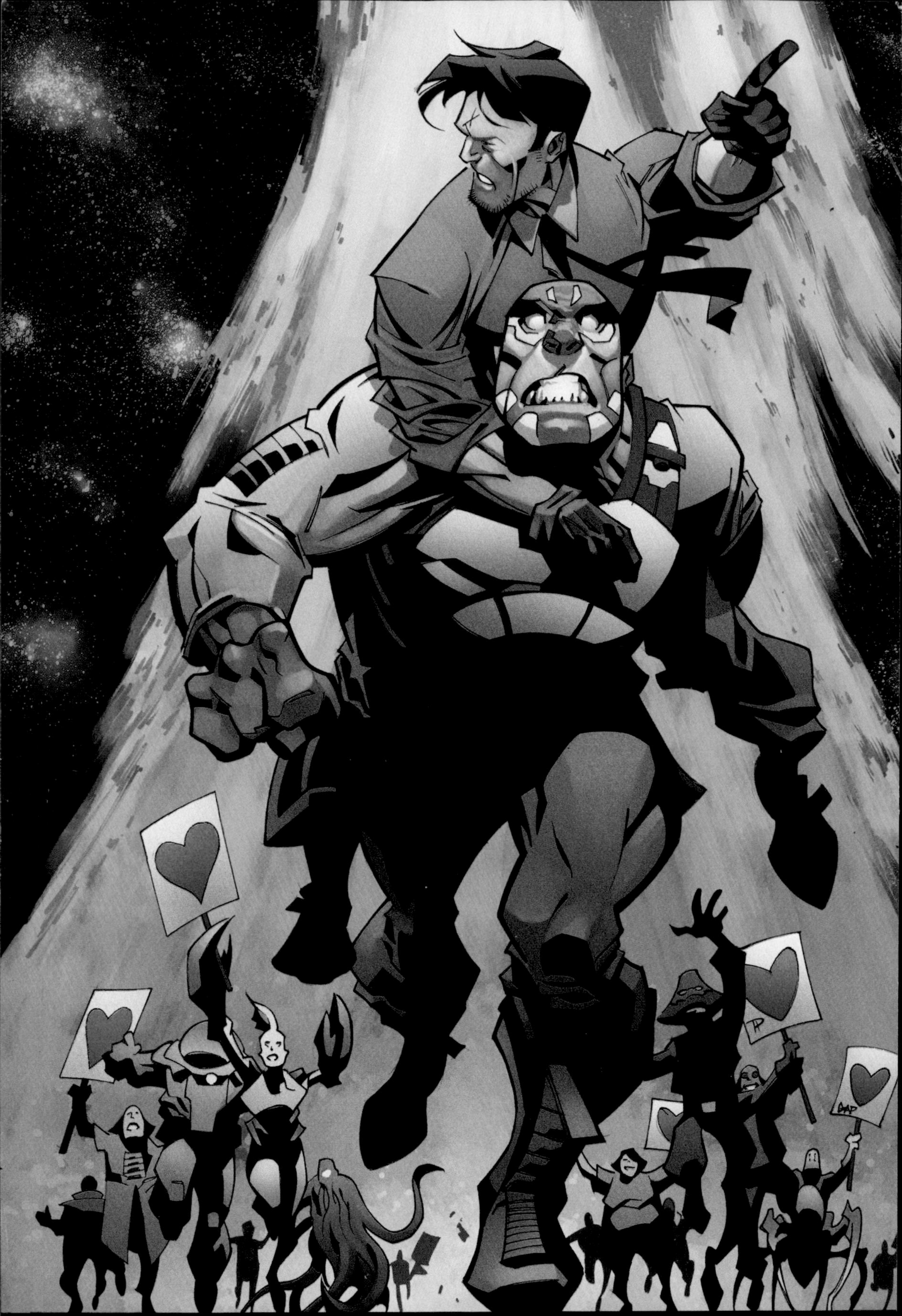

issue 1
variant cover
PHIL HESTER

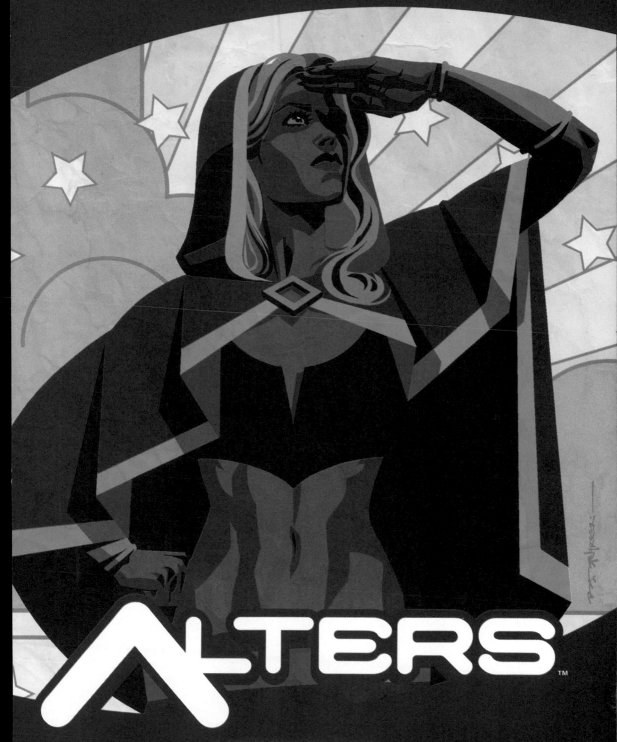

The saga of a young woman who can only really be herself...whenever she is not herself.

# ALTERS ™

**A NEW SERIES FROM**

**PAUL JENKINS** (WOLVERINE: ORIGIN, SENTRY)
**LEILA LEIZ** (NVRLND)

## RESERVE THIS AFTERSHOCK SERIES TODAY!

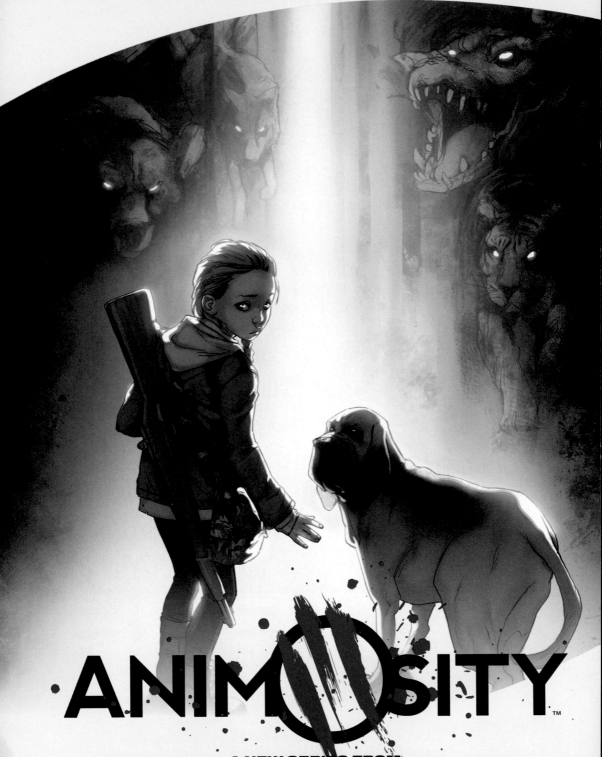

**One day, for no damn reason, the Animals woke up. They started thinking. They started talking. They started taking revenge.**

# ·ANIM(Ø)SITY™

### A NEW SERIES FROM
## MARGUERITE BENNETT (INSEXTS)
## AND RAFAEL DE LATORRE (SUPERZERO)

### RESERVE THIS AFTERSHOCK SERIES TODAY!

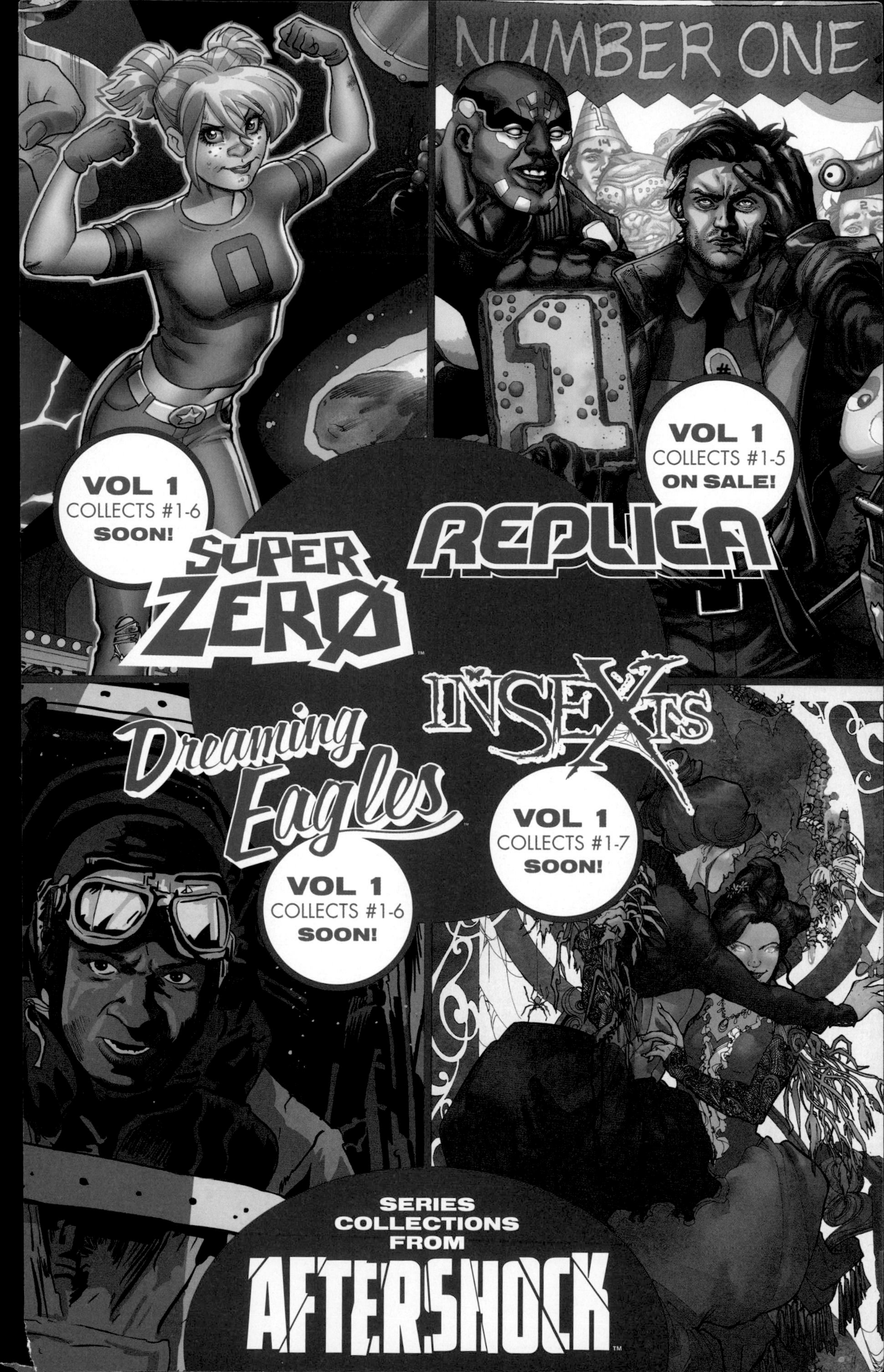

NUMBER ONE
VOL 1
COLLECTS #1-6
SOON!
SUPER ZERØ™
VOL 1
COLLECTS #1-5
ON SALE!
REPLICA™
INSEXTS™
Dreaming Eagles™
VOL 1
COLLECTS #1-7
SOON!
VOL 1
COLLECTS #1-6
SOON!
SERIES
COLLECTIONS
FROM
AFTERSHOCK™

## PAUL JENKINS writer
🐦 @mypauljenkins

Paul Jenkins has been creating, writing and building franchises for over twenty years in the graphic novel, film and video game industries. Over the last two decades, Paul has been instrumental in the creation and implementation of literally hundreds of world-renowned, recognizable entertainment icons.

From his employment with the creators of the *Teenage Mutant Ninja Turtles* at the age of 22, to his preeminent status as an IP creator, Paul has provided entertainment to the world through hundreds of print publications, films, video games and new media. With six Platinum-selling video games, a Number One MTV Music Video, an Eisner Award, five Wizard Fan Awards, and multiple Best-Selling Graphic Novels, Paul Jenkins is synonymous with success. He has enjoyed recognition on the New York Times bestseller list, has been nominated for two BAFTA Awards and has been the recipient of a government-sponsored Prism Award for his contributions in storytelling and characterization.

Paul's extensive list of comic book credits include *Batman* and *Hellblazer* for DC Comics; *Inhumans, Spider-Man, The Incredible Hulk, Wolverine: Origin, Civil War: Frontlines, Captain America: Theater of War* and *The Sentry* for Marvel Comics; and *Spawn* for Image Comics.

## ANDY CLARKE artist

Andy began working in comics in 1998 with writer Dan Abnett on *Sinister Dexter* for 2000AD. He made modest contributions to *Judge Dredd* (including a newspaper strip), worked on *Nikolai Dante* and *Shimura* with Robbie Morrison and with Kek-W on *Rose O'Rion*. He co-created *Thirteen* with Mike Carey and teamed up with Andy Diggle for *Snow/Tiger*. Since 2005, he has been very fortunate to work with some of the best writers on a small number of titles in the US: *Aquaman, R.E.B.E.L.S.* and *Batman* for DC and a *Mystique/Logan Legacy* one-shot for Marvel. He's also done the odd cover here and there.

## MARCELO MAIOLO colorist
🐦 @MMaiolo

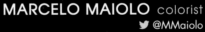

Marcelo Maiolo is best known for his work at DC Comics on such titles as *I, Vampire, Green Arrow, Demon Knights, Constantine, Green Lantern Corps, Teen Titans* and most recently, *Batman Beyond*. His work for other publishers includes *True Blood* for IDW, *King* for Jet City Comics, *Pacific Rim* for Legendary and *All-New X-Men* and *Old Man Logan* for Marvel. He lives and works in Brazil.

## DAN BROWN colorist
🐦 @danbrowncomics

Hailing from the frozen prairies of central Canada, Dan Brown has been a colorist for every major publisher for the past 23 years. Dan is thrilled to be working with Mike Marts (who gave him his first coloring gig at Marvel, lo those many moons ago) and the rest of the fantastic AfterShock team to bring the next level in comic book entertainment!

## CLAYTON COWLES letterer
🐦 @ClaytonCowles

Clayton Cowles graduated from the Joe Kubert School in 2009 and has been lettering full-time ever since. In addition to lettering for Marvel Comics, he works on the acclaimed Image titles *Bitch Planet, Phonogram, Pretty Deadly,* and *The Wicked + The Divine.* He lives in upstate New York with his cat.